NATIONALISM IN A NON-NATIONAL STATE

EDITED BY

WILLIAM W. HADDAD AND WILLIAM OCHSENWALD

NATIONALISM

IN A NON-NATIONAL STATE

The Dissolution of the Ottoman Empire

Ohio State University Press : Columbus

Copyright © 1977 by the Ohio State University Press
All Rights Reserved.
Manufactured in the United States of America

Library of Congress Cataloguing in Publication Data
Main entry under title:
Nationalism in a non-national state.
   Includes index.
   1. Near East—History—1517–   2. Nationalism—
Near East—Addresses, essays, lectures. I. Haddad,
William W. II. Ochsenwald, William.
DS62.4.N36   320.9'56   77-1253
ISBN 0-8142-0191-1

This book is respectfully dedicated to

Sydney Nettleton Fisher

Contents

Foreword

This volume was compiled to honor Professor Sydney Nettleton Fisher upon his retirement from the Ohio State University. In this endeavor, we have, hopefully, abided by one of the major lessons Professor Fisher taught his students —the necessity for clarity of expression and unity of purpose. In his textbook *The Middle East: A History* (New York, 1959, 1968), the most widely read general study in the United States, Fisher admirably followed these principles, as he did in his other works, in the books he edited, and in his pungent reviews.

Picking a common theme for the present volume has meant, unfortunately, that some of his former students could not participate. Nevertheless, it allowed a number of his friends and colleagues to make possible a more coherent and, perhaps, a more valuable book to show our respect and gratitude.

While resisting the urge to follow T. E. Lawrence's famous advice to ignore consistency in transliteration, we have chosen to attempt consistency in certain items. The names of individuals and place names mentioned in more than one essay have been spelled in the same way. In general, Ottoman Turkish institutions and names have been transliterated according to current Turkish usage except that "sh" and "ch" have been employed and the undotted "i" has not been shown. Arabic words follow the U.S. Library of Congress system with modifications, most notably the deletion of subscript and suprascript diacritical marks. With other languages we have followed authors' preferences.

In a sense this volume is dedicated not only to Sydney Fisher but also to his wife Elizabeth. Her hospitality and help to us over the years have been too great to be described in a short space.

Prof. Fred Kohlmeyer read the entire manuscript and offered advice that was gratefully accepted. We also owe our thanks to the History Departments of Virginia Polytechnic Institute and Illinois State University and in particular to Carolyn Alls, Diane Williams, Anita Crowe, Debra Adcock, Micki Schultz, Dorothy Haeffele, and Sharon H. Boswell for their assistance in typing and otherwise preparing this manuscript for publication. Billie D. Tyner and Alfred H. Ward probably bankrupted their firms making copies of our drafts. Weldon Kefauver, Director of the Ohio State University Press, has shown an unusual amount of forebearance in the face of repeated delays.

Most important of all have been Barbara Baker Haddad, Barbara Kaiser, and Charles Kaiser. They provided the encouragement, sustenance, understanding, and love which made this book a reality.

NATIONALISM IN A NON-NATIONAL STATE

William W. Haddad

Nationalism in the Ottoman Empire

Some years ago Professor Sydney Fisher first provided the clue to the subject we are considering while reviewing M. S. Anderson's *The Eastern Question* (New York, 1966). He noted that Anderson's topic (the diplomatic partition of the Ottoman Empire) "need not be done for another century." In other words, it was Dr. Fisher's opinion that, from the European point of view, the question of what was to be done with the "sick man of Europe," had been fully answered by Anderson and others. This portion of European diplomatic history could be laid to rest. Western scholars had carefully examined and reexamined their own archives; they had asked Western questions about the reasons for the demise of the Ottoman Empire and had reached Western conclusions.

But Professor Fisher added a rather disquieting note to his review of Anderson's book. He pointed out that Anderson was not familiar with the government of the Ottoman Empire, nor was he acquainted with Ottoman sources. What was needed, to quote Dr. Fisher, was "a book on the Western question." Implicit in this statement was his belief that future examination of the decline and partition of the empire had to be done from Balkan, Middle Eastern, Crimean, and North African points of view. How did the peoples of the Ottoman Empire—be they Turk, Serb, Tatar, Arab, or whatever—view the events occurring around them at the time of their leaving the empire? How did they react to the changed situations and apply them to the different problems facing them?

In answering these questions, I feel a revision of the interpretation of nationalism advanced by most Western historians and social scientists is urgently needed. Their approach to a study of nationalism frequently betrays a serious degree of Western ethnocentrism. They tend to view the nation-building process as inevitable, immutable, and desirable. "The nation-state may all too seldom speak with the voice of reason. But it remains the only serious alternative to chaos."[1] In two sentences all of humanity's history, except the last two hundred years, becomes a void, and the future must not be changed for fear of anarchy. Nonetheless, we believe the impact of two world wars, the threat of a third, and the movement toward regional economic integration have created a timely need for reviewing the basic assumptions concerning the phenomenon known as nationalism.

European military power either destroyed national entities or led to the evolution of powerful national states during the nineteenth and twentieth centuries. There seemed to be no alternative to the dynamic, expansive spirit of nationalism. However, the political systems of certain non-national states offered a major alternative to Western European methods of organizing large geographical territories and diverse groups of people. The shortcomings of Western-style nationalism have become all too apparent. Chauvinism, a word that originally signified extreme, uncritical national loyalty ("my country, right or wrong"), has become a term of opprobrium, e.g., "male chauvinism." Thus it is necessary to try to obtain a new and more informed historical perspective of the non-national states.

The Ottoman Empire was among the most important of the

non-national states. Closest to Europe, lasting more than six centuries, spanning three continents, its durability and extent provide a major instance of a dynastic and religiously based alternative to secular, populist European nationalism.

Western interpretations of the growth of nationalism in the Ottoman Empire may be divided into three phases: (1) acceptance and presentation of the national, anti-Ottoman groups' claims and their own account of their historical relationship with the Ottoman Empire;[2] (2) a revisionism that attempted to correct what were perceived to be the factual errors of the first phase;[3] (3) the beginning of syntheses based on detailed revisionist monographs.[4]

Western scholars of the second phase have not been negligent in the use of indigenous sources. In fact, one aspect of the impact of the West on the Middle East has been thoroughly covered—the problem of nationalism as a political philosophy. Sylvia Haim's *Arab Nationalism: An Anthology* (Berkeley, Calif., 1962), interprets the writings of over twenty Arab authors. Gustave Von Grunebaum in his *Modern Islam* (Berkeley, Calif., 1962), deals with the confrontation of Islam with Western ideas. Revisionist work in religio-political history has considered a few leaders, especially Jamal al-Din "al-Afghani" and his followers.[5] Other works have appeared, often scattered in journals.

Yet all these books, however great their value, have dealt only with ideas, without coming to grips with the question of how or why these ideas became manifest. Even the outstanding work of Bernard Lewis, *The Emergence of Modern Turkey* (London, 1961, 1968), tends to separate idea from action. Several chapters of his book deal with the ideological revolution that was occurring among the Ottoman populace in the nineteenth century. He then proceeds to discuss the formation of the Kemalist Republic. There seems to be little transition between the two. Obviously, the background and formative years of the establishment of all the successor states of the Ottoman Empire should be examined in greater detail. Furthermore, the writings of Western historians seem to imply that the intellectual ferment of the late nineteenth century and early twentieth century was monolithic and the major cause of change. It is my belief that this was not so. I believe that there were divergent, as well as convergent, ideologies in the Middle East and that geographic, economic, social, and Great Power influences played a greater role than did nationalist ideology.

The study of anti-Ottoman nationalism and the pro-Ottoman resistance to it needs to be brought together, to be more carefully scrutinized and coherently assessed.

The purpose, then, of this volume is not to reexamine the Western impact on the Middle East from a Western point of view but to begin to examine the various groups there, emphasizing the use of indigenous sources in an attempt to answer the following questions:

1. What were the hopes and aspirations of the various proto-national groups when confronted with Western power and Ottoman weakness?

2. What were the economic, social, and internal political bases of anti-Ottoman nationalism, or did they even exist?

3. How were (or were not) these bases made manifest? What was the form of action to achieve national goals? What was the reality, not the ideology, of the nationalisms of the Ottoman Empire?

These questions will probably remain unanswered when the reader finishes this book. Even to pose them is to sketch a perhaps overambitious task. It is my modest hope that the mere raising of the issues may provoke the detailed monographic work that will test the validity of the answers that follow.

Before the reader travels farther along the path we have prepared, a few additional words about what he may expect to find are in order. The chapters that follow will be concerned

with the attempts of various peoples to be free and independent, both during and after Ottoman rule. For some the
outcome was successful; for others, only partially so; but in
virtually every case one will behold a situation of bewilder-
ing complexity involving a diversity of causes and forces,
internal and external, religious, political, economic, ethnic,
and so on. The contributors to this volume will clearly demonstrate how intricate the motivating factors and goals of
these struggles for independence were. These movements
have been viewed in the West, and quite naturally so, in terms
of the concept of European secular nationalism. Our findings
are that the conventional interpretation of nationalism is much
too narrow to be applied to the subject peoples and provinces
of the Ottoman Empire. At least four meanings of *nationalism* can be discerned: nationality, nation, nation-state, and
nationalism.

The term *nationality*, as commonly used today, denotes
citizenship. However, nationality, as it was originally en-
visaged in Western Europe, carried with it certain characteristics that defined a group of people. These characteristics
included the belief in a common descent, the same language,
the same territory, a political entity, religion, customs, and
traditions. Such a conglomerate of people possessing the
same nationality was called a *nation*. This group of people
did not have to possess *all* the characteristics that defined a
"nationality" in order to call themselves a "nation." Thus,
one may speak of the United States of America as a nation,
though it is not racially homogeneous; and of a Palestinian
nation, even though the latter does not now possess a finite
territory. The term *nation* may be used synonymously with
the word *people*. In contemporary usage the term *nation-
state* has come to mean the political and territorial expression
of the nation. Actually, the idea of nation and nationality are
quite old, dating back to the times of the Greek and Hebrew
peoples. However, the contemporary idea of the secular nation-state was not fully developed until late in the eighteenth
or early nineteenth century. Before that time one found reli-

gious, dynastic, or multinational states. Nonetheless, by the nineteenth century, the ideal political entity came to be identified in the West as the single-nationality state.

This concept, emerging in Western Europe, began to sweep the world. It was a liberal one in its day and rejected Rousseau's concept of the primacy of the individual, substituting for it the idea that the best objectification of a people's political aspirations was in the nation's forming a nation-state. This nation-state would also serve to preserve and enhance each nation's nationality. This belief has formed the basis for a definition of the last concept, *nationalism*. Nationalism arose in Western Europe largely as a result of the bourgeois French Revolution. Nationalism is a state of mind. It is undoubtedly the greatest motivating force in the world in the twentieth century. It has as its basis the transfer of the primary loyalty of human beings from religion to the political entity, the nation-state. It is also prideful, believing each nation is unique, excellent, and has a historical mission to fulfill in the world. The concept of nationalism carries with it the alleged right of each nation to territorial self-determination and, therefore, is often viewed as an aggressive philosophy, as opposed to the idea of patriotism, which by definition is defensive. With the rise of Western nationalism, one sees different nations competing in their irredentist claims. Thus in Europe the Bulgarians, the Serbs, the Greeks, and the Turks all call Macedonia and Thrace their own. As Carlton J. H. Hayes said:

> Nationalism as a religion inculcates neither charity nor justice; it is proud not humble; and it signally fails to universalize human aims. . . . Nationalism's kingdom is frankly of this world, and its attainment involves tribal selfishness and vainglory, a particularly ignorant and tyrannical intolerance—and war. . . . Nationalism brings not peace but war.[6]

In trying to understand the emergence of nation-states out of the territories of the Ottoman Empire, we, as Westerners, have imposed our theoretical framework on an Eastern setting. Perhaps we should not be too harsh on ourselves in trying to view the history of an alien area in terms of our own perceptions. The Western concept of nationalism was the only framework for reference that we had. As Arnold Toynbee wrote several decades ago, "For us, in our time and place, it was not within our power to start from anywhere else; for the national community is the social prison-house in which our modern Western souls are incarcerated."[7]

The attempt by Western sociologists and historians to interpret the causes for the dissolution of the Ottoman Empire, using largely this framework, has led to serious academic controversies in the twentieth century. George Antonius, in his book *The Arab Awakening*, which perhaps has had the most influence on attitudes toward the rise of Arab nation-states, wrote, "The story of the Arab national movement opens in Syria in 1847, with the foundation in Beirut of a modest literary society under American patronage."[8] Antonius, a Christian Palestinian educated in the West, argued that this literary movement eventually infected the entire Middle East with the Western idea of national self-determination, that it was eventually fused with the Arab revolt under the sharif of Mecca, Husayn Ibn 'Ali, and resulted in a measure of freedom for the Arabs after World War I. This point of view, which was widely accepted for numerous years, in the past decades has been challenged by others, most notably Zeine N. Zeine, C. Ernest Dawn, and George Kirk. Dawn refuted Antonius's main argument about the effectiveness of the intellectual movement centered in Beirut. He argued that most Arabs remained pro-Ottoman until 1918.[9] Kirk also argued that, in World War I, the Arabs were more interested in fighting hunger than the Turks.[10]

As for the European Ottoman provinces, the same arguments persist. Hans Kohn wrote, "The Greeks were the first successfully to raise the banner of nationalism and liberalism. With their 'war of independence' the age of nationalism in Eastern Europe was established."[11] H. A. R. Gibb disagreed with this view and said that the Greeks were not nationally oppressed but economically oppressed, and therefore they revolted against the Ottomans. "The Greek rebels had a common bond of language and religion, but they were not consciously affected by national ideas."[12] This view was opposed by Elie Kedourie, who argued that "Greek and Armenian nationalism arose among populations which were generally more prosperous . . . than their Ottoman Muslim overlords."[13]

The numerous and often contradictory explanations of events in Asia and Eastern Europe (the Maghrib was simply ignored) in terms of the Western experience led Hans Kohn to formulate, in numerous books with wide influence, a series of complex theories that attempted to explain the differences between the rise of nationalism in the West and in the East. He wrote that in the West the nation-state preceded both nationalism and the nation. The most famous example of this was England, which emerged as a state before there was an English people. The opposite was true in Central and Eastern Europe and in Asia, where the nationality was clearly identified by the nation before the nation-state emerged. As a result, the nations in those regions had to fight to gain their "historic" lands, as in the German case.

In the West the nation-states that emerged were more tolerant and pacific because they did not have to fight for territorial sovereignty. In the remainder of Europe and Asia, these peoples more warlike and tribal. Emile Marmorstein, commenting on this appparent phenomenon, wrote that England and France "are more tolerant of individualistic tendencies and sectional differences. On the other hand, the German, Italian, Czech, and Arab nations, for example, were prevented from becoming states by dynastic conquests. They therefore stressed the attributes of a nation, language, race, common history, and traditions. Deprived of the experience of Statehood until the development of the nation, they tended to concentrate on unity at the expense of liberty."[14] Presumably, Marmorstein and Kohn would argue that the result in the West was the development of more humanistic and rational attitudes that were neither aggressive nor repressive. On the other hand, in those areas of the Ottoman Empire that gained their independence after World War I, the tendency has been to build the nation-state on myths of the past and to be more warlike, elevating the state to an end in itself rather than a means for improving the conditions of its citizens.

Even granting the validity of Hans Kohn's and others' arguments on the evolution of Western nationalism and its Eastern manifestations—and these generalizations are certainly questionable—it is perhaps more incumbent on Westerners looking at the Middle East to reexamine the dissolution of the Ottoman Empire in terms of what the indigenous populations thought of that process and how they acted upon those thoughts.

As we shall see, Western secular nationalism was not the greatest motivating force in the breakup of the Ottoman Empire. In the former Arab provinces, for example, "the absence of a specific ideology of Arab nationalism until the end of World War I is indeed noteworthy. It was not until the 1930s that a serious attempt was made to define the meaning of Arab nationalism and what constitutes the Arab nation."[15]

The Ottoman Empire, when its central government and rulers were strong, was a powerful suzerain over its provinces. One rarely finds instances of rebellion aimed at denying the legitimacy of Ottoman overlordship. The reasons for the generally quiescent nature of the provinces were largely positive: the Turkish-speaking administrators who ruled the multireligious empire were generally more capable than preceding conquerors; the military was ordinarily firm and impartial in meting out justice; and, most important, the Ottomans did not attempt to destroy the culture and mores of the peoples they conquered.

By the mid-nineteenth century this process had changed. The main reasons for the decline and eventual breakup of the Ottoman Empire were, in part, internal unrest, often religious, combined with European intrigue. It was a multi-

religious empire, divided into numerous millets that tended
to be the storehouses from which nascent nationalism could
draw. The assertion that there was little chance the empire
would have fallen had it been composed only of Muslim
Ottomans is an eminently defensible one. Different religious
groups and the support, especially in the Balkans, for these
groups by European religious champions was a prime cause
for the eventual break-up of the Ottoman Empire. It would
have been impossible for all of the Balkans to have gained
their independence by World War I had it not been for European aid. Although nationalism, as it was promulgated in
the nineteenth and twentieth centuries, was secular, there
was an attempt to elevate the national churches, to venerate
them as the national souls, and to incorporate them into the
budding nationalist movements. The church was viewed as
the repository of national identity in the period prior to the
rise of modern nationalism.

Other reasons for the internal decline of the Ottoman
Empire are familiar, and we need only summarize them here.
In brief, they were the following: Mahmud II's destruction
of the Janissary corps, which had served as a check on the
sultan, and economic weakness as a result both of increased
industrial imports from Europe and the decline of agriculture.
There was also a lack of openness to secular education as
the result of the primacy of the religiously educated elite.
Also, by the eighteenth century, military weakness resulted
in many provinces being virtually independent. This permitted European incursions into Ottoman territory, and in
geographic Syria, for example, gave rise to highwaymen. The
net effect of all these weaknesses was the fractionalizing of
the empire into numerous parts as local ruling individuals or
groups began to take control from a weak central government. The great majority of people allowed this to happen
for the same reason that they had welcomed Ottoman control centuries earlier: local rulers provided greater security,
stability, and autonomy. Although this process would provide the basis for the later growth of nationalism, it was not

nationalism. It was, rather, a demand to safeguard local political and social interests. One European visitor of the nineteenth century to the Ottoman provinces noted,

> Everywhere, I say, I have found the expression of an indelible and universal sentiment, the hatred of the Turks. . . . The plan for concerted action among the diverse factions of the great Arab family, to throw off the detested yoke, is gradually progressing.[16]

Though it may be tempting to interpret this statement to show the growth of nationalism, this would be a Western perception. Nonetheless, it does portray a disintegrative process to which the Ottomans were not blind. They were both part and cause of it and so responded with occasional repression, tactical retreat, and nominal reform.

The Ottoman response, most notably in the Arab provinces, was self-defeating. It was seized upon by a twentieth-century generation of Arab nationalists who had been nurtured by their decentralizing parents and who had partaken of imported Western ideas. Eventually, when the West violated its own maxim, self-determination, and colonized the Middle East, the nationalists gained new supporters who demanded freedom. The events that resulted in the formation of nation-states in the territories of the Ottoman Empire were not uniform, however, and differed according to their geographic settings. Those provinces whose borders were contiguous to European Christian states were naturally more exposed to Western ideas, and their struggles for independence more closely resembled Western conceptions of national independence movements. They also found themselves in the midst of European intrigue and power politics. As a result, their separatist aspirations were aided and abetted by the various Christian European countries. Sometimes the end result was worse than the original condition.

The Crimean khans, of all the Turkish vassals, felt the most similar to the Ottomans because of their common descent. The Crimean Tatars often had fought well for the Ottomans and had served as a buffer state against Russian and Polish-Lithuanian expansion at Ottoman expense. However, the attempt on the part of the Ottomans to interfere internally in Crimean affairs in the eighteenth century increased hostility on the part of the vassal khans of the Crimea. This growing irritation was seized upon by the Russians and encouraged by their agents not for Crimean benefit but for Russian imperial interests. They sought to instill in the Crimean people a sense of their former independence and to encourage the khans to disapprove of Ottoman interference in succession questions. The result was ephemeral Crimean independence, which lasted only a decade until the peninsula was incorporated into Russia. Crimean scholars afterward looked back with regret at this "independence" and often longed for the possibility of the reintegration of the Crimea into the Ottoman Empire

In the Hellenic-Balkan areas, too, the people were aided by the European powers in gaining their nominal freedom. The formation of pan-Hellenic societies in the West, the breakdown of feudal societies in Eastern Europe, and the increasing intellectual and economic intercourse with the West, as a result of the growth of Western demand for Balkan agricultural goods, resulted in a growing national awareness in the Balkan provinces of the Empire. Western Europe perceived positively the stirrings of these nascent national groups, whose identities had been kept alive by the failure of the Ottomans to integrate their subjects because of the millet system. This view held that the partial breakup of the Ottoman Empire and the freeing of the Christian provinces were favorable occurrences. The infusion of Western nationalism into various portions of the Ottoman body was "the injection of something entirely new, modern Western civilization, into something entirely different, Ottoman Moslem civilization, and that its effect was to give new life to something which was dead—or rather, to replace what was dead by something new and living."[17] The net effect was to see all of the European provinces torn from the Turkish body by World War I.

A similar scenario was being played in Asia Minor with the Christian Armenians. The Armenian millet was known as the "loyal nation" (*millet-i sadika*); and some have argued that though other proto-national groups had revolted periodically, the Armenians "remained the most pacific of all ethnic elements in the empire."[18] The Armenian nation, too, because of its Christian background, was exposed to Western knowledge, largely as a result of missionary work. This new awakening was accentuated by the repressive regime of Abdülhamid II. The sultan, recognizing the weaknesses of his empire, chose to interpret reform to mean, in part, the centralization of power in Istanbul, a process that had begun with Mahmud II and that was anathema to the Armenian millet. He further saw Western reform as the adaptation of Western technology to repressive ends, for example, by using his secret police and improved communications to maintain control over the disparate parts of the empire. The Armenian millet was unusual in that it was a nation that was partly European in orientation while at the same time it reflected events that were occurring among other proto-national groups in geographic Syria. What made it similar to other communities in the European provinces was its Western outlook and contact with the West as a result of its religion. But the Armenian millet was, at the same time, Asian in the sense that its nationalism appeared later chronologically, its revolt against the Ottomans was of less interest to Europe, and its eventual independence was questionable.

The Armenians, like the Arabs, joined in the general rejoicing occasioned by the overthrow of Hamidian repression in 1908-9 and hoped for a happier existence in a more liberal regime. This dream was short-lived when the Young Turks turned to pan-Turanism. The Armenians renewed their rebellion with disastrous results. The "Armenian Question" was raised in earnest after the death of hundreds in Cilicia and northern Syria beginning in April 1909. The intermittent warfare, in which both sides suffered heavily, culminated in the death of scores of thousands of Armenians in World War

I and later in 1920-22, resulting in their flight to Syria, Lebanon, and Palestine. Thus the imperfectly articulated Armenian desire for a nation-state was virtually destroyed, only to be revived with the formation of an Armenian Soviet Socialist Republic under Russian protection.

It should be noted that the heightened national awareness in the Christian provinces, the resulting European intrusions into these areas, and the resulting struggles for political control of the Balkans by several peoples led to increased strife in the early twentieth century and was a cause of World War I.

That war and the resulting destruction of the Ottoman Empire led to the flowering of Turkish nationalism. The Turks loved their new nation-state, which arose in the provinces of the old empire where they formed a majority. Their feeling was heightened by the allied occupation after World War I and, particularly, after the Greek occupation. In the renascent Turkey the Ottoman sultan-caliph was viewed as a puppet of the Allied victors and a betrayer of Turkish popular sovereignty. According to Mustafa Kemal (Atatürk), "It was by violence that the sons of Osman acquired the power to rule over the Turkish nation and to maintain their rule for more than six centuries. It is now the nation that revolts against these [Ottoman] usurpers, puts them in their right place and actually carries on their sovereignty."[19] Because the Osmanli dynasty was unable to impede either the growing Western pressure or the rise of national identity as the primary loyalty of the individual, the Turks turned against their former masters by stripping the Ottomans of their temporal power in the declaration of the Turkish republic in 1923. Their spiritual power was lost in 1924 with the abolition of the caliphate.

The Arab provinces of the Ottoman Empire differed significantly in their struggle for independence from the Christian European provinces. They were farther removed geographically from Western influence and, therefore, were not of as great interest to Europe; also they were predominantly of a different religion and thus did not need "protection." This comparative lack of interaction thereby retarded the introduction of Western nationalism. Further, the overwhelming majority of Arabs did not comprise a separate millet since they were Muslim. Their theoretical equality with the dominant Muslim Turks had both positive and negative points. They could rise to many of the highest Muslim offices in the empire and had a revered position as the race that produced the Prophet. But they had no formal institutions that could preserve an Arab identity that was neither Islamic nor Ottoman. As a result, the Arabs' knowledge of their past had virtually disappeared, only to be partially revived by several nineteenth-century movements.

The impact of the unitarian Wahhabi movement in the Arabian peninsula in the eighteenth and early nineteenth centuries was not nationalistic; it was religious. It aimed at making the Arab world sectarian, not secular. Still it would be wrong to disregard the influence of the Wahhabis on the Arab national consciousness. As a result of considering the Wahhabi phenomenon, many Arabs began to become aware of their own past and to ask questions about their future. So, too, would it be incorrect to characterize Jamal al-Din "al-Afghani" as an Arab nationalist. He was quintessentially a pan-Islamist. He felt that the deterioration of the Muslim world, epitomized by the caliphate in Istanbul, was a result of Muslim deviation from the laws of Islam. He called not for the formation of a secular Arab nation but rather for the reintroduction of Muslim values into all the Islamic world in order to stave off the attacks of the Christian West. But he too served to awaken Arab self-examination, and his disciples aided the growth of a national consciousness among the Arab people.

Neither should we view the career of Mehmed Ali in Egypt in the first half of the nineteenth century as nationalistically motivated. It was more a case of personal ambition. Mehmed Ali was not an Arab, and the fact that he attempted to form an Arab kingdom was simply a geographical accident. He wished to form a personal empire and perhaps ultimately to place himself in the sultanate in Istanbul. Nonetheless, he and his son Ibrahim, and the latter's conquest of geographic Syria in the 1830s, changed the Middle East. Ibrahim's espousal of the Arab cause and the opening of geographic Syria to Western thought greatly aided the modest literary movement that was to help the growth of the Arabs' self-awareness of their past.

Opening geographic Syria to Western influence caused a subsequent influx of Christian missionaries into that area. The literary revival that their arrival engendered was centered on Lebanese Christians. It was not supported by, nor did it widely influence, the majority of Arabs, the overwhelming number of whom were Muslim. It would therefore be wrong to view the numerous rebellions in the Arab provinces after the arrival of the missionaries as being national. It would also be a mistake to view the Christian Lebanese awakening as an Arab nationalist event. It would be better characterized as a Lebanese separatist movement dominated by Maronites, who looked to the West, especially France, for protection from the sectarian strife that racked Lebanon throughout the latter half of the nineteenth century. "The anti-Turkish movement in Lebanon in the nineteenth century was in general Lebanese Maronite and it cannot be considered a national Arab revolution in the Arab East against Turkish rule. The great majority of Muslims in the states ruled by the Sultan did not wish at that time to leave the Islamic government and overthrow it."[20]

Muslim Arab energies were largely spent on interpreting new means of establishing a strong Islamic state to ward off European incursion. Loyalty to Istanbul was strong while the empire was strong, despite the presence of some officials from Istanbul, like the insensitive censor, who often did more damage than good to Ottoman-Arab relations. Even when the empire declined and the Arabs felt this weakness, the Muslim Arabs did not wish to substitute European control for Ottoman control. The Muslim Arabs were aware of

European colonial activities, especially of the conquest of North Africa, which began in 1830 in present-day Algeria. They were also aware of the European role in defeating Mehmed Ali's government of geographic Syria in 1841. Nuri al-Sa'id wrote, "None of us thought of separation from the Ottoman Empire. Our thinking was directed toward obtaining a local Arab administration, the recognition of Arabic as an official language, and Turkish-Arab association in the administration of the general policy of the state. . . . Some Turks, among them Mustafa Kemal [Atatürk] . . . , were supporting this idea."[21] There was no such thing as Arab nationalism in the Hijaz, though it may well be argued that loyalty to Istanbul decreased after the 1870s with the bankruptcy of the empire and the subsequent decrease in imperial subventions to that province. There was no such thing as Palestinian nationalism until Zionism became a threat to that proto-nation. Indeed, as late as the 1940s, Palestinian children were singing songs extolling the virtues of the Syrian fatherland. Certainly there was no such thing as Transjordanian nationalism before World War I. Nationalism only emerged there after negotiations between Winston Churchill and 'Abd Allah Ibn Husayn resulted in the creation of the nation-state in 1923.

If one excludes the Lebanese movement, centering almost exclusively on Christian intellectuals, all of geographic Syria and the Arab peninsula remained quiet and thought little of separation from the empire until the institution of pan-Turanism after 1908. "In fact it is no exaggeration to say that the rule of Cemal Pasha in Syria during World War I was one of the determining factors in the attitude of the majority of the Arab Muslim leaders toward Turkey. It eliminated all reluctance and made them decide on complete separation from Turkey."[22] The policy of pan-Turanism, the personal ambition of the Hashimites, the power of Britain, and the desire to restore "Arab," that is, "Islamic," glory were the forces behind the Arab revolt, not nationalism. Even then the Arabs were in most instances reluctant to take this final step. The success of the revolt and its subsequent betrayal by Europe through the institution of the Sykes-Picot Agreement and the incorporation of the Balfour Declaration as part of the colonial settlement created the detached Arab nation-states. Nationalism grew in response to this activity.

Most of the Arab world, since the fall of the Umayyad Empire in 750 A.D., has been dominated by non-Arabs. So the rise of nationalism in the twentieth century in the Arab world should not be viewed in the context of revulsion over the rule by aliens, for this was a common occurrence, but because these aliens were Europeans. The nation-state was created in the Arab East in the twentieth century by the European West; and slowly various nationalisms, as in Western Europe, grew to identify with these boundaries originally drawn in red, blue, and brown on the maps of the British and the French. The idea of nationalism was brought with the Europeans, with their ideas on government, constitution, and popular sovereignty. It is no coincidence that the centers of Arab nationalism were Damascus, Baghdad, and Cairo —capitals of colonized countires—and not Riyadh or Mecca, the dominant cities of an independent state. Who is to say, however, that the nation-building process has reached its final stage? Since Islam has been a way of life, why may it not return to dominate politics in the Muslim world? Though the thesis is tenuous, some would argue that this is exactly what is happening and must be fought.[23]

It is widely recognized that a nation, a nation-state, and nationalism can be created. The United States has discovered this in Panama, and the Arab peoples see it in themselves. Contemporary Lebanon, a creation of France, with its population divided between Muslim and Christian, is still not a nation. Yet the dichotomy between the Arab peoples' view of themselves as one nation and the rise of regionally focused nationalisms has led to an attempt to assert both aspects of their character. Thus we have the *Hashimite* Kingdom of Jordan, the Syrian *Arab* Republic, the *Arab* Republic of Egypt, and so on. On the one side there is the assertion of

the Arabs as a predominantly Islamic people and on the other
the growth of secular nationalism. The former leads to the
dream of Arab unity, whereas the latter represents, as was
stated earlier, the primary motivating force in recent world
history. As long as nationalism remains the greater force,
the dream of Arab unity will most likely remain unattain-
able. It was, perhaps, predictable that the attempted unions
of Jordan and Iraq; Syria, Egypt, and Yemen; Libya and
Egypt; and Tunisia and Libya would all fail.

In North Africa the emergence of nation-states followed a
quite different pattern from the Ottoman provinces of Europe
and Asia. This difference was a result of at least two factors.
First, there was the distance from Istanbul to Africa, which
allowed independent Barbary states to emerge along the
coasts and in the urban areas of Tunis, Tripoli, and Algiers.
Second, the West began the conquest of North Africa in 1830,
a process that was started by the French and was completed by the eve of World War I with the subjugation of
Libya (to Italy) and Morocco (to France).

Prior to the coming of the West, the Ottoman period in
North Africa was generally ameliorant. By the eighteenth
and nineteenth centuries, under the leadership of men such
as Muhammed Ibn 'Ali al-Sanusi, North African national
identification began to emerge as a fusion of Arab and
Berber values. However, the coming of Western influence,
epitomized by the Tunisian Organic Law of 1857, which defined the obligations of both the governors and the governed
for the first time in non-Islamic terms, was the herald of a
new era in North African history. The Maghrib basically never
revolted against the nominal control of a distant Ottoman
state. It did revolt against European colonialism. Largely as
a result of these revolts and two world wars, North Africa
began to emerge at the end of World War II as extensions
of the city-states that it had been earlier.

Egypt usually is separated from the Maghrib. Her long
civilization has made her unique in the history of North
Africa. In the study of nationalism in the Ottoman Empire,

she also stands alone because of the founding there of the Albanian-Turkish dynasty, which lasted a century and a half, and her seventy-six-year occupation by the British.

Although Mehmed Ali was not a nationalist, his rule in Syria and Egypt is important because for the first time there were planted the "seeds of a new national thought which began to grow within the framework of Islam, guided by Western principles."[24] Perhaps the first true Egyptian nationalist was Colonel 'Urabi, an Egyptian army officer whose origins were from the *fallahin*. His movement was crushed by the British landing in Alexandria in 1882. The rule of Evelyn Baring, later Lord Cromer, began the seventy-four years of British sojourn there. This prolonged period of British domination in Egypt, the non-Arab monarchy, the importance of the Suez Canal, the growing knowledge of the technologically superior West, and the increasing awareness by the Egyptians of their enforced inferiority led to a heightened desire to be free. The rise of nationalist leaders and their intrigues against the khedive and the occupiers did not bode well for the latter two. Largely as a result of this Egyptian national awakening, combined with the Suez fiasco of 1956, the British wrote an end to their colonial presence in Egypt.

In summary, the history of the dissolution of the Ottoman Empire is a complicated one. Very different forces at work in each of the three distinct areas of the empire eventually led to its destruction. The European provinces of the Ottoman Empire, because of their proximity to Western Europe, first discovered secular nationalism. This, combined with European aid, resulted in their separation from Istanbul.

Arab Asia gained its independence later than the Balkan areas. It was divided after World War I in order to enable the Europeans to rule more easily. In this area the resulting mandates over geographic Syria meant that the nation-state preceded secular nationalism. One should not view the Arab revolts of the nineteenth century and the Arab Revolt of World War I as being primarily nationalistic movements.

North Africa had a long history of allegiance to the Ottomans under their semi-independent rulers. Nationalism did not grow until the arrival of the Europeans and the division of North Africa among the British, French, Spanish, and Italians. Once again the nation-state preceded nationalism. North African nationalisms were not a factor in the dissolution of the Ottoman Empire.

Though each of the nation-states of the fallen Ottoman Empire became independent at a different time, all were influenced by secular, European nationalism. One may argue that the rise of this virulent nationalism is a primary cause for the strife and hostility in the former provinces: Turk against Greek, Kurd against Iraqi, Israeli against Palestinian, Egyptian against Libyan, to mention only the more obvious. Those of us who are students of the area sometimes secretly wish the Ottoman Humpty Dumpty could be put together again. Perhaps a more realistic hope is that nations will become more benign and that other philosophies may emerge to replace the xenophobic one we call nationalism. In any case, it is my desire that the series of essays presented here will open up new interpretations of the conflicts within the Ottoman Empire in the late nineteenth and early twentieth centuries, and that they will enable the reader to gain a broader view of the events that shook, and still shake, the Mediterranean and the Balkans.

1. David Calleo and Benjamin Rowland, *America and the World Political Economy* (Bloomington, Ind., 1973), p. 191.

2. Perhaps the two most important examples are the translations of the Turkish nationalist Ziya Gökalp (e.g., *The Principles of Turkism* [Leiden, 1968], trans. Robert Devereux) and George Antonius, *The Arab Awakening*, published in London in 1938, reissued in 1946, and now available in the United States in paperback. A naïvely anti-Ottoman point of view also pervades the film *Lawrence of Arabia*.

3. Some examples of careful revision of earlier nationalist claims may be found in Z. N. Zeine, *Arab-Turkish Relations and the Emergence of Arab Nationalism*, published in 1958, and his second edition of this work entitled *The Emergence of Arab Nationalism* (Beirut, 1966); C. Ernest Dawn, *From Ottomanism to Arabism: Essays on the Origins of Arab Nationalism* (Urbana, Ill., 1973); and Elie Kedourie,

The Chatham House Version, and Other Middle-Eastern Studies (New York, 1970).

4. Kemal Karpat, ed., *The Ottoman State and Its Place in World History* (Leiden, 1974), is an example.

5. Two of the more recent examples are Nikki R. Keddie, *Sayyid Jamal ad-Din "al-Afghani": A Political Biography* (Berkeley, Calif., 1972), and William L. Cleveland, *The Making of an Arab Nationalist: Ottomanism and Arabism in the Life and Thought of Sati' al-Husri* (Princeton, N.J., 1971).

6. Carlton J. Hayes, *Essays on Nationalism* (New York, 1937), p. 125.

7. Arnold Toynbee, *A Study of History* (London, 1939), 5:373.

8. George Antonius, *The Arab Awakening* (London, 1945), p. 13.

9. C. Ernest Dawn, "From Ottomanism to Arabism: The Origin of an Ideology," *Review of Politics* 23 (1961): 400.

10. George Kirk, "*The Arab Awakening* Reconsidered," *Middle Eastern Affairs* 13 (1962): 162-73.

11. Hans Kohn, *The Idea of Nationalism* (New York, 1961), p. 537.

12. Royal Institute of International Affairs, *Nationalism* (London, 1939), p. 91.

13. Elie Kedourie, *Nationalism in Asia and Africa* (Cleveland, 1970), p. 20.

14. Emile Marmorstein, "The Fate of Arabdom: A Study in Comparative Nationalism," *International Affairs* 25 (1949): 475.

15. Sylvia Haim, *Arab Nationalism: An Anthology* (Berkeley, Calif., 1962), p. 35.

16. Denis de Rivoyre, *Les Vrais Arabes et leur pays* (Paris, 1884), pp. 294-95.

17. Albert Hourani, *A Vision of History* (Beirut, 1961), p. 36.

18. Avedis Sanjian, *The Armenian Communities in Syria under Ottoman Dominion* (Cambridge, 1965), p. 275. This statement is probably incorrect. The Jewish *millet* was more pacific.

19. Kemal Atatürk, *A Speech Delivered by Ghazi Mustapha Kemal* (Leipzig, 1929), p. 578.

20. Z. N. Zeine, *Nashu' al-Qawmiyah al-'Arabiyah* [The Growth of Arab Nationalism] (Beirut, 1972), p. 47.

21. Nuri al-Sa'id, "Muhadarat 'an al-Harakat al-'Askariyah li al-Jaysh al-'Arabi fi al-Hijaz wa Suriya" [Lectures on the Military Movements of the Arab Army in the Hijaz and Syria] (mimeographed pamphlet, Baghdad, 1947), p. 5.

22. Zeine, *Nashu' al-Qawmiyah al-'Arabiyah*, p. 122.

23. Bernard Lewis, "The Return of Islam," *Commentary* 61 (January 1976): 39-49.

24. 'Abd al-Ghani al-Bushri, *al-Harakah al-Qawmiyah al-'Arabiyah* [The Arab Nationalist Movement] (Cairo, 1964), p. 134.

Roderic Davison

Nationalism as an Ottoman Problem and the Ottoman Response

Nationalism is a Western invention. Like another Western invention of the later eighteenth century, the steam engine, it has been a creative and unifying force. Nationalism has also been an immensely disruptive force. The Near East in modern times has found nationalism in its twin aspects to be favorable at times and also to be inimical. The Ottoman Empire, embracing within itself nearly the whole of the Near East through most of the nineteenth century, profited not at all from nationalism. It suffered. In the end, the empire was torn apart by nationalism's explosiveness.

The nationalist impulse was first felt within the empire in the period of the French Revolution and Napoleon. Nationalism thereafter made its way in the Ottoman lands from west to east, affecting peoples in approximately this chronological, as well as geographical, order: Greeks, Serbs, Romanians, Bulgarians, Armenians, Albanians (an exception to the geographical trend), Arabs, Kurds. The time span of this geographic peregrination of an ideology ranges from the last quarter of the eighteenth century to the first quarter of the twentieth. The Turks were among the last to be affected by nationalism. A few individuals felt its urgings in the late nineteenth century, but not until after 1908 and in all probability not until 1913 did many Turks think of themselves as Turks, or nationalists.

By that time the Russo-Turkish War of 1877-78 and the first Balkan War of 1912-13 had taken away all the empire's European lands except Istanbul and a strip along the Straits. Then the war of 1914-18 and the Arab Revolt it spawned tore away most of the Asian lands, leaving only Anatolia in Turkish possession. The Osmanli dynasty was not finally deposed until 1923, but the empire it had created and ruled was mostly gone by 1918. Great Power diplomatic and military intervention and outright war had unquestionably played a crucial role in the empire's dismemberment. But had there been only Turks within the empire, had there been no non-Turkish nationalities, had there been no anti-Turkish nationalisms, the probability of such dismemberment would have been far smaller. In the end, the Ottoman Empire was killed by its own heterogeneous nature and by the nationalisms that developed within it.

In a steadily losing struggle, Ottoman rulers and statesmen fought against both the prospect of dismemberment and, from time to time, its actual occurrence. Before the last quarter of the eighteenth century, the Ottoman domains had already dwindled significantly—Hungary, Transylvania, the Crimea, and much of the northern shore of the Black Sea had been lost. The Ottomans acknowledged these losses in the treaties of Karlowitz (1699) and Küchük Kanarji (1774). These defeats by Hapsburg and Russian military power preceded the age of modern nationalism. Then came the Greek revolt, followed by other nationalist movements for autonomy and independence. The new movements posed enormous problems for Ottoman statesmen, who were already engaged in efforts, sporadic and inadequate though they proved to be, to strengthen the empire. Domestic reform and reorganization were essential, in their view, so that the empire could better

confront the external and internal threats. Now the Ottoman
statesmen had to face nationalist separatism too.

The problem can profitably be examined as it presented
itself to Ottoman statesmen in the mid-nineteenth century,
and specifically in the two or three decades following the end
of the Crimean War. By that time the Ottoman Empire had
thrice been saved from destruction by the intervention of
European powers: in 1833 and again in 1839-41, when the
ambitious expansionism of Mehmed Ali of Egypt had been
thwarted, and in 1854-56, when the Russian military threat
had been checked by the Anglo-French alliance with the
Ottoman Empire, joined also by Piedmont. By 1856, then, the
Porte had some respite from the menace of the local strong
man and the outside invader, and could turn its attention
to the still-growing nationalist revivals among various minority peoples, as well as to reforms intended to strengthen the
whole empire. By 1856 Greece alone had gained complete
independence from the sultan, and it was a small Greece
that included only a portion of the Greeks who were under
the Porte's rule. In Serbia and in the Romanian principalities of Moldavia and Wallachia, each of which enjoyed a large
degree of autonomy, the nationalism of Serbs and Romanians
grew apace. Newer stirrings arose also among Bulgarians
and Armenians.

The natural instinct of Ottoman statesmen in this situation
was to reaffirm the integrity of the empire. In the first article
of the Constitution of 1876, this nineteenth-century Ottoman leitmotiv was most succinctly stated: "The Ottoman Empire is a unit, including its present territories and parts and
privileged provinces, which can be divided at no time and
for no cause whatever."[1] But simple affirmation was, of course,
insufficient. It stated only a principle, not a program or a plan
of action.

In fact, it did not even define the problem posed by rising
nationalisms. What, in fact, was the situation of the Ottoman Empire that made nationalism so great a problem?
Only against the background of that situation can the re-

sponses of the Ottoman statesmen to nationalism be understood. Perhaps by examining the diverse population of the
empire we can find an answer. The Ottoman Empire at about
mid-century is usually considered to have had a population
of between 35,000,000 and 36,000,000.[2] A semi-official estimate of 1867 put the total population at 40,000,000.[3] A rea-
sonably careful calculation of 1876, based on whatever figures
had been published officially and unofficially for the 1860s and
the early 1870s, produced a total of approximately 38,500,000.[4]
In the absence of any general census based on scientific
principles, and even of accurate local counts for most areas,
such intelligent approximations must suffice, though the general margin of error may be 20 percent and, in individual
areas, greater. The census of 1844 for conscription purposes,
with all its recognized faults, served as the usual basis for
the estimates, supplemented by occasional later counts in one
locality or another. There was in the Ottoman Empire a strong
tendency to hide from the census-takers, because people believed—correctly—that taxation and military conscription would
follow; the 36,000,000 figure may therefore be low. On the
other hand, the Ottoman Empire was not yet experiencing
the extraordinary growth rates that had come to Western
Europe in the later eighteenth and especially in the first half
of the nineteenth centuries. For comparison, at mid-century,
the population of Great Britain was 22,000,000; European
Russia's was 60,000,000.[5]

Ottoman census figures did not, however, reveal nationality
or linguistic differences, excepting in unusual cases and where
there was some coincidence between linguistic and religious
dividing lines. The count was made by geographic locality
and by religion. This is clear in Enver Ziya Karal's description of what he calls the first attempt at a census on modern
lines, in 1831—not of the whole empire, but of Anatolia and
Rumelia together. It was a count of males for conscription
purposes (as well as a census of property). Gypsies and
nomadic tribes were tallied separately within totals for
Islam, but Christians were tallied neither by race nor by lan-

guage as a rule.[6] Figures on nationalities within the Ottoman Empire therefore usually are derived from estimates by
Europeans, who sometimes, because of economic or political
interest or religious or humanitarian sympathy, tended to
accept the largest possible estimates put forth by representatives of one or another national group within the empire.[7]
Nevertheless, such estimates have to be used as the basis for
outlining the nationality problem.

The calculations of Ubicini and Pavet de Courteille as of
1876 are as careful as any for the mid nineteenth century,
and are reproduced in table one to illustrate the division
of the empire's peoples into nationalities. These authors actually use the term *race*, an even fuzzier concept than that
of nationality, but what they mean by it is groups set apart
by language and by historic origin and common tradition.
They are really, then, speaking of nationalities, which they
try to group by linguistic kinship.[8]

TABLE ONE

FIGURES ON NATIONALITIES WITHIN THE OTTOMAN EMPIRE

Turkish group (14,020,000)	Ottoman Turks	13,500,000
	Turkomans (including Yürüks)	300,000
	Tatars	220,000
Greco-Latin group (3,520,000)	Greeks	2,100,000
	Kutzo-Vlachs (Tsintsars)	220,000
	Albanians (Ghegs and Tosks)	1,200,000
Slavic group (4,550,000)	Serbo-Croatians	1,500,000
	Bulgarians	3,000,000
	Cossacks	32,000
	Lipovans (Old Believers)	18,000
Georgian group (1,020,000)	Circassians	1,000,000
	Lazes	20,000
Indian group (212,000)	Gypsies	212,000
Persian group (3,620,000)	Armenians	2,500,000
	Kurds	1,000,000
	Druze, Mutawälis, Nusayris, and Yazidis	120,000
Semites (1,611,000)	Jews	158,000
	Arabs (a pure guess)	1,000,000
	Syrian-Chaldaeans	160,000
	Maronites	293,000

To these figures must then be added the populations of
the so-called privileged or tributary provinces—Moldavia and
Wallachia, with 4,425,000, mostly Romanians; Serbia, with
1,215,000, almost entirely Serbs; Egypt with 3,350,000 and
Tunis with 950,000, in both cases mostly Arabs.[9] The totals
shown in table one would then be altered for Serbs and Arabs
to read 2,715,000 Serbo-Croatians and 5,300,000 Arabs.[10]
The authors, relatively favorable to the Turks, may have
selected figures indicating a larger Turkish population and
a smaller count of other nationalities than some others would
agree with. Perhaps the Turkish population was between ten
and twelve million only. Their estimate is in itself, however,
of value in helping to see the nationality picture through
Ottoman eyes.

The figures show that no nationality group was a majority
within the empire. The Ottoman Turks were 35 percent of the
total population of 38,493,000. The next largest groups, in
descending order, were Arabs (13.8 percent), Romanians (11.4
percent), Bulgarians (7.8 percent), Serbo-Croatians (7 per-
cent), Armenians (6.5 percent), Greeks (5.5 percent), Albanians (3.1 percent), Kurds (2.6 percent), and Circassians (2.6
percent). These nine minorities, with the Ottoman Turks,
constituted most of the empire's population, and the other
fourteen nationalities in the table together formed only about
five percent. The diversity of peoples within the empire of
the Ottomans was as great as that within the empires of the
Romanovs and the Hapsburgs.

It was not only the number and diversity of nationalities
that rendered the Ottoman situation complex, but also their
geographic distribution. Had each of the nationalities been
grouped in a compact mass, intermixed with no other, the
situation would in some ways have been simpler—although the
tendency for each nationality to become autonomous or independent might in that case have been speeded up. But com-
pactness was the rule only in some provinces. There were
fairly large areas in European Turkey where Serbs, Romanians, Bulgarians, Albanians, and Greeks lived in compact

groups. But Turks formed large minority groups in some localities, and Tatar and Circassian refugees from Russian persecution formed other enclaves. Fringe areas were very mixed, as for instance where Albanian met Greek. The classic example of population mixtures is Macedonia, so varied that its name has become enshrined in European menus to mean a total mélange—"une salade Macédoine," or "una Macedonia di frutta." Here Turks, Bulgars, Greeks, and Serbs vied for dominance, along with some Vlachs. The empire's capital, Istanbul, was itself a huge mixture—perhaps a million people, including the suburbs, of whom about half were Turks, followed in numbers by Armenians, Greeks, Jews, Hellenes (citizens of Greece), and Europeans.[11]

Anatolia, unlike the Balkan peninsula, had a Turkish majority, but here again intermixture was prevalent. Large numbers of Greeks lived in western and northern coastal regions, especially around Izmir. In a number of eastern districts, the largest single nationality group was either Armenian or Kurd, although in many cases this largest group was still a minority of less than 50 percent. The mixing process had come about through immigration, warfare, settlement of tribes, migration within Anatolia, and forced or planned resettlement carried out by earlier sultans. Sir Edwin Pears, a resident of the empire for over thirty years, wrote in 1911 of an earlier visit to a town of about 10,000 population named Bardizag that was purely Armenian, located in Anatolia near Ismid, far from the Armenian highlands where most of that people lived. He recalled another experience:

> Riding over the Bithynian hills a quarter of a century ago with two Turkish friends, we found in a remote mountain valley a fairly thriving Armenian village called New Town, or Yenikeuy, of probably three thousand persons. Neither at Bardizag nor at Yenikeuy were we able to obtain definite information as to how colonies of Armenians were found in such isolated places. The only answer obtainable was that their ancestors had been brought there many generations ago by the Turks.[12]

With such a distribution of nationalities, no clear lines could be drawn to separate them. Strife among them would be disastrous, both to them and to the empire. Obviously the duty of an Ottoman statesman would be to find means to obviate such strife and, if possible, to repress or to moderate the stirrings of national consciousness among the nationalities.

But what was a nationality? Some of the smaller groups in the table above appear to be, primarily, religious groups rather than nationalities. Furthermore, many of the individuals counted in a national group, particularly among the larger ones, often could not or did not speak the national language; yet language is the single most important criterion in determining nationality. "In Crete, Greek is the only language spoken, even by the Turks," reports Ubicini.[13] Were they then Turks? Many Armenians and Greeks, on the other hand, spoke only Turkish. Were they then not Turks? An American missionary working among these two peoples in western Turkey estimated that a good half of the Greeks and Armenians did not know their own languages.[14] "The Armenians generally speak Turkish," says Ubicini, or an Armenian heavily loaded with Turkish words; only the literate and the schools use pure Armenian.[15] This is the evidence of the 1870s. Though in both the Greek and the Armenian communities there was a revival of learning and education in the vernacular during the nineteenth century, especially in its second half, and though the use of the Armenian and Greek languages increased, ignorance of them was still widespread in the early twentieth century. Pears noted that "there are many Armenian villages where only Turkish is spoken, and many Greek villages where the inhabitants have forgotten the speech of their race."[16] An experience of his about 1905 makes the point more vivid. At a village near Iznik, the historic Greek-Byzantine city of Nicaea, Pears attended a Greek Orthodox church service. The service was, of course, in Greek. Then the congregation went outdoors, where the priest conducted a special prayer service for rain. The prayers were in Turkish, read by the priest from sheets of paper.

Later the priest explained to Pears that "his flock could not understand Greek." The Greek liturgy they knew, through long familiarity, but anything unusual had to be translated from Greek into Turkish so they could understand.[17] Since Pears was himself a Greek scholar, rather Hellenophile and anti-Turkish, his testimony is even more significant.

The point is, of course, that the parishioners called themselves Greek because they were of the Greek religion. Their church was the Greek Orthodox church. In the Near East the traditional dividing lines among people were religious, not national. The millet, the religious community, to which an individual belonged was the determining factor in his self-identification and in his identification by others. If there was any "nation" or "nationality" to which an individual belonged, it was his millet. Non-Muslims were Armenians, Greeks, Jews, Catholics, or Protestants. The millet groupings were political as well as religious. From the time of Mehmed the Conqueror, the millet had become institutionalized in the Ottoman Empire as a quasi-autonomous civil unit that had its own legal, judicial, fiscal, and educational as well as charitable and religious functions. The Greek and the Armenian patriarchs of Istanbul, and the grand rabbi of the same city, were recognized by the sultan as heads of their communities—civil communities defined by religious persuasion. Final authority always remained in the hands of the sultan and his government, but the quasi-autonomy of the non-Muslim millets continued until the empire's demise. It is significant that the meaning of the word millet itself began to change in the nineteenth century, almost imperceptibly, until in the twentieth it came to mean nation and nationality. Religion and nation, sect and nationality, were thoroughly confused and intertwined.[18]

Experience in the mid nineteenth century shows the confusion. There were numerous instances of individuals leaving one millet and joining another for essentially political reasons—to flee oppression by the millet hierarchs, to escape a trial for misdeeds, or to avoid taxation.[19] Terminology of the

same period also shows the confusion. Both Europeans and
Ottoman subjects frequently used the term *nation* to desig-
nate a millet. Various Kizilbash "have repeatedly requested
to be received into the 'Protestant nation'," reported an
American missionary.[20] A local Armenian notable at Siirt
planned to lead 130 families from the traditional church to
make a "Protestant nation."[21] In 1857 an Ottoman Armenian,
who had been to college in New York, wrote with scorn
of the Levantines in Beyoğlu—"the race of Perotes," as he
called them—who thought that their Catholicism made them
Europeans on "the Oriental principle that religion and nationality are synonymous."[22] He recounted the story of an
Armenian from Ankara who went to Trieste, then in Hapsburg Austria, on business. "On his arrival there, he was asked
by the officer of the quarantine what nation he belonged to.
His unsophistical and prompt answer was 'Catholic.' The
officer, somewhat puzzled at this novel nationality, reminded
him that they were also all Catholics there, but called themselves Austrians or Italians—now, what is your nation? There-
upon our worthy friend unflinchingly reiterated that he was a
Catholic; nothing else but a Catholic; for they now had,
through the interference of the French ambassador, a Patriarch of their own, and were recognized as a nation!
meaning a community."[23] An Armenian Catholic millet had
in fact been recognized by the Porte in 1830; the pope was
its religious head, but a patriarch in Istanbul was the civil
head of the community.[24] In this sense, then, the Armenian
at Trieste was correct—his nation was the Catholic Armenian
nation. He was, of course, also an Ottoman subject, which
is what the quarantine officer wanted to know. What he did
not say is most significant: he made no claim that his nationality was Armenian.

   The mixture of languages and religions among the peoples
of the empire was even more complex than has so far been
indicated, for two reasons. First, few inhabitants of the empire
were of pure racial stock; successive waves of invasion and
migration over millennia had produced many mixtures.[25] In

addition, there were religious combinations, syncretisms of all kinds, and different varieties of crypto-Muslims.[26] The Ottoman Empire was an altogether amazing conglomeration of peoples. What held it together?

The key to whatever unity the Ottoman Empire possessed was the Ottoman government. By the nineteenth century the Osmanli dynasty had ruled for five centuries over the heterogeneous empire. It was served by an Ottoman military organization and by an Ottoman bureaucracy. Members of this ruling group thought of themselves not as Turks, nor as supporters of a Turkish state, but as Ottomans who served state and religion—the Ottoman state and the Islamic religion. The state was never called "Turkey" except by Europeans; it was known as the *devlet-i aliye*, the "exalted state," or the *memalik-i osmaniye*, the "Ottoman dominions," or by other equally non-national names. Although the dynasty was of Turkish origin, and although Ottoman Turkish was the basic language of the empire, the ruling group used the term *Turk* as one of opprobrium, to indicate a boorish or uneducated person. The Osmanli elite was infused over the course of centuries with non-Turkish blood from many quarters, particularly through the system of slave administrators that selected only non-Muslim boys as its recruits. The best of them rose by ability, training, and performance—and also by favoritism and corruption as time passed—to the highest military and civil posts. An analysis of the origins of a group of Ottoman elite, the 215 grand vezirs of the empire, showed 78 Turks, 31 Albanians, 11 Bosnians, 11 Georgians, 9 Abkhasians, 4 Greeks, 3 Circassians, 3 Croats, 2 Armenians, 2 Italians, and one each from several other peoples, plus many doubtful or unknown. Among the doubtful, three were perhaps Arabs.[27]

To the non-national elite of the Ottoman Empire, the rest of its inhabitants were traditionally, before the nineteenth century, the *reaya*, the subjects. The term included peoples of all languages and all creeds, Muslim and non-Muslim. They were not differentiated by language or nationality, in official eyes. The *reaya* were taxed, but the ruling class, the *askeriye*, were not. As late as 1774, the whole mass of subjects was still labeled *reaya*.[28] But even then the use of the term was changing, and by the early nineteenth century, it denoted only the non-Muslim subjects of the sultan, with more bitter connotations of second-class status than it had had before.[29] Still, though non-Muslims were now lumped together as a group in the eyes of the elite, there was no distinction made among them by nationality. Keeping the *reaya* distinct from the people of Islam was, however, in the eyes of Ottoman statesmen, an important aspect of good government; for the classical rules of government postulated that all classes of people should stay in their places. In the early nineteenth century, the *reaya* had freedom of worship, they could be educated, they could grow rich, but they were not to be confounded with the Muslims. Various outward marks kept the lines clear. An English resident of Istanbul reported in the 1830s: "The various nations that compose the population of Turkey are all distinguished by peculiarities which are not left to their option, but which are strictly prescribed to them, that there may be no amalgamation, and the Osmanli may be marked everywhere by separate and distinct characters from their Rayas. Not only the manner of their turban and the colour of their slippers distinguish them from their masters, but the hue of their houses."[30]

Whatever distinctions the Osmanli ruling elite made among the *reaya* were along the familiar religious lines. There was a tacitly accepted order of precedence among the major millets. After the Muslims, sometimes referred to as the *millet-i hakime*, or "ruling millet," came first the Greeks, then the Armenians, and then the Jews.[31] The millet system was a part of good government, in the Ottoman view; it provided for each group of people its proper place. It gave each group its civil identity, kept them separate, and helped eliminate quarreling among the *reaya*.

In the nineteenth century, instead of recognizing nationalist groups, the Porte recognized additional millets, several of them splinter Catholic groups in communion with Rome (uniates). In addition to the Armenian Catholic millet (1830) already mentioned, to which were attached for civil purposes the Chaldaean church and the Uniate Syrians (1844), the Greek Uniates (Melkites) were recognized in 1847 with their own patriarch, and a small church of Bulgar Uniates was also recognized in 1860 by the Porte. The Latin (Roman Catholic) millet was recognized in 1840 with its own civil head, and the Protestant millet similarly in 1850.[32] The growing number of separate millets did not completely avoid intestine quarrels that bothered the Ottoman government as well as the millet involved. One such was the Hassunist controversy that split the Armenian Catholics, in the years after 1869, over the issues of papal infallibility and control from Rome. Another was the Bulgarian agitation, at about the same time, to secure a church organization separate from the Greek. Nevertheless, the millet system was a workable system. It helped maintain Ottoman stability.

The millet system was workable, within the Ottoman system, because it was suited to the mosaic pattern of peoples. Members of the Greek Orthodox millet could live in Belgrade, Rhodes, Istanbul, Trabzon, Beirut, or Alexandria—it did not matter; millet rules applied to them. It may seem curious that in the nineteenth century, at least until 1878, the Porte dealt with the millets through the Ministry of Foreign Affairs —almost as if they were foreign nations.[33] That also did not matter, for these "nations" did not require solid blocks of territory where the communicants could live in a contiguous mass. It was enough that they had the same church and the same law, which touched them as persons, not as residents of a given circumscribed area.

Modern nationalism, however, could not coexist with a millet system. Instead, it required one territory—usually viewed in emotional terms as "homeland" or "sacred soil" —and one law. Karl Renner, the Austrian Social Democrat, at about the beginning of this century, proposed that nationalities in the Austro-Hungarian Empire be treated like churches; each citizen could choose whatever nationality he wanted to belong to and could send his children to schools of that nationality.[34] Such a policy would make nationalities into millets, but in neither the Hapsburg nor the Ottoman domains were nationalistic peoples likely to be content without a country of their own. This was the challenge that the Ottoman statesmen faced. Unless they could check it, nationalism would not simply lop one or two outlying pieces off the empire. Nationalism, carried to its logical conclusion of separate national states, would tear pieces out of the Ottoman mosaic. It would destroy the government of the Ottoman dynasty and elite. It would rend Istanbul and kill the empire.

The nineteenth-century Ottoman statesmen were aware of the danger; but how fully they comprehended the nature of modern nationalism, irrational and emotional as it was, is a question that cannot be precisely answered. One gets the impression from Ottoman documents and histories that they did not fully understand, even though they well knew that national feeling helped to carry Piedmont along to the unification of Italy, and Prussia to the creation of Germany. But within their own dominions, they saw nationalist protests or actual risings in terms of insurrection or rebellion, *isyan* or *ihtilal*. This is quite natural. There is little evidence that the Ottomans understood the powerful nationalist ferment in the revolts. They tended to see them, often quite rightly, as discontent with local conditions or officials. Sometimes they used the names of the peoples involved, more often of their districts—Bulgaria, Serbia, Montenegro, Bosnia, Herzegovina; but when lumping the peoples together, they spoke of "Christians" rather than of nationalities. They knew what Panslavism was and referred to Slav sentiments. But in this, as in all nationalist ferment, they usually saw the work of outside agitators—Russians, Greeks, or Austrians very often. Even the Polish and Magyar refugees who flooded into the Ottoman Empire and were accorded asylum were regarded, evidently, less as nationalists than as anti-Russians. The welcome and protection granted them gained great glory for the Islamic millet, said the historian and statesman Cevdet Pasha; he did not see the event in national terms.[35] Perhaps Kechecizade Mehmed Fuad Pasha did understand. He was the most Europeanized of the top-ranking statesmen of the mid nineteenth century, followed nationalist developments in Europe, and wrote a memorandum on the danger that such concepts posed to the Ottoman Empire. But Fuad was one of the few, or perhaps unique. What most statesmen saw was Christian discontent, Great Power intrigue, or rebellion fueled by agents from without.[36]

In the face of the danger of dismemberment, whether or not it was conceptualized as a nationalist danger, Ottoman statesmen developed a number of responses. One may classify seven of these, some more important than others; also, several could be used in combination. Although no Ottoman statesman was ever conscious that he had seven responses at his command, our somewhat artificial analysis may be helpful in unraveling complex historical events. A concrete example at the end will attempt to reweave the strands in an actual historical situation.

The first and most important Ottoman response to nationalism was the effort to combat separatist movements by proclaiming the equality of all Ottoman subjects regardless of creed. This doctrine of Ottomanism, *Osmanlilik*, had originated in the era of Sultan Mahmud II, but found its most formal expression in the *Hatt-i Sherif* of Gülhane of 1839. Reaffirmed and broadened in the *Hatt-i Hümayun* of 1856, the concept of *Osmanlilik* was a little more rapidly, though rather erratically, translated into fact during the ensuing two decades. Restrictions on the dress of non-Muslims were removed, the foundations of secular legal and judicial systems that would apply to all subjects were laid, non-Muslims became regular members of governmental advisory councils, and a few secular schools accepting Muslims and non-Muslims on an equal basis were opened. The term *reaya* itself was now forbidden in official usage.[37] Differences of

religious belief and practice were respected; but before the
law and in opportunity for public employment, all Ottoman
subjects were, in theory, to be equal. Fuad Pasha, among
others, believed, or tried to believe, that equal rights and
opportunities for all would thwart separatist nationalisms.[38]

The culmination of the drive for *Osmanlilik* came with the
adoption of a written constitution setting up a chamber of
deputies, to include representatives of all peoples of the empire. For some time a small group of dissident writers had
advocated such a parliament. Namik Kemal, the most prominent spokesman for these New Ottomans, as they called themselves, argued that a parliament would work to the salvation
of the empire even if it contained representatives of seventy-
two different languages, with varied backgrounds and interests.[39]

By 1876 some top-ranking statesmen, led by Midhat Pasha,
elaborated the constitution at a time when open revolt had
again broken out in the Balkans. Article 8 stipulated that
all subjects of whatever religion or sect were to be called
Osmanlis, without exception. The constitution then went on
to elaborate the rights of all Osmanlis.[40] This progress toward
formal equality of all Ottoman subjects in a legal and political
sense was accompanied by an effort to inculcate a more
emotional attachment to the empire. Its people were so
diverse that one could hardly speak of Ottoman nationalism
as a possibility, but Ottoman patriotism was perhaps possible. Some of the leading statesmen and journalists of the
1870s encouraged devotion to the common fatherland.[41]

A second response by the Ottoman statesmen was to confirm and even to extend the rights and privileges of minority
groups—but treating them as millets and not as nationalities.
"All the privileges and spiritual immunities" formerly promised to Christian and other non-Muslim religious communities were reaffirmed in the *Hatt-i Hümayun* of 1856.[42] More
than that, each millet's internal structure was to be reformed
to make it more responsive to its members and, conversely,
less subject to autocratic control by its clerical hierarchy.

Such reforms were carried out in the Greek, Armenian, and Jewish millets in the 1860s.[43] It seems strange that lines of religious distinction among the empire's peoples should thus be retraced and reemphasized at exactly the same time as the doctrine of *Osmanlilik* attempted to promote a secular equality among adherents of all creeds. The contradiction is due in part to unresolved conflicts of attitude among Ottoman statesmen and in part to the pressure of European powers on those statesmen for reconfirmation of the rights of Christians within the empire. But it is obvious that the statesmen hoped to forestall any greater discontent among non-Muslims, and thus any separatist moves, by reaffirmation of religious freedom and millet privileges.

This reaffirmation of religious rights is closely connected to the third Ottoman response, which was to try to prevent the European powers from meddling in Ottoman domestic affairs. Such meddling was a major problem for Ottoman statesmen. The Great Power interference often came in the form of diplomatic representations or demands in favor of religious minorities in the empire. The religious minorities were actual or potential nationalities. Although France, Austria, and Britain had often intervened in Ottoman affairs on the grounds that they were securing justice for a religious minority, the greatest transgressor on this score was Russia. Her claims to the right to protect all Greek Orthodox subjects of the sultan—claims based on enormous stretching of clauses in the 1774 treaty of Küchük Kanarji—had in the Ottoman view been the direct cause of the Crimean War in 1853. To avoid this sort of situation in the future, the Ottoman statesmen agreed to issue the *Hatt-i Hümayun* of 1856, guaranteeing Christian privileges. They hoped to secure in the peace treaty an explicit renunciation by Russia of all pretensions to a right of protection or intervention, but this they were unable to do.[44]

One article of the Paris peace treaty of 1856, however, gave Ottoman statesmen a diplomatic weapon that they used thereafter as effectively as they could to ward off foreign intervention. Article 9 mentioned the *Hatt-i Hümayun*, and then stated that the communication of the reform decree "cannot, in any case, give to the said Powers the right to interfere, either collectively or separately, in the relations of His Majesty the Sultan with his subjects, nor in the internal administration of his Empire."[45] From 1856 onward the invocation of article 9 was a standard Ottoman response to the Great Powers when they threatened to intervene in support of a religious or national group within the sultan's domains.[46]

A fourth Ottoman response, parallel but separate, consisted of a series of efforts to curb foreign embassies and consulates in their practice of extending protection to individual Ottoman subjects by issuing to such subjects an official patent of protection (*berat*) or a foreign passport. This sort of interference in favor of individuals had the effect of granting to members of minority groups in the empire extraterritorial exemption from many Ottoman laws and taxes—exemption that was properly allowed under the capitulations granted only to foreigners or to Ottoman subjects who were genuine employees of foreign embassies or consulates. The practice of issuing such *berats* had become so common as to be a formidable abuse of the capitulatory system. It afforded a privileged sanctuary for crime, and even for political and nationalistic agitation. A British consul, judge of the supreme consular court in Istanbul about the time of the Crimean War, later wrote his impression that there were "little short of a million" in the Levant who were "so-called British protected subjects."[47] This is a fantastic figure, very likely too high, yet it indicates the magnitude of the problem. An American diplomat estimated that 50,000 individuals, born Ottoman subjects, had acquired foreign nationality in Istanbul alone.[48] Ottoman statesmen and patriotic reformers were understandably bitter about the foreign protégés among Ottoman subjects.[49]

Beginning in the 1860s, the Porte tried to curb the abuse by issuing regulations concerning the protégés of foreign powers and also by asking each foreign consulate in Ottoman territory for a precise list of its nationals and protégés. When the Greek consul at Izmir failed to provide the list, claiming lack of instructions and a large number of nationals under his care, the Porte complained that "it is precisely this Consulate which is prodigal in issuing certificates of protection" to Ottoman subjects.[50] These measures were followed by a new law on nationality in 1869. In addition to setting up modern secular criteria for nationality, it stipulated that all persons with domicile in Ottoman territory would be considered Ottoman subjects in the absence of proof to the contrary, and that no Ottoman subject could acquire foreign citizenship without the Porte's consent.[51] The new law became a potent weapon in the Porte's arsenal of defenses against nationalism. Shortly, a commission was created to inquire into the status of those who claimed foreign protection.[52]

A fifth response was the Porte's effort to counteract the influence of one of the Great Powers in support of autonomy or independence for a nationality by siding with one or more of the other powers. The Porte was not strong enough militarily to play one power against another, but it could try to use the natural divisions among the powers to its own advantage. Generally, in the post-Crimean period, this meant opposing Russia by reliance on Britain, Austria, or France. On occasion France also endangered Ottoman integrity, and Britain or Austria would be the main Ottoman resource. But when the Great Powers found themselves in agreement, the Porte was left helpless.

There are numerous examples of the foregoing Ottoman tactic. In 1856-57, the Porte relied on Austria and Britain for aid in combatting the Romanian nationalist separatism, which was favored, for varying reasons, by Russia, France, Prussia, and Piedmont. The desire of Romanians in the two principalities of Moldavia and Wallachia for "union and a foreign prince" seemed at first to have been thwarted. Then when the governments of Queen Victoria and Napoleon III composed their differences, the Turks had no option but to agree, in 1857-58, to two autonomous and separate but "United

Principalities," which were in fact the kernel of a soon-to-be independent Romania.[53] In 1876-78 this scenario of Great Power disagreement followed by unity was virtually reversed. After anti-Turkish nationalist risings in the Balkans, the Naval Arsenal Conference[54] of the Great Powers at the end of 1876 unanimously elaborated a plan for Balkan administration that included a very large autonomous Bulgaria composed of two segments. When the Turks rejected the plan in 1877, they were left without support in the face of a Russian attack designed to impose it (and more). But while the Turks held up the Russian advance for half a year, British and Austrian views changed, so that in 1878 the Porte received backing from those two powers in reducing the size of the self-governing Bulgaria created for this renascent nationality. The Ottoman tactic was then to court Britain, when the powers were split, and to seek her aid at the Berlin Congress.[55]

Ironically, the Porte should not even have needed to solicit aid from Britain, or from France or Austria, for that matter, when Ottoman integrity was threatened. For these three powers had in 1856 signed a treaty undertaking to "guarantee, jointly and severally, the independence and the integrity of the Ottoman Empire."[56] None of the three powers honored its word in the crisis of 1875 to 1878, when the empire was under severe attack from within and without.

Retreat, strategic or final, was a sixth Ottoman response in the face of nationalist movements. As indicated above, it was most likely to occur when the Porte could find no backing among the Great Powers. Examples are many. In 1859, for instance, the Porte was unable to void the cleverly contrived election of one and the same prince by each Romanian principality, but had to accept it. By 1862 the Porte had to concede the merger of the two Romanian legislative assemblies into one. Strategic retreat and acceptance of the accomplished fact at least kept the united principalities within the empire; a confrontation, if provoked, might have brought enough Great Power support for the Romanians to cut all ties between themselves and the Porte.[57] Similarly, when the autonomous Bulgaria and the separate Eastern Rumelia, created by the Congress of Berlin, declared their union under Prince Alexander Battenberg in 1885, the Porte did not dare annul the union even though it had the military strength to do so.[58] There were also occasions when a direct threat by a Great Power provoked an Ottoman retreat: thus the armistice to save the Serbs, imposed by Russian ultimatum in the fall of 1876, just when the Ottoman army was thrashing the rebellious Serbian principality.[59] Discretion prevailed over valor in such cases.

Whenever possible, however, the Ottoman answer to nationalist subversion was to repress it with whatever force was necessary. This, the seventh response, was sometimes augmented by granting extraordinary powers, for civil and administrative reform as well as for military action, to a special high commissioner sent out from the capital. The use of force was of course not confined to the repression of nationalist movements, but extended to the repression of rebellion that occurred because of the ambitions of a local strongman, because of local grievances against provincial administrators, because of tribal discontent, or for whatever reason. Sometimes, an insurrection arising solely from local grievances took on nationalist overtones as it spread. Ottoman histories of the nineteenth century are full of stories of rebellion and their repression, both in Arab areas and in Balkan lands. But until the War of 1914, Arab risings were local rather than nationalist in character, or were the work of politically ambitious individuals. In the Balkans, by contrast, local grievances and nationalist sentiment were often intermingled. The latter became stronger and more frequently dominant in the post-Crimean period. Whatever the case, the Porte used its armed forces against rebels—against Montenegrins, Herzegovinians, Bosnians, Serbs, Bulgars, and Greeks. As a rule, regular troops were used, but irregulars were occasionally employed also. In 1876, in the supression of revolutionary Bulgarian terrorism, the Porte used some *bashibozuks*, whose devastating actions became known in Europe as the "Bulgarian massacres." Sometimes the Porte was slow to act, as against the rising in Bosnia and Herzegovina in 1875, or the Bulgar rising in 1876. Sometimes action was stopped by the Great Powers, as when the Turkish advance into Serbia was halted in 1876. As a rule, however, the Porte fought back whenever it could.[60]

There were, then, seven identifiable Ottoman responses to nationalism—seven veils that attempted to clothe decently a body politic entirely made up of ethnic minorities. None of the responses proved sufficient by itself or in combination with others, and the empire disintegrated ultimately into its national components.

Yet at times the combined Ottoman responses to nationalism were at least partially effective. The events of 1866 to 1868 offer an example. The situation then was serious in many ways. First, the Romanian principalities moved a step closer to independence by electing, without Ottoman consent, a foreign prince, Karl of Hohenzollern, who left Germany in disguise and stole across Austria to Bucharest. Then, Prince Michael of Serbia secretly hatched a scheme for an anti-Turkish Balkan alliance and publicly mobilized Serbian and European sentiment to press the Turks to evacuate the last of their garrison from Belgrade. Thereafter, an actual revolt, though not well planned, broke out among Bulgarians. A much larger revolt, meanwhile, erupted among Greeks on the Island of Crete. It was fed by money and volunteers from independent Greece, and some of the rebel leaders demanded *enosis* with that country. Sentiment in Greece became so aroused that irregular and regular armed forces from Greece began to raid nearby Turkish frontier areas. Greeks within and without the Ottoman Empire began again to dream their *megali idea*, the creation or re-creation of a great Greek state like the Byzantine Empire. European powers also were concerned by these events. Two of them, France and Russia, pressed the Porte vigorously for extensive concessions to Christian minorities and even for the outright cession of Crete and other provinces. The solution advanced by Russia called for carving the empire into autonomous nationality-based regions.

In the face of these challenges, the Porte's responses were varied. First and continuously, through statements and reform measures, it made more emphatic than ever the doctrine of *Osmanlilik*, of equality among all the empire's peoples. The most remarkable expression of this policy was in a memorandum written for the guidance of the government in 1867 by Ali Pasha, the grand vezir, wherein he advocated the "fusion" of all Ottoman subjects so that the only remaining distinctions among them would be in purely religious matters.[61] Ali's reasoning was based not only on principle but explicitly on remedying the situation in which the empire found itself. At the same time the Porte reaffirmed its observance of all special privileges of the non-Muslim millets. This second Ottoman response was enshrined in a memorandum, sent to the Great Powers in 1867 by Fuad Pasha, that reaffirmed the observance of millet rights and went on to adduce evidence of the principle of *Osmanlilik* in practice![62]

With these responses came diplomatic efforts to prevent the intervention of foreign powers in any of the domestic Ottoman troubles, and especially in the Cretan revolt. Article 9 of the Treaty of Paris of 1856 was invoked early; as Ali Pasha wrote to the Ottoman chargé d'affaires in Saint Petersburg, it "formally forbade all immixtion into the internal affairs of the Empire" outside of matters specifically designated in the treaty.[63] Further, to ward off intervention, Sultan Abdülaziz undertook the first trip ever made outside his dominions by an Ottoman ruler, except at the head of an army. His visits in 1867 to Paris, London, and Vienna successfully brought the reinforcement of personal diplomacy, exercised largely through his accompanying foreign minister, Fuad Pasha, to the campaign to ensure that article 9 was respected.[64] Throughout the crisis period the Porte sought the backing of the British government, and generally received it. Though London also urged the Porte to further reform measures, it discouraged the extreme Franco-Russian positions.

The British support came principally on the Cretan question and the curbing of Greek belligerence.[65]

In two other areas where the Porte's ability to exercise control was minimal and where it did not get effective foreign backing, it decided on the tactic of retreat. The advent of Prince Karl in the Romanian principalities was protested, but then accepted after a formula was worked out with Karl defining his position and stating that the principalities formed an "integral part" of the Ottoman Empire.[66] Likewise the Porte decided to yield to the Serbian demands for evacuation of the last Turkish troops from the Belgrade fortress, employing a formula that emphasized the loyalty of Serbia and its prince to their Ottoman suzerain.[67]

Thus, late in 1866 and early in 1867, the decks were cleared for armed combat in the two other areas. The Bulgarian insurrection was expeditiously suppressed by units of the Ottoman army, and followed up by vigorous Ottoman judicial proceedings against the Bulgarians punishing the guilty and perhaps some innocent as well.[68] The Ottoman army was also engaged in Crete in what turned out to be a campaign of something over two years before the rebel guerrilla forces were totally subdued. Ömer Pasha, the Porte's best general, was finally given the command there. Ali Pasha, the grand vezir, dispatched himself to the island on a special mission in 1867 and produced a report that led to reorganization of the island's administration in the following year.[69] Greece received a series of stern warnings from the Porte, and the Great Powers were early put on notice that the Ottoman Empire was prepared to go to war with Greece if she did not heed appeals to reason.[70] The Greco-Turkish border was quieted, and finally the outsiders from Greece who had nourished the Cretan rebellion were expelled from the island.

Temporarily, then, the Porte achieved some success against nationalism by combining reform, retreat, and resistance. None of the accommodations reached in 1866 to 1868, however, lasted beyond 1878, a year that ended another period of more reform, more retreat, and more—but largely futile—resistance.

It is barely possible, though not likely, that a different response—an eighth—might have kept the empire together better and perhaps longer. This was federalism. In Europe of the 1850s and 1860s, federalism was very much in vogue, both as a concept and as a practice. Various permutations of federative polity, if this be understood as the sharing of elements of sovereignty horizontally among more or less equal associates instead of the vertical thrust of power and authority downward from one central source, were even more widespread.[71] Sovereignty in the Ottoman Empire was, in fact, already somewhat diffused. Tunis, Egypt, Lebanon, Serbia, the Romanian principalities, Montenegro, and the island of Samos all enjoyed special regimes with varying degrees of autonomy that, in some case, amounted almost to independence. The sultan was suzerain but not completely sovereign. The other provinces of the empire, however, including many where nationalist feelings were rising, were incorporated within the new provincial administration system of 1867, the *vilayet* system, in which Porte-appointed officials exercised direct control. Perhaps some kind of federalism, provincial or regional, might have produced enough flexibility combined with uniformity to hold the far-flung pieces of the empire together.

There were a number of federalist proposals in this period. One, highly suspect because it came from the traditional enemy, was the Russian plan of early 1867 for the division of the Ottoman Empire into autonomous regions, based on nationality.[72] Put forth at a time of growing pan-Slavic sentiment and Balkan nationality crisis, it was probably designed to hasten the dissolution of the sultan's empire. Fuad Pasha, the Ottoman foreign minister, said he told the Russian ambassador that the plan would create "La Monarchie de la République des Etats non unis de la Turquie."[73] At almost the same time, a group of moderate Bulgarian nationalists proposed a dual monarchy for the Ottoman Empire; the Ottoman sultan should be also the czar of a self-governing Bulgaria, which would have its own national assembly. The plan was obviously fashioned after the Ausgleich of 1867, which gave Hungary autonomy, the Hapsburg monarch being emperor of Austria and king of Hungary. The Porte was less than enthusiastic, and the Bulgarian suggestion also bore no fruit.[74]

One federal scheme did enjoy brief consideration at the top level of Ottoman government. It was apparently the idea of Midhat Pasha, the reform-minded Ottoman provincial governor who became grand vezir in 1872, and his foreign minister, Halil Sherif Pasha. Their inspiration was the German Empire created by Bismarck the year before. The Romanian principalities and Serbia, in this scheme, would be tied to Istanbul as Bavaria and Württemberg were tied to Berlin. Their military strength would be at the disposition of the imperial ruler. The plan naturally evoked protests from Serbia and Romania, as well as from the Russian ambassador to the Porte.[75] This plan too disappeared without a trace.

During the reign of Sultan Abdülhamid II (1876-1909), there was indeed further dilution of the sultan's sovereignty in various Ottoman provinces that yet remained in the empire: Bosnia and Herzegovina came under Austrian administration; Cyprus and Egypt fell under British administration; a foreign-officered gendarmerie kept order in Macedonia; Crete received from the powers a special regime with the Greek king's son as governor; and a self-governing Bulgaria absorbed Eastern Rumelia. But these twilight zones of sovereignty in areas where (except for Egypt) nationalist ferment was at work were the haphazard result of imperialism and Great Power politics rather than of any rational federal scheme. Only with the rather loose-jointed ideas of Prince Sabaheddin's League of Administrative Decentralization and Private Initiative about 1906 did something approaching a federalist plan again come to the surface; and it was a plan proposed by an exile, a rebel against the sultan.[76]

Given its experience with the ever growing separatist tendencies of its nationalities, the Ottoman government could hardly be expected to welcome any developments likely to subtract yet another province from the empire. Federalist plans that provided for a generous extension of autonomy would surely be suspect. "The autonomous form . . . ," wrote Ali Pasha in 1867, "is in other words the dismemberment of the Empire. It would be impossible to prevent it from becoming rapidly and generally contagious."[77] In fact, the very concept of nationality was not really accepted by the Porte at all. In the case of the Cretan rebellion, the official Ottoman documents speak of insurrection, rebels, brigands, Cretans, Cretan people (both Greeks and Turks), outside agitators from Greece, covert Russian intrigue, but not of nationalism or nationalists. They speak also of Cretan Christians and, more broadly, just of Christians, but not of Greeks in a national sense. The "Greeks" who are mentioned are outside agitators from independent Greece. The Ottoman terminology is not necessarily inaccurate but is sometimes exaggerated and, in avoiding nationality altogether, insufficient. Ali Pasha used the word *nationalities* at least once, but only to belabor Russia's professed concern for the rights of nationalities who were Ottoman subjects by pointing out how Russia treated her Poles and other subject nationalities of her own empire.[78]

It is impossible to know to what extent this refusal to recognize the concept of nationality was deliberate policy or simply the result of the traditional view that religious dividing lines were the real ones. Certainly, at times the blindness must have been intentional. When Prince Karl was finally recognized in the Romanian principalities of Moldavia and Wallachia, for instance, he spoke in his letter to the Porte of "the Romanian population." The Porte in its letter spoke, in provincial rather than national terms, of "the Moldo-Wallachian population."[79] Ottoman policy could not, any more than could Austro-Hungarian policy, afford to admit such a thing as a principle of nationality or of national self-determination. Fuad Pasha, penning an eloquent defense of Ottoman policy in the Cretan affair, called into question the whole principle of what he termed "the agglomeration of races."[80]

It was, however, natural for Ottoman Turks to think in non-national terms. To the end of the empire, despite the loss of more lands to nascent nations and despite the increase among Turks themselves of Turkish nationalist feeling, the concept of Ottomanism persisted. The last Ottoman parliament of 1920, voting the National Pact that was actually the charter of the Turkish nationalist movement, insisted that there should be "an Ottoman Empire and an Ottoman nation."[81] Yet in 1920 it was obvious that war and nationalism had killed the Ottoman Empire, and that Ottomanism had been unable to save it. It remained for Mustafa Kemal, the supreme realist, to lead the Turks away from the "Ottoman nation" and toward the Turkish nationalism of today.

1. A. Sheref Gözübüyük and Suna Kili, *Türk Anayasa metinleri Tanzimattan bugüne kadar* (Ankara, 1957), p. 25.

2. See, on sources for statistics, Charles Issawi, ed., *The Economic History of the Middle East* (Chicago, 1966), p. 17 and n. 1, who thinks the above figure high; Roderic H. Davison, *Reform in the Ottoman Empire, 1856–1876* (Princeton, N.J.: 1963), pp. 414–15; Ibrahim Hakki Akyol, "Tanzimat devrinde bizde coğrafya ve jeoloji," in *Tanzimat* (Istanbul, 1940), p. 549, who selects for inclusion figures for mid-century evidently from Viquesnel, which, as he points out, are added incorrectly to give 36,334,105; the figures given actually total 34,834,105.

3. Salaheddin Bey, *La Turquie à l'Exposition universelle de 1867* (Paris, 1867), pp. 210–14.

4. Abdolonyme Ubicini and Pavet de Courteille, *Etat présent de l'Empire Ottoman* (Paris, 1876), combining information on p. 18 and n. 1 and p. 69.

5. William L. Langer, *Political and Social Upheaval, 1832–1852* (New York, 1969), p. 15.

6. See Karal's *Nizam-i Cedit ve Tanzimat devirleri (1789–1856)*, 3d ed. (Ankara, 1970), pp. 155-56.

7. Edouard Scrosoppi, *L'Empire Ottoman au point de vue politique* (Florence, 1874), 1:257–77, with greatly inflated figures on Greeks, Armenians, and Arabs, to prove that Turks were nowhere a majority, is an example.

8. Ubicini and de Courteille, op. cit., p. 69.

9. Ibid., p. 18.

10. Some Greeks and Arabs had been lost in 1830, owing to the establishment of the independent Greek kingdom and to the French seizure of Algeria from the Ottoman Empire.

11. Lorenz Rigler, *Die Türkei und deren Bewohner* (Vienna, 1852), 1:141, gives figures that add up to about 813,000, based on an 1846 census; Ubicini, *Letters on Turkey*, trans. Lady Easthope (London, 1856), 1:24, gives 891,000 for Istanbul and

its environs; an American missionary resident there reported in 1857 that the usual estimates of 600,000 were far too low, with 800,000 as a conservative estimate for the city proper and 1,200,000 to 1,300,000 a conservative estimate including the suburbs: Goodell to Perry, Constantinople, 3 April 1857, American Board of Commissioners for Foreign Missions, Archives (hereafter ABCFM), Armenian Mission, V, no. 166. See the varying estimates through the nineteenth century and into the twentieth, with the accompanying nationality map, in Clarence R. Johnson, ed., *Constantinople Today* (New York, 1922), pp. 14–19.

12. *Turkey and Its People*, 2d ed. (London, 1912), p. 29.

13. *Etat présent*, p. 27.

14. ABCFM, Western Turkey Mission, III, no. 21, 11 August 1874.

15. *Etat présent*, p. 41.

16. Op. cit., p. 317.

17. Ibid.

18. Namik Kemal, the patriotic Ottoman writer, criticized the Porte in 1868 for using *millet* in the sense of *nation*, for which he specified *ümmet*. *Millet* he kept only for *religious community* (Ihsan Sungu, "Tanzimat ve Yeni Osmanlilar," in *Tanzimat*, p. 840 n. 103).

19. American missionaries reported many cases, especially of Armenians who left their millet to become Catholics, or who asked to become Protestants, for such worldly reasons: ABCFM, Armenian Mission, VIII, no. 392, Van Lennep in 1857 Tokat report; Armenian mission, V, no. 298, Hamlin to Anderson, Bebek, 24 September 1859, are examples.

20. ABCFM, Armenian Mission, VIII, no. 57, Schauffler to Anderson, Bebek, 16 February 1857.

21. Ibid., no. 291, 1858, Trowbridge, p. 136.

22. C. Oscanyan, *The Sultan and His People* (New York, 1857), pp. 387–88.

23. Ibid., p. 409.

24. George Young, *Corps de droit ottoman* (Oxford, 1905–6), 2:98–99.

25. William M. Ramsay, "The Intermixture of Races in Asia Minor: Some of Its Causes and Effects," *Proceedings of the British Academy*, 1915–16, pp. 359–422; Eugene Pittard, *Les Peuples des Balkans* (Paris, 1920), pp. 21, 101, 229–30.

26. See F. W. Hasluck, *Christianity and Islam under the Sultans*, ed. Margaret M. M. Hasluck, 2 vols. (Oxford, 1929), passim; Andreas D. Mordtmann, *Anatolien: Skizzen und Reisebriefe (1850–1859)*, ed. Franz Babinger (Hanover, 1925), pp. 123–24; Henry J. Van Lennep, *Travels in Little-Known Parts of Asia Minor* (London, 1870), 1:30–31.

27. I. H. Danishmend, *Izahli Osmanli tarihi kronolojisi* (Istanbul, 1947–55), 4:528. Danishmend's estimates are thought by some scholars to be too high on the Turkish side. On the Ottoman state and slave system, see Halil Inalcik, *The Ottoman Empire: The Classical Age, 1300–1600* (New York, 1973), pp. 65–69, 76–88.

28. See the text of article 2 of the treaty of Küchük Kanarji in *Muahedat Mecmuasi* (Istanbul, 1294–98) 3:255.

29. Joseph von Hammer-Purgstall, *Des osmanischen Reiches Staatsverfassung und Staatsverwaltung* (Vienna, 1815), 1:181, where he says, "The name Raaja or subject is . . . a term of abuse, which carries with it all the insult and oppression of a conquered people given over to the caprice of the conqueror."

30. Robert Walsh and Thomas Allom, *Constantinople* (London, ca. 1839), 1:65.

31. Cevdet Pasha, *Tezâkir*, ed. Cavid Baysun (Ankara, 1953–67), 1:68.

32. Ubicini and de Courteille, *Etat présent*, list these millets, pp. 185–90, and discuss them on pp. 190 ff. in more detail. The official *salname*, or yearbook, of the empire, as they note, listed only the major millets, omitting Latins, Protestants, and Bulgar Uniates. When they wrote, there was also a Bulgarian Exarchate split off in 1870 from the Greek Orthodox. The Nestorian and Jacobite churches continued to be attached to the Armenian patriarchate for civil affairs. Sephardic and Ashkenazi Jews were also in one millet despite their quite different racial and cultural characteristics. Compare the list of millets in 1914 as given in Nasim Sousa, *The Capitulatory Regime of Turkey* (Baltimore, 1933), p. 89 n. 2.

33. See evidence in Abraham Galanté (Bodrumlu), *Histoire des juifs d'Istanbul* . . . (Istanbul, 1941), 1:251 ff. Sesostris Sidarouss, *Des patriarcats. Les Patriarcats dans l'Empire ottoman* . . . (Paris, 1906), p. 282, says that after 1878 the millets were tacitly put under the Ministry of Justice.

34. Oscar Jaszi, *The Dissolution of the Habsburg Monarchy* (Chicago, 1929), pp. 178–80.

35. Cevdet, op. cit., 1:11. For examples of the Ottoman view on revolts, see (on Crete), Ali Fuad Türkgeldi, *Mesail-i mühimme-i siyasiye*, ed. Bekir Sitki Baykal (Ankara, 1957-66), 3:10-11; Ahmed Rasim, *Resimli ve haritali Osmanli tarihi* (Istanbul, 1328-30), 4:2135 (Panslavism); Mahmud Celaleddin, *Miraat-i Hakikat* (Istanbul, 1326), 1:43 (1875–76 Balkan revolts).

36. Orhan Köprülü, "Fuad Pasha," *Islam Ansiklopedisi*, cüz 36, p. 679, citing a holographic memorandum by Fuad in a private collection.

37. See Roderic H. Davison, *Reform in the Ottoman Empire, 1856–1876* (Princeton, N.J., 1963), chaps. 1–3, 5–7, on details of these and other reforms.

38. Köprülu, op. cit.

39. In *Hürriyet*, no. 35, 10 Zilkade 1285/22 February 1869, quoted in Sungu, op. cit., p. 847.

40. Text in Gözübüyük and Kili, op. cit., p. 26.

41. Sherif Mardin, *The Genesis of Young Ottoman Thought* (Princeton, N.J., 1962), pp. 326–32, 398.

42. Text in Karal, op. cit., p. 259.

43. Davison, *Reform*, chap. 4.

44. Roderic H. Davison, "Ottoman Diplomacy at the Congress of Paris (1856) and the Question of Reforms," *VII. Türk Tarih Kongresi . . . 1970 Kongreye Sunulan Bildiriler* (Ankara, 1972-74), 2:580–84.

45. English text in J. C. Hurewitz, *Diplomacy in the Near and Middle East* (Princeton, N.J., 1956), 1:154.

46. Davison, "Ottoman Diplomacy," p. 586.

47. Edmund Hornby, *Autobiography* (London, 1928), p. 93.

48. United States National Archives, State Department Records (hereafter USNA, State), Turkey 16, Williams to Cass, no. 98, 17 September 1860.

49. See, for example, Ziya's strictures in *Hürriyet*, no. 48 (12 Safer 1286/24 May 1869), in Sungu, op. cit., pp. 787–89.

50. Bashbakanlik Arshivi (Istanbul), Yildiz tasnifi, kisim 33, evrak 37/26, zarf 71, Karton 94, Ali to Photiades (Athens) 25 June 1863, nos. 7672/92. Regulations enclosed in USNA, State, Turkey 19, Morris to Seward, no. 61, 14 August 1863.

51. Text of law in *Düstur* (Istanbul, 1289), 1:16–18; Grégoire Aristarchi, *Législation ottomane* (Constantinople, 1873–88), 1:7–8.

52. Text of law, *ibid.*, 3:99–102.

53. T. W. Riker, *The Making of Roumania . . . 1856-1866* (London, 1931), chaps. 2-6, is detailed on this, although his account is from a European and not an Ottoman point of view.

54. To the Ottomans, this is the Tershane [Dockyard, Naval Arsenal] Conference, from the place of its meeting. Europeans have always called it the Constantinople Conference.

55. M. S. Anderson, *The Eastern Question, 1774-1923* (New York, 1966), pp. 406-7, gives an introduction to the vast literature on this crisis.

56. English translation in Hurewitz, *Diplomacy*, 1:156.

57. Riker, op. cit., chaps. 7-11.

58. William L. Langer, *European Alliances and Alignments*, 2d ed. (New York, 1950), p. 349.

59. Anderson, op. cit., p. 187.

60. A survey of risings between 1856 and 1876 and Ottoman reactions is in Enver Ziya Karal, *Osmanli tarihi* VI-VIII (Ankara, 1954-1962), 6:29-96; 7:3-101; 8:14-24.

61. Text in Ali Fuad, *Rical-i mühimme-i siyasiye* (Istanbul, 1928), pp. 118-27, and in German translation in *Augsburger Allgemeine Zeitung*, 18 September 1876.

62. "Considérations sur l'exécution du Firman Impériale du 18 février 1856," printed in Ubicini and de Courteille, *Etat présent*, pp. 243-54.

63. Ali to Comnenos, 18 October 1866, no. 17803/112, conf., Dishishleri Bakanliği Hazine-i Evrak (Istanbul) (hereafter DB), karton S6, dosya 11.

64. See Davison, *Reform*, pp. 235-38, on the trip.

65. Ottoman diplomacy from 1866 to 1869, including the Ottoman-British relationship, is a subject I shall explore separately, in a further study on the basis of the Porte's diplomatic documents.

66. *Aus dem Leben König Karls von Rümanien* (Stuttgart, 1894), 1:132-35.

67. DB, karton S41, dosya 28, telegram to Hayder Efendi (Vienna), no. 18509/9, 28 February 1867; Grand Vezir to Prince Michael Obrenovich no. 18557/1, 3 March 1867. Fortunately for the Porte, Michael was assassinated in 1868 and his alliance schemes died.

68. Ali Haydar Midhat, *The Life of Midhat Pasha* (London, 1903), pp. 42-45; Alois Hajek, *Bulgarien unter der Türkenherrschaft* (Stuttgart, 1925), pp. 235-36.

69. Copy of the ferman on reorganization in Public Record Office (London) (herafter PRO), FO 195/893, dated 15 Ramazan 1284 (10 January 1868).

70. DB, karton S7, dosya 13, Ali to ambassadors in Paris, London, and Saint Petersburg, no. 18208/53, 26 December 1866.

71. Robert C. Binkley, *Realism and Nationalism, 1852-1871* (New York, 1935), chapters 8-11, explores these forms as they evolved in Europe.

72. The Russian memorandum of 18 April 1867 is in I. de Testa, *Recueil des traités de la Porte Ottomane* (Paris, 1864-1911), 7:446-55.

73. PRO, FO 78/1960, Lyons to Stanley, no. 200, conf., 22 May 1867.

74. Text of the Bulgarian petition in *Le Nord* (Brussels), 26-27 March 1867. More than forty years later, a secret Arab society proposed a similar dual monarchy, Turk-Arab: Z. N. Zeine, *Arab-Turkish Relations and the Emergence of Arab Nationalism* (Beirut, 1958), pp. 80-81; George Antonius, *The Arab Awakening* (New York, 1946), p. 110. The two authors differ on which society held this view.

75. N. P. Ignatyev, "Zapiski Grafa N. P. Ignatyeva (1864-1874)," *Izvestiia Ministerstva Inostrannykh Diel*, 1915, 1:170-72; Nicholas Iorga, ed., *Correspon-*

dance diplomatique roumaine sous le roi Charles Ier (1866–1880) (Paris, 1923), pp. 95–99.

76. E. E. Ramsaur, Jr., *The Young Turks* (Princeton, N.J., 1957), pp. 84–86.

77. DB, karton S6, dosya 11, Ali to Musurus, tel., 16 January 1867.

78. Ibid., Ali to Comnenos, private, no. 18450/9, 10 February 1867. There must be other instances. Bernard Lewis, "Ali Pasha on Nationalism," *Middle Eastern Studies* 10 (January 1974): 77–79, reprints from Cavid Baysun's article in *Tarih Dergisi* 5 (September 1953), pp. 125–37, a private letter by Ali to Cemil of 18 September 1862 in which Ali speaks of "nationalities" and "national aspirations" in the Balkans.

79. *Aus dem Leben König Karls*, 1:133 and 135.

80. DB, karton S6, dosya 11, Fuad to Ottoman ambassadors in Paris and London, no. 18523/15, 27 February 1867.

81. This is the official French translation in *Histoire de la République Turque* (Istanbul, 1935), p. 46 n. 1. The original Turkish is "an Ottoman sultanate and society" [bir Osmanli saltanat ve cemiyeti]: *Tarih IV, Türkiye Cumhuriyeti* (Istanbul, 1934), pp. 45–46 n. 1.

Alan Fisher

Crimean Separatism
in the Ottoman Empire

Strivings for national identity or national conscious-ness usually contain both positive and negative characteristics. On the one hand are the attempts to provide a new social and political framework for the nationality in which it is able to make manifest its own identity. Of equal importance are attempts to eliminate the existing social and political conditions in which nationality plays a subordinate or nonexistant role. By concentrating on the first characteristic at the expense of the second, historians have come to view national movements as at least normal political developments, and even inevitable. However, the Ottoman Empire and its breakup in the nineteenth and twentieth centuries provide a set of historical cases where the second aspect of nationalism is even more important than the first.

To deal in a sophisticated manner with nationalism and separatism in the Ottoman Empire, one must first analyze the existing social and political conditions against which the nationalists or separatists were acting. Almost everywhere one looks in the Ottoman Empire, the relationships between a

province and the center were different—the Danubian principalities, the North African amirates, the Egyptian Mamlukes,
the Anatolian derebeyliks, the Caucasian shaykhdoms, and
the Crimean khanate. Where one finds voevodas, amirs, sultans, beys, shaykhs, and khans, one also finds very different
sets of ties between province and center. One could even
make the point that Istanbul itself was governed as an adjunct
to various government departments and later as a province,
not as an imperial center. And if, as it seems clear, these
relationships were very different from the start, might not the
movements to change these conditions also take on very different characteristics?

In considering this question, an examination of the Crimean
khanate is of special significance. Of all the Ottoman provinces, the khanate maintained more of its independence and
sovereignty than any other. And though its territory was not
the first that the Ottomans lost, it was in fact the first self-
contained province to break away from the empire (albeit
with Russian help and encouragement) at a time when
"nationalism" and "national consciousness" had scarcely
emerged anywhere else. Finally, it was the first Muslim land
to be lost irrevocably by the Muslim Ottoman sultan. To
understand the significance of the Crimean separatist movement and the effect that its loss had upon the Ottoman
government, we must first attempt to describe and analyze
the realities of Crimean-Ottoman relations in the period before the 1770s, when the break occurred.

Halim Giray Sultan's *Gülbün-ü hanan yahud Kirim tarihi*
[The Rose Garden of the Khans], published in Istanbul in
1909 but written in 1811, is the best known of the Tatar
histories or chronicles to deal with Crimean affairs independently of Ottoman events. It was composed during a period
when Crimean Tatar identity was apparently disappearing,
when the Tatar homeland (the Crimea) was being heavily
resettled by Russian and Ukrainian colonists and large numbers of Tatars were fleeing to Istanbul. Halim Giray Sultan's
book is understandably bitter toward the Russians, the Otto-

man government, and also those of his own Tatar brothers who worked hard for "separatism" and independence in the last half of the eighteenth century. It is particularly the Girays and clan leaders who ruled in the 1760s and 1770s who bear the brunt of his criticism, and his arguments do seem to strike at the heart of the ultimate failures of the separatist movement. This was the inability of the Tatar leaders to see that the ideal of Tatar independence would have to be tempered by the realities of the power of both the Ottomans (on the decline) in the south and that of the Russians (increasing) in the north. The Tatar leaders either refused or were unable to take into consideration these power shifts when they embarked upon what Halim Giray Sultan termed their "adventure in folly."

In addition to his bitterness, the historian Sultan's writing reveals a good deal of sadness or sentimental reflection on what might have been. He realizes clearly that the ideas of Crimean separatism, which, when put into practice, virtually eliminated the Crimean Tatars as a distinct entity, did not make a sudden and unexpected appearance; that they had centuries of tradition and experience behind them; that really almost from the beginning of the Crimean khanate, the seeds of this separatism had existed, appearing more or less strongly at different times. He admits that his criticism has to be aimed at all Crimean history; thus the format of his work is a thumbnail sketch of the reigns of various Crimean Giray khans. It is this background to the overt movement toward separatism, not its outcome, that will be the primary concern of this chapter.[1] Halim Giray Sultan would not know, of course, that his book would have a great impact on a new leader of Tatar nationalism within the Russian Empire, Ismail Bey Gasprinsky, whose intellectual movement would attempt to relate Tatar and Islamic traditions with modern non-Islamic nationalist movements.

In the royal palace of the Crimean Giray khans near Bahchesaray, there used to be an inscription over the main entrance that stated: "Kirim Giray Khan, son of his ex-

cellency Devlet Giray, the source of peace and security, wise
sovereign, his imperial star rose above the glorious horizon.
His beautiful Crimean throne gave brilliant illumination to
the whole world."[2] The inscription, which dates from the
second third of the eighteenth century, includes some unusual terminology when one recalls that the khanate had been
a vassal state of the Ottoman Empire for three centuries,
that the period of the khanate's grandeur had ended long
before, and that Khan Kirim Giray, like many of his predecessors, had in fact been appointed by the Ottoman sultan,
in his case, Osman III. Words such as "sovereign," "imperial
star," and "throne" seem out of place in an account of the
characteristics of a vassal of the Ottoman ruler. A century
earlier the Crimean khan bore the following title: "Of the
Great Horde, and Great Iurt, of the Kipchak Steppe, Crimean
State, of the innumerable Tatars and Nogays, Great Sovereign, His Excellency Giray Khan."[3] Again one meets "sovereign," but with the addition of "state."

In both the inscription and title, one finds elements of the
real nature of Crimean politics in the sixteenth through the
eighteenth centuries and clues to the reality of Crimean
Tatar-Ottoman political relations during this period. Did the
Ottomans and Crimeans themselves look upon their relationships as those between sovereign and vassal, sovereign and
subjects, sovereign and sovereign?

The basis for the political relationships between the Crimean Tatars and the Ottomans had two ingredients: historical
tradition and geopolitical necessity. To understand the nature
of later Crimean separatism, and the effect of the actual
separation of the Crimea and the Ottoman Empire in the
eighteenth century on both parties, we must first establish
the main characteristics of these two aspects of their relations.

Ottoman political ideology by the middle of the sixteenth
century combined three distinct traditions, all of which were
incorporated within the official titles of the sultans, to wit:
Islamic (protector of the Holy Places), Byzantine-Roman

(emperor of the two seas), and Central Asian Turkic (khan, and padishah-i Desht-i Kipchak). It was the last of the three that was significant for Ottoman-Crimean relations. Feridun Bey provides one document where the sultan, in a letter to the Polish king, even claimed to be padishah of the Tatar lands of Kefe, Krim, Desht-i Kipchak, and Dagestan.[4] In the historical chronicles written by both Crimean and Otto-man authors, political descent from Chingiz Khan was used to provide legitimacy for suzerainty over large parts of the Turkic world.[5] And in their relationship to Chingiz Khan, the Crimean khans of the Giray clan could go even further than the Ottomans, since they believed themselves directly de-scended, not only politically but physically, from the khan of the Great Horde.[6] In this belief the Ottomans concurred, using the epithet *cingiziye*, when referring to the Girays, in almost all correspondence from Istanbul to Bahchesaray. It was this claim of genealogical descent from the Mongols that made the relationship between the khans and the sultans a special one, in which each often viewed the other as a sovereign. Sultan Sülcyman I, when writing to Khan Mehmet Giray I, used for the latter the title "Descendant of Crimean Sultans and of Chingizid Hakhans" (Halif-ul selatin-ul Kirimiye ve sheref-ul Khavakin-ul cingiziye).[7]

In the seventeenth and eighteenth centuries, there was a widespread belief in Western Europe, apparently shared also by some officials in Istanbul, that this special relationship had been formalized in an agreement by which the Giray khans would be eligible to mount the Ottoman throne if the House of Osman should become extinguished.[8] But A. D. Alderson has effectively disposed of this idea, suggesting that "their claims were purely legendary, had no legal foundation whatsoever, and had probably been fabricated by different travellers out of local gossip."[9] That such a theory could have many supporters, especially in the eighteenth century when the Crimea was in its terminal period of decline, is evidence, however, that the special relationship between the Girays and the Ottomans was well known.

In the realm of geopolitical necessity as well, the Ottomans and the Crimean Tatars had a special relationship. Back in the sixteenth century, on occupying the steppe area between the Ottomans and two powerful, ambitious, and growing states, Poland-Lithuania and Muscovite Russia, the Crimeans allowed the Ottomans to concentrate their defense efforts on the borders with the Hapsburgs and the Safavids. It had been the steppe region where the Mongols had ruled, where the part of the Great Horde called the Golden Horde had derived the main sources of its strength; and it was the late sixteenth and seventeenth centuries' struggle for control of the steppe that presented the greatest challenges to the maintenance of close relations between the Girays and Ottomans.

In practical terms the Crimeans served as military supports for the Ottomans on this northern frontier, for which service they received handsome financial and social rewards. I have elsewhere discussed in greater detail the financial arrangements that the Ottomans made to ensure continued Crimean participation in their military campaigns, arrangements that came to cost the Ottomans dearly in the eighteenth century.[10] First, the Giray khans received annual payments called *saliyane* that in the seventeenth and eighteenth centuries ranged from 2.5 million *akches* to 9.5 million.[11] In receipt of *saliyane* the Girays maintained a similar arrangement to that of the Mamluk sultans of Egypt and also the *deniz ümerasi* (naval leaders of the *eyalet* of the *Kapudan Pasha*).[12] Second, upon their accession to the throne in Bahchesaray, the khans received a large sum of money, which amounted to almost a million *akches*.[13] The sum, called *teshrifat akchesi*, was evidently granted only to the khans, setting them apart from all other Ottoman subjects or vassals.

Third, the khans were assigned personal revenues from the Ottoman *hass* administration, a common occurrence for most members of the Ottoman upper class. But what set the khans apart was the fact that their *hass* was always inscribed in the *defters* for the royal family. The names of the Giray khans (and former khans), in the *defters* that I examined, were placed just after that of the *Valide Sultan*.[14] Fourth, the khans were given a special military guard account to pay the expenses of the personal guard corps assigned to Bahchesaray, the *sekban akchesi*.[15] One could argue that the *sekbans* of the khans were, in reality, representatives of the sultan, assigned to the Crimea as assurance of Crimean co-operation. And it is true that on occasion they participated in the deposition of a khan and the installation of another. But the khans themselves included the expenses of the *sekbans* in their lists of income and thus considered such revenues as grants from the Ottomans along with all the others.

Fifth, and most important for our discussion of Crimean separatism, was the custom of allowing the Crimean khans to collect an annual tribute from the Danubian principalities, a tribute assigned and collected by the khan's own representatives. The tribute, called *tiyish*, was a holdover from the pre-Ottoman practice of the Golden Horde's requiring the annual payment of a tribute from all of its subject provinces.[16] The Crimeans also collected such tribute from both Muscovite Russia and the kingdom of Poland-Lithuania. Such payments continued through the seventeenth century and represented, for payer and payee alike, a recognition of the political rights on the steppe that the Crimeans had inherited from their predecessor there, the Golden Horde.[17] Lastly, the Ottomans sent to the Crimean khans, with every invitation to participate in a military campaign, a large sum of money called the *tirkesh baha* ("quiver price").[18] That it was always considered an "invitation" and not a command provides further substance to the view that their affairs were conducted in a special manner.

In return for the *tirkesh baha*, the Ottomans expected the khans to provide loyal military service for the sultan, although it was not always forthcoming. The Ottoman contribution of the *teshrifat akchesi* and the *sekban akchesi* allowed the Ottomans to interfere directly in internal Crimean politics, especially those concerned with the deposition and installation of khans. It was this practice, which occurred more and more frequently during the last years of the seventeenth and throughout the eighteenth centuries, that led most historians to suspect that the khans were no more than vassals of the Ottoman sultans.[19] The physical force of the *sekbans* and the monetary influence (which could be spread around as bribes) gave the Ottomans the ability to interfere, but this practice was never codified or given a legal foundation. On the contrary, such increased meddling in affairs that many Crimean leaders considered purely of internal Crimean interest provided much of the impetus for Crimean separatist movements in the eighteenth century.

Although the major manifestations of Crimean "separatism" emerged only in the second half of the eighteenth century, it should then have been no surprise to anyone that the foundations for such a movement had always existed in the Crimean khanate since 1475, when the Crimea "entered under Ottoman protection."[20]

First, both the Crimeans and the Ottomans, in mutual correspondence, treated the other as a sovereign entity. Rather than the more usual *buyrultu, hüküm, berat,* or *ferman,* which were used when sending communications from the sultan to his servants and vassals, the common form for correspondence between Topkapi Saray and Bahchesaray was the *name-i hümayun* or *name-i sherif.* Except for the Crimean case, the *name-i hümayun* was a piece of diplomatic correspondence from the sultan to the head of another state.[21] The following examples are typical of the subject matter included in such Ottoman *name-i hümayuns* to the Crimean khans. In 1687 Sultan Süleyman II sent to Khan Selim Giray I his recognition of the khan as sovereign in the Crimea and accompanied this statement "with the traditional presents."[22] In 1688 Khan Selim Giray I sent a *name-i hümayun* to Sultan Süleyman II, confirming this receipt of the sultan's recognition and affirming "his loyalty to the leader of the world of Islam" but without any apparent acknowledgment of *political* loyalty to the House of Osman.[23] In 1689 the sultan sent to Khan Selim Giray money to pay for his campaigns in

Bosnia.[24] Another, in 1692, from Sultan Ahmed II to Khan Safa Giray, accompanied by presents for the khan and his notables, invited him to enter a military campaign.[25] And finally, in 1696, a *name-i hümayun* from Sultan Mustafa II to Khan Selim Giray provided recognition of his "outstanding service" with a financial reward to be shared with his *Kalga* and other notables.[26] On one occasion Devlet Giray was called only "Emir of the Province of the Crimea, sincere and loyal friend of our Throne."[27]

From *their* direction, too, the Crimean khans corresponded with the sultans in a manner unusual for Ottoman vassals with their sovereign. The Girays refused to surrender their early pretensions to be lords of the steppe, pretensions inherited from the Golden Horde and, even earlier, from Chengiz Khan. Among the *cingiziye* symbols of steppe sovereignty was the right to use an official signature on their documents called the *tamga*, similar in use but not in form to the Ottoman *tuğra*. First used by the Uygurs, the *tamga* was heavily utilized by the Giray khans in the sixteenth and seventeenth centuries on virtually all their documents, which included those sent to Istanbul. In the later seventeenth and through the eighteenth centuries, the khans even used their own *tuğras*, accompanied by a special pear-shaped seal bearing the name *cingiziye* to signify their sovereignty.[28]

Unlike all other Ottoman vassals and government officials in the provinces, the Giray khans also conducted their own independent diplomatic relations with those states bordering on the steppe and over whom the khans claimed some form of traditional suzerainty. Although these claims were not officially admitted by the other states in question, the khans were successful in having their representatives recognized in Moscow, Warsaw, and even in Iran.[29] In the seventeenth century in Moscow, the *Prikaz* of Foreign Affairs provided permanent housing for Crimean diplomats, as they did for most other foreign states. Interestingly though, no such housing was available for Ottoman envoys. The *Krymskii Dvor*, as the Crimean "embassy" was called, was occupied almost continuously by Tatar envoys during the seventeenth century. It was used not only for the conduct of usual diplomatic discourse between the Girays and the czars, but also as the place where the annual Muscovite tributes were paid to the khan's envoys. This tribute, called *tiyish* in Tatar and *pomimok* in Russian, was in reality only the annual payment that the czars made in the hopes of both ransoming Slavic prisoners held by the Tatars for future sale as slaves, and preventing the Tatars from making new raids into Muscovite territory. But it is interesting that the names used for this tribute were the same terms employed by both the Muscovites and the leaders of the Golden Horde for the annual tax and tribute payments made in the years when the Horde was the actual sovereign in the Russian lands.[30]

The Ottoman government, very interested in Tatar diplomacy, especially in Poland and Muscovy, was constantly kept abreast of its direction and accomplishments, but seems never to have tried to prevent the khans from conducting their own relations with foreign states. In the *Mühimme Defteri* one can find innumerable copies of reports from Crimean envoys sent to Istanbul, not for approval (there is no such request or response in the reports found there) but merely for the information for the sultan's own officials.[31]

Thus, from the sixteenth through the eighteenth centuries, the Crimean khans acted in steppe politics as virtually independent sovereigns, carrying on their own diplomatic relations, sending and accepting envoys from Poland, Muscovy, and Iran; they were treated by the Ottoman bureaucracy more as allies than as subjects, at least so far as diplomatic affairs went. In two other areas the khans evidenced their claims to traditional sovereignty. First, the khans continued to mint their own coins until the annexation of the Crimea in 1783.[32] And second, until the Treaty of Karlowitz in 1699, the khans issued *iarliks* for land-holding in many areas of the Ukraine and southwestern Muscovy.[33]

A second major area in which the khans manifested a conception of separateness, even independence, was in the realm of succession to the Crimean throne. Of course, it is one of the basic requirements of an independent people that they be allowed to choose their own leaders, according to their own traditions and without outside interference. The Crimean khans and almost all their subjects believed that the Crimean throne derived directly without any break from that of Chengiz Khan, and that Crimean and Golden Horde traditions should govern the transition from one khan to the next. According to the Ottoman succession traditions, the eldest legitimate son of the ruler would inherit the throne. On the other hand, the Crimean traditions required the reigning khan to appoint his eldest brother to the position of kalga, which was that of the heir apparent.[34] The existence of this conflict allowed or encouraged the Ottomans to try to interfere in the succession process in Bahchesaray more and more frequently during the later years of the seventeenth and eighteenth centuries. That the Ottomans were able to find individual Girays willing to counter the traditional Crimean methods of succession so as to support their own claims did not overcome the more general Crimean feeling that their own, and not Ottoman, laws of succession should be followed. In the late eighteenth century, when the separatist movement succeeded in actually separating the Crimea from Istanbul, it was the question of Ottoman interference in internal succession matters that was to be one of the main battle cries of the independence movement.

Third, Crimean historians, chronical writers, and intellectuals in general had paved the way in the sixteenth and seventeenth centuries for the ideological justifications of Crimean separatism as it developed in the eighteenth century. In many nationalist movements it is the intellectuals who are the leaders, the groundbreakers, the consciousness-raisers, whose activities precede those of the politicians and the economic interests. In the Crimea, on the contrary, the historians and writers were apparently reflecting deeply held beliefs in supporting the claims for the Girays and their subjects to have a long history of independence. Indeed, Crimean historians from the very beginning never accepted the idea of Crimean Giray *subjection* to the Ottomans in the political field, but only in the religious.

The earliest sixteenth-century Crimean historians were deeply concerned with Tatar separateness, with Tatar identity, and with traditions that were exclusively Tatar. In the first of these, the *Tarih-i Sahib Giray Khan*, written soon after the death of the khan in 1551, no pain is spared to support the historical tradition that the Giray clan is second to none in legitimacy and longevity. The author points out that the khan is "the descendant of Chengiz Khan; his ancestors have been Khans for seventy-two generations." And further, "Unless he abdicates his own power, one cannot depose the Khan of the Crimea; for generations he has been the master of power, named in the public prayers and possessing the right to mint coins." We must remember that this is written in the reign of Süleyman I.[35]

A second Crimean Tatar history, the *Tevarih-i Desht-i Kipchak*, written between 1623 and 1640 by a Tatar living in Kefe, speaks of the sovereignty of the khans emerging from "time immemorial" and of the fact that the khans deal with the sultans as genealogical equals and that the sultans approve of the Crimean choices for succession to the throne "mütad üzere". (No mention is made of Ottoman dictation of these choices.) Those Crimean khans who acted especially independently, such as Mengli Giray, at the beginning, and Devlet Giray, whose sabotage of the Ottoman Astrakhan campaign in 1556 helped cause its failure, are treated as the real heroes of Crimean history.[36]

A later chronicle, *Üchüncü Islam Giray Khan Tarihi*, composed by Kirimli Haci Mehmed Senai in the early 1650s, makes the same points as the first two about the descent of the Girays from the Chingizids and the khans' possession of all of the political characteristics of the former "Hakhans" of the Golden Horde. In its introduction, however, an inconsistent argument states that the Giray ancestors of Islam Giray had been under the "sovereignty of the Ottoman throne" and received from the Ottomans an annual payment (*saliyane*) for their services. The over-all thrust of the history, though, points to Giray and *cingiziye* traditions and glory, and plays down the connections and "sovereignty" of the Ottoman sultan.[37]

Fourth, in the 1750s Seid Muhammed Riza wrote a chronicle entitled *Asseb' o-sseiiar'*.[38] This is the most interesting and enlightening of the four chronicles written during the existence of the Crimean khanate. It is by far the longest and most detailed. (Perhaps for this reason it provided the foundations for the two masterful volumes on Crimean history by V. D. Smirnov.)[39] As in the second chronicle, Riza emphasizes, almost to the point of excluding other khans, those who acted according to the interests of the Chingizids. Such khans pursued a Crimean political policy independent of, or at least separate but parallel to, that of the Ottomans. His greatest hero is again Devlet Giray, who not only refused to endanger Crimean interests in the Ottoman Astrakhan campaign, but in opposition to Ottoman demands, conducted several major raids against Moscow. Once, in 1571, he actually was able to enter the city of Moscow and lay it waste. On more than one occasion, Riza describes Ottoman participation in the Giray succession crises as "interference."[40] Additionally, in devoting the first quarter of his history to the period of Mongol domination of the steppe, Riza is not content merely to mention the Chingizid origins of the Girays, but presents their entire history as flowing directly from that of the Golden Horde.

Thus we arrive at the fifth and last of the major Crimean Tatar histories, that of the aforementioned Halim Giray Sultan, and the major criticisms that he made of the foundations of the Crimean separatist movement.[41] Sultan argues that the Crimean leaders, some of them members of Giray clan, but especially leaders of the other major clans such as the Shirin and Barin, acted irresponsibly and, for Tatar national identity, disastrously, in pressing for separatism in the 1760s and 1770s during the Russo-Ottoman war in those years. He alludes to the cleverness of Russian diplomacy and the Russians' ability to persuade many of the Crimean leaders that the time had come, now that the Ottoman Empire was suffering a major military defeat, to declare once and for all their separation from the sultan. Russian diplomats, acting under orders from Empress Catherine II, conducted negotiations with some dissident members of the Giray family, especially Kaplan and Shahin Giray, and with leaders of some of the Tatar hordes under the suzerainty of the Girays. First concentrating on the Nogay horde that roamed the steppe of the western shore of the Black Sea, Catherine's agent from the Zaporozhian Cossacks was able to persuade Can Mambet Bey to sign a "treaty of friendship and alliance" with the Russians in 1770. This "treaty" was more a declaration of "independence" from the Ottomans than one of alliance with the Russians, and included the following statements:

> The Yedisan Nogay horde will remain for all eternity, free and separate from the Turkish yoke. They will become an independent people, under the authority of their own particular laws and administration.

> The Yedisan and Bucak hordes of Crimeans, through agreement made among themselves, have now broken away from their subjection to the Ottoman Porte, and have entered into eternal friendship and alliance with the Russian Empire.

> We have sworn on the Quran never to give aid to the Turks or to the Khan of the Crimea, and not to recognize the Khan unless he should submit to the same conditions, that is, to live peacefully under the protection of Russia and to renounce the sovereignty of the Porte.[42]

In first approaching the Nogays and both the Yedisan and Bucak hordes, the Russians were attacking what they perceived to be weak spots in the Crimean administration. For a long time attempts by Crimean khans to impose ever stricter authority over the nomadic Nogays had resulted in growing dissatisfaction with the Girays. It was not surprising that in this, their first attempt, the Russian diplomats were so successful.

As the progress of the war left the Ottomans in more and more desperate straits, the Russians quickly followed up their Nogay successes with attempts at "subversion" of some of the Crimean leaders themselves. In a series of letters to Khan Kaplan Giray, General Petr Panin, who had been in charge of the Nogay negotiations, wrote that "the Sultan has incorporated the Crimeans and all of the Nogays within his authority, not by the result of war or of succession, but by his various tricks."[43] Kaplan Giray replied almost immediately in late 1770 that "we, the Crimean Khan, and other leaders of the Crimean state and Shirin mirzas, instead of obeying the Ottomans, at the present time want to take an oath to a government such as yours which is friendly to us, and which will allow us to follow our ancient political traditions."[44]

The Ottoman government, quickly learning of Kaplan Giray's "treason," sent as a Giray replacement for him Selim Giray, who had been living in the Giray yali in Büyükdere, in Istanbul. For a short while, in the early months of 1771, Selim Giray, with Ottoman troops at his disposal, was able to "restore order" in the Crimea and to stop, for the moment, overt Russian diplomatic activity there. But not for long. General Dolgorukii, at the head of a large army, invaded the Crimea in the spring of 1771 and immediately issued a manifesto that was publicized by Crimean supporters of independence. It stated:

> The Yedisan, Bucak, and Cambuluk Hordes, according to the most basic of human rights, have thrown off their Turkish subjection and have taken an oath to live independently of any people, under their own ancient traditions and laws, and to enter into eternal friendship with the Russian Empire. . . . My Sovereign, Her Imperial Majesty, has granted them permanent protection. . . . I guarantee to all of the inhabitants of the Crimea no harm from my army if they break away from the slavery of the Porte. . . . As Cingiziye you were inde-

pendent; now you are under the rule of the Ottoman state; they appoint and depose Khans as they do their own *valis*. If you act in conjunction with us, we will provide you with your former independence.[45]

The manifesto, as we can see in the light of our knowledge of Tatar interest in their past and *cingiziye* traditions, was an unqualified success. Almost all of the Giray and clan leadership agreed to support the call for independence from the sultan; and, when the Ottoman negotiators met with the Russians at Küchük Kanarji in 1773 and 1774, they were presented with a *fait accompli*, the establishment of a Crimean independent State.[46] By emphasizing "former independence" under the great khans of the past, by pointing to the *cingiziye* heritage, and especially by reminding them of Ottoman interference in the Crimean succession process, the Russian manifesto had mentioned all the points that were important to Crimean sensibilities.

This "independence" lasted only for eleven years, to 1783, when Catherine II formally and totally annexed the Crimean peninsula to her state and reformed it into *Tavricheskaia guberniia*. Halim Giray Sultan remarks bitterly in his history that the result was a foregone conclusion. The Girays and the Crimeans with them could have preserved their national identity only as part of the Ottoman Empire, in which they had been able to maintain their special relationships with the Sultans. The Girays were "shamefully fooled" by the clever words of Russian diplomats into believing the "nonsense" of Crimean glory in the past as an independent state. Halim Giray Sultan concludes that whatever "glory" the khans of old had possessed was directly related to their connections with the Ottomans; it had been the Ottomans, he reminded his readers, who had permitted the Girays so much independence of actions. This they forgot completely in the wartime years of the late 1760s, and it brought them to the tragedy of the 1770s.

The annexation of the Crimea by the Russian Empire was

not the end of Crimean aspirations for identity, however. Substantial numbers of Tatars emigrated from the Crimean peninsula in several waves (1783–85, 1812–14, 1826–27, and 1854–62) to Anatolia and Rumelia, many of them settling in the suburbs of Istanbul.[47] Within the Ottoman Empire, the Crimean Tatars continuously pressed for Ottoman support for their return "to their homeland" and did not seem to be easily assimilated into Ottoman society. Those Tatars remaining in the Russian Empire, despite vigorous attempts by the government to deny their national identity, to convert them to Orthodoxy, and to move them around the empire to break their hold on their lands, retained at least a germ of national consciousness, which was renewed and which grew into a flourishing national movement in the late nineteenth century and the beginning of the twentieth.[48] And it was to be Tatar nationalist leaders, both in Russia and in Turkey, who were to have such an impact on the growth of Turkish nationalist aspirations at the end of the century.

1. The author wishes to thank the All University Research Fund of Michigan State University for financial assistance in the preparation of this essay.

2. A. Borzenko and A. Negri, "Bakhchisaraiskaia arabskaia i turetskaia nadpisi," *Zapiski odesskogo obshchestva istorii i drevnostei* (1848), 2:495.

3. A. Skal'kovskii, "Zaniatie Kryma v 1783 g," *Zhurnal ministerstva narodnago prosveshcheniia* 30 (1841): pt. 2, p. 3.

4. Bernard Lewis, *The Emergence of Modern Turkey* (London, 1961), pp. 10–14; Feridun Bey, *Münsheat-i Selatin* (Istanbul, 1849), 2:419–25, 529.

5. Among the Ottoman chronicles that discuss Chengiz Khan as an Ottoman predecessor, see Müneccimbashi Ahmet Dede, *Müneccimbashi Tarihi* (Istanbul, 1913), 2 vols.

6. See Hasan Ortekin, *Kirim Hanlarinin Sheceresi* (Istanbul, 1938), and Abulgazi Bahadir Khan, *Shecere-i Türk* (Kazan, 1874)

7. Feridun Bey, op. cit., 1:502.

8. H. A. R. Gibb and H. Bowen, *Islamic Society and the West*, vol. 1, pt. 1 (London, 1950), p. 25; Paul Rycaut, *The Present State of the Ottoman Empire* (London, 1668), p. 58.

9. A. D. Alderson, *The Structure of the Ottoman Dynasty* (Oxford, 1956), p. 151. See also Joseph von Hammer-Purgstall, *Geschichte der Chane der Krim* (Vienna, 1856), pp. 36–37, who raises some doubts about this theory.

10. Istanbul, Bashbakanlik Arshivi, *Cevdet: Eyalet-i mümtazim*; see my ar-

ticle, "Les Rapports entre l'Empire Ottoman et la Crimée: l'aspect financier," *Cahiers du monde russe et soviétique*, XIII/3 (1972), pp. 368–81.

11. Fisher, op. cit., pp. 377–81, for lists of such *saliyane* payments.

12. Stanford Shaw, *The Financial and Administrative Organization of Ottoman Egypt, 1517–1798*, (Princeton, N.J., 1962), pp. 185–88.

13. Mehmed Ağa Silahdar, *Silahdar Tarihi* (Istanbul, 1928), 1:395; 2:99, 132, 682.

14. Istanbul, Bashbakanlik Arshivi, *Cevdet: Hariciye*, no. 4646; *Cevdet: Eyalet-i Mümtazim*, no. 675; *Maliyeden müdevvere defterleri*, no. 14, 525.

15. Mehmet Rashit, *Rashit Tarihi*, 2d ed. (Istanbul, 1865), 2:523; 4:217.

16. Endoxiu de Hurmuzaki, *Documente privitoare la istoria romanilor*, suppl. 1, vol. 1 (Bucharest, 1886), pp. 55–56; and I. H. Uzuncharshili, *Osmanli Tarihi*, 2 (Ankara, 1964): 434.

17. See my "Muscovy and the Black Sea Slave Trade," in *Canadian-American Slavic Studies* 6 (1972): 575–94, for the connection between the Polish and Muscovite *tiyish* payments and the slave traffic in the steppe.

18. Ozalp Gökbilgin and Dilek Desaive, "Le Khanat de Crimée et les campagnes militaries de l'Empire Ottoman—fin du XVII*e* début du XVIII*e* siècle," *Cahiers du monde russe et soviétique* 11 (1970): 110–17.

19. I. B. Grekov, *Ocherki po istorii mezhdunarodnykh otnoshenii vostochnoi evropy XIV-XVIvv.* (Moscow, 1963), p. 153, who states flatly that "the Crimea became a vassal of the Ottoman Empire, was subject to the desires of the Sultan's will, and became one of those means by which the Ottomans began to interfere in East European politics." V. D. Smirnov, *Krymskoe Khanstvo pod verkhovenstvom otomanskoi porty do nachala XVIII veka* (St. Petersburg, 1887), p. xxxi, says that "the Crimea was a vassal not only in theory but in practice."

20. Halil Inalcik, "Yeni vesikalara göre Kirim hanliğinin Osmanli tabiliğine girmesi ve ahidname meselesi," *Belleten*, vol. 8, no. 31 (1944), pp. 185–229, where the evidence seems to show that the Crimea "entered under Ottoman protection," not "subjection."

21. Dilek Desaive, "Le khanat de Crimée dans les Archives Ottomanes: correspondence entre khans de Crimée et padichahs ottomans dans les registres des name-i hümayün," *Cahiers du monde russe et soviétique* 13 (1972): 560–83; see also Jan Reychman and Ananiasz Zajaczkowski, *Handbook of Ottoman-Turkish Diplomatics* (The Hague, 1968), pp. 135–37, for a discussion of different types of Ottoman documents.

22. *Name-i hümayün defter*, 5:1–2 (in Istanbul, Bashbakanlik Arshivi).

23. Ibid., pp. 23–25.

24. Ibid., pp. 87–89.

25. Ibid., pp. 130–32.

26. Ibid., pp. 188–90.

27. Chantal Lemercier-Quelquejay, "Les Expéditions de Devlet Giray contre Moscou en 1571 et 1572," *Cahiers du monde russe et soviétique* 13 (1972): 555.

28. Reychman, op. cit., pp. 157–58; O. Akchokrakly, *Tatarskie tamgi v krymu* (Simferopol, 1927); A. Spitsyn, "Tatarskiia baisy," *Izvestiia Imperatorskoi Archeologicheskoi Komisii* 29 (1909): 130–41.

29. B. Kutukoğlu, *Osmanli-Iran Siyasi Münasabetleri* (Istanbul, 1962); and C. M. Kortepeter, "Gazi Giray II, Khan of the Crimea, and Ottoman Policy in Eastern Europe and the Caucasus," *Slavonic and East European Review* Vol. 44, no. 102 (1966): p. 140.

30. "Istoricheskoi i diplomaticheskoe sobranie del proiskhodivskikh mezhdu Rossiiskimi Velikimi Kniaziami i byvshimi v Kryme tatarskimi tsariami s 1462 po 1533 god," *Zapiski odesskago obshchestva istorii i drevnosti* 5 (1863): 277–78, 379–80; S. Belokurov, *O posol'skom prikaze* (Moscow, 1906), pp. 78–79.

31. For example, the report of the Crimean envoy to the Polish king (1564) sent to Bahchesaray, with copy to Istanbul, Istanbul, Bashbakanlik Arshivi, *Mühimme Defteri*, vol. 6, doc. 97. See also Ozalp Gökbilgin, *1532-1577 Yillari Arasinda Kirim Hanliğinin Siyasi Durumu* (Ankara, 1973), for a discussion of this general problem.

32. Ananiasz Zajaczkowski, *La Chronique des steppes kiptchak* (Warsaw, 1966), p. 82; C. M. Kortepeter, *Ottoman Imperialism during the Reformation: Europe and the Caucasus* (New York, 1972); see also Mehmed Mubarek, *Meskukat-i Kirimiye* (Istanbul, 1900), which is a catalogue of existing Crimean coinage.

33. Petrun', "Khansiki Iarliki na Ukrains'ki Zemli," *Skhidnie Svit* (Kharkov, 1928), 2:170-87.

34. V. D. Smirnov, op. cit., pp. 309–11; and A. Bennigsen and Chantal Lemercier-Quelquejay, "La Moscovie, l'Empire ottoman et la crise successorale de 1577-1588 dans le Khanat de Crimée," *Cahiers du monde russe et soviétique*, 14 (1973): 453, 487.

35. Ozalp Gökbilgin, ed., *Tarih-i Sahib Giray Han* (Ankara, 1973), pp. 20-21, where it states: "Ali Chengiz Hanidir. . . . Kirim Hanlari ma'zul olmaz eba'an ced sahib-i saltanat ve sahib-i hutbe ve sahib-i sikke padishahlardir."

36. The text as well as French translation was published by Ananiasz Zajaczkowski, op. cit., and discussed in Ananiasz Zajaczkowski, " 'Letopis' kipchakskoi stepi' kak istochnik po istorii kryma," in A. S. Tveritinova, *Vostochnye istochniki po istorii narodov iugo-vostochnoi i tsentral'noi evropy*, (Moscow, 1969), 2:10–28.

37. See the published Polish edition: Hadzy Mehmed Senai z Krymu, *Historiu Chana Islam Gereja III*, ed. Olgierd Gorka and Zbigniew Wojcik (Warsaw, 1971) for citations above, pp. 89–91; Turkish text, pp. 1–3.

38. The Tatar text was edited and published by Adiunkt-Professor Mirza Kazembek as Seiid Mukhammed Riza, *Asseb' o-sseiiar' ili sem'planet'* (Kazan, 1832).

39. V. D. Smirnov, op. cit.; and *Krymskoe khanstvo pod verkhovenstvom otomanskoi porty v XVIII stoletii* (Odessa, 1889).

40. Riza, op. cit., pp. 87 (katl elchi-i cingiz), 131–32, 201–2.

41. I have not included the work edited and published by Ismail Hikmet Ertaylan, *Gazi Geray Han, Hayati ve Eserleri* (Istanbul, 1958), which is claimed to be a real "history" but which is in fact a series of poems written during the reign of Gazi Giray; nor the so-called "Tatar National Epic" published by A. Lebib Karan (in Tatar): *Tatarlarning Tupchigishi* (Istanbul, 1962), since its only claim to legitimacy rests on the oral traditions maintained by the Crimean Tatar exile community in Istanbul.

42. *Arkhiv Gosudarstvennago Soveta*, vol. 1, part 1 (St. Petersburg, 1869), p. 56; A. Skal'kovskii, "O Nogaiskikh tatarakh, zhivushchikh v Tavricheskoi gubernii," *Zhurnal Ministerstva Narodnago Prosveshcheniia* (1843), 2:123; E. I. Druzhinina, *Kiuchuk-kainardzhiiskii mir 1774 goda* (Moscow, 1955), p. 108.

43. Boris Nolde, *La Formation de l'Empire Russe*, (Paris, 1953), 2:59.

44. Necati Effendi, "Zapiski Mukhammeda Nedzhati-Efendi," *Russkaia Starina* (March 1894), p. 132.

45. *Sbornik imperatorskago russkago istoricheskago obshchestva*, 97:245-46.

46. Fisher, op. cit., for a more complete account of these first months of Crimean independence.

47. See Mark Pinson, "Russian Policy and the Emigration of the Crimean Tatars to the Ottoman Empire, 1854–1862," *Güney-Doğu Avrupa Arashtirmalari Dergisi* (Istanbul, 1972), 1:37–56 (to be continued in a later volume) for a discussion of the last of these emigrations.

48. Ethem Feyzi Gözaydin, *Kirim: Kirim Türklerinin Yerleshme ve Göchmeleri* (Istanbul, 1948); Alexandre Bennigsen and Chantal Lemercier-Quelquejay, *La Presse et le mouvement national chez les musulmans de Russie avant 1920* (Paris, 1964); Serge A. Zenkovsky, *Pan-Turkism and Islam in Russia* (Cambridge, 1960); and Cafer Saydahmet, *Gaspirali Ismail Bey: Dilde, Fikirde, Ishte Birlik* (Istanbul, 1934).

Carole Rogel

The Wandering Monk and the
Balkan National Awakening

The nineteenth century saw the Balkan peoples, who had been growing increasingly conscious of nationality, participating in rebellions against Ottoman rule. Some had been under foreign domination for five centuries; yet when it came to national awareness, these Balkan nations seemed not to be especially behind other peoples. Even Western Europe had just begun sorting itself into national units; both German and Italian unification were realized only after the middle of the nineteenth century. The national groups of the Hapsburg Empire, quick to be fired with the political ideals of German romanticism, had to put off until World War I a "national" resolution of their affairs. Some of the Balkan nations achieved independence even before the creation of an Italian kingdom or of a German empire; and all were freed before 1914.

A decaying Ottoman administration and the burgeoning imperialism of major European powers assisted the cause of Balkan nationalists. Indeed, without the encouragement of the great European states, it is unlikely that the Balkan nations could have succeeded so quickly in their nationalistic pursuits. These peoples, after all, were largely comprised of peasants—with certain notable exceptions among the Greeks and Romanians—and were by Western standards backward in almost every way. Still, when the powers engaged in various skirmishes with the Ottoman Empire in the nineteenth century, the Balkan nations joined them in the name of liberation for their respective peoples. More important, some understood "nation" in the modern, secular sense of the term. How may this be explained?

Some historians have suggested that the national consciousness of Albanians, Bulgars, Greeks, Romanians, and Serbs was a feature of their medieval inheritance that had survived the Ottoman period. It had been transmitted orally from generation to generation largely through the vehicle of the folk epic. The medium was rich, filled with the exploits of "national" heroes or the glories of medieval empires. The Ottoman system contributed to the survival of this sense of national identity. It did not encourage literacy or imperial political allegiances; it tended instead to isolate the peoples of the empire. The divisions generally followed religious boundaries and for decades separated Muslim towns from Christian countryside and later Muslim guilds from Christian guilds. That the Ottoman regime continued to rule according to traditional and religious bases served more than anything else to sustain Balkan national individuality. In reality, though, this was a "national" awareness rooted in the past. It was content with unfulfilled reveries, occasional millenarianism, and, in times of stress, sporadic peasant or brigand (*hajduk, haidut, klepht*) rebellions against local administrators.

The national consciousness that began to appear in the eighteenth century was another matter entirely, although at first it was not particularly distinguishable from the earlier expression. What made it in time distinct was that it did not draw exclusively upon native roots or derive from the epic past. That newer national awareness drew its spirit from Western European modes of thought; its adherents came to constitute an element in Balkan society that, not always deliberately, projected national feeling into a more modern, secular framework.

If we are to explain this phenomenon, we must investigate non-Muslim Balkan society from within. This is a difficult task, given the dearth of source material; moreover, a scholar dealing with Balkan-wide developments must contend with a babel of languages. Some studies have succeeded. The most impressive works produced on this transitional period have to do either with the appearance of the wandering native merchant or with those intellectual transformations that seem to have been linked with his emergence.[1]

Seventeenth- and eighteenth-century economic factors produced a native merchant class in Southeastern Europe.[2] The impetus came initially from a demand in Western and Central Europe for Balkan agricultural products—cotton and grain, especially maize. The feudal landlord began to require his peasants to produce these crops.[3] The sale and transport of these agricultural commodities was left to the non-Muslim sector of Balkan society. Jews, by the eighteenth century, had virtually ceased to be important as a commercial class in that part of the empire;[4] but the number of Balkan Christians who were outlaws or itinerants had been increasing. The Christians began to find occupation as traveling merchants since they could rarely establish entry into the town economy, where Muslim craft guilds restricted membership. They transported the goods produced by the Balkan peasant by mule, then by ship, to markets in the West. As merchants and shippers, the Greeks were leaders, but Romanians and Serbs, Albanians and Bulgars also produced a merchant class in the eighteenth century.[5] Soon these Balkan Christian merchants established permanent contacts and, later, colonies and even churches outside the empire. Their chief centers were in Vienna, Trieste, Leipzig, Livorno, Naples, and southern Russia. In these places the Orthodox merchant prospered, and was exposed inevitably to Western thinking and Western ways; many would say he was greatly impressed with what the West had to offer.[6]

Central to the understanding of Balkan development during

that period is the changing nature of East-West interaction.[7]
Until the eighteenth century, contacts between Balkan Christians and Western Europe had been irregular. The Ottomans
had not favored it; they tolerated it when military or diplomatic
interest required. The leadership of the Orthodox church de-
plored it; the West for them was Rome, bastion of ideological
error. Granted, just prior to the conquest of Constantinople,
the Eastern church under pressure from the Byzantine emperor
had effected a rapprochement with Rome; but after 1453 that
faction which opposed union had easily prevailed. Wishing to
avert a united Christian coalition against themselves, the Ottomans befriended the opponents of union and made them custodians of the Eastern church. In practical terms this meant
that after 1453 the church, dominated by anti-unionists, that is,
anti-Westerners, became a supporter of the regime. The
patriarch assumed the position of a high-ranking official in the
Ottoman administration.[8] Substantive East-West dialogue was
virtually terminated, not to resume for nearly three centuries.

When East-West contacts were resumed in the seventeenth
and eighteenth centuries, Rome had ceased to be the major
symbol of Western thought. In its place the authority of science had gained impressive weight. And it was the emerging
Balkan commercial class that developed an affinity for Western
ways and the new Western thought. Stavrianos has put it very
aptly: "So long as Western civilization was essentially Catholic and Protestant, it was unacceptable to the Orthodox peoples." However, "when it became primarily scientific and secular, it was acceptable and even desirable."[9]

The Eastern merchant, by the eighteenth century had come
through his commercial contacts in Central Europe to respect
the technological and material advances of the West. He also
came to envy the Europeans the regimes under which they
lived and to envy them their enlightened monarchs, who not
only promoted commercial development (and often invested
themselves), but seemed to have a forward-looking, compre-
hensive view of the needs of the state. From this view were
derived the enlightened economic, social, legal and even reli-

gious reforms of the eighteenth century, which in turn favored business growth. In this context the Hapsburg Joseph II, to some extent Maria Theresa, Russia's Catherine II, and even Peter the Great were viewed as monarchs whose policies created a benevolent climate for such advancement. These could be contrasted with the Ottomans, whose governing not only impeded progress but seemed to lack direction altogether.

As his contacts outside the Ottoman Empire increased, as his wealth accumulated, the Balkan merchant was led to inquire into the thoughts and the ideas of Europeans, for these seemed to be at the root of European successes. He wanted to know about things one could not learn in the Ottoman world, for there were few or no secular schools or printing presses and little dissemination even of contemporary technological and scientific information. So Balkan merchants learned foreign languages and bought foreign books. They brought printed material home with them and sent their sons to schools abroad. Some became, as a result, quite radical in their thinking; and merchants or sons of merchants, having absorbed Western enlightened political thought, even joined revolutionary societies in the early nineteenth century. And they were greatly responsible for one other development—making information available in the vernacular. If Balkan Christian society was to be truly revolutionized, it needed to be educated in the ways of more advanced societies and even about its own past—and this in its own tongues. Toward this end Balkan merchants became patrons of those who were learned and had facility with languages or those who wished to write in their own words about the history or cultural heritage of their people. Merchants readily subsidized publication in the vernacular, though at times perhaps for the gratification of seeing their names in print. Advance subscribers were always prominently listed at the back of the book.[10]

The native merchant class, however, was not the only element in non-Muslim Balkan society to contribute to an intellectual awakening in the late seventeenth and early eighteenth centuries. The Balkan monk played a significant role in opening the region to new ideas. Little has been written about this subject, partly because it is more difficult to establish the monk's relationship to a secular or national outlook than it is to associate the merchant with it. But it seems that monks did prepare the way, perhaps unwittingly at first, for a more worldly intellectual climate. Though much work needs to be done on the subject, two valuable sources have suggested some interesting possibilities for investigation. One is a detailed inventory of the Serbian monasteries of Fruška gora, dated 1753; the other, a collection of seventeenth- and eighteenth-century documents housed in Russian archives and relating to Serbian-Russian church contacts.[11] The sources deal primarily with Serbian monks, but much of what will be said of them might be applied to other monks in the Balkans. There was much intermingling, not only at Mount Athos (the Holy Mountain), where all the Eastern Orthodox peoples were traditionally represented in its numerous monasteries, but throughout the area of Southeastern Europe. In that period of intellectual awakening, Balkan monks led similar kinds of lives, and were able to compare experiences and exchange ideas whenever they came together.

This investigation of monks and their involvement in the Balkan national awakening was prompted by the fact that the first national histories and early studies of national language and culture so often were produced in monasteries or by clerics. Every Balkan people lists members of the monastic clergy among its national-spiritual forefathers. For the Bulgarians, it is Paisii Hilandarski (that is, Paisii of Hilandar monastery on Mount Athos) who is credited with giving impetus to a national regeneration. Paisii in 1762 did this by completing a Slaveno-Bulgarian history.[12] His work was carried on by another cleric, Sofronii, bishop of Vratsa. Romania boasts a trio of national forefathers—Gheorghe Şincai, Petru Maior, and Samuel Clain—all at one time students of Uniate theological seminaries in Transylvania. In the second half of the eighteenth century, they produced fundamental works on Romanian history, language, and culture.[13] The Serb nation, like the Bulgarian and Romanian, had monks among its national awakeners. Two of these were Jovan Rajić (1726–1801) and Dositej Obradović (1742–1811). The former is noted for his history, entitled, "Istorija raznyh slavenskih narodov naipače Bolgar, Horvatov, Serbov."[14] His initial interest had been the geography of the Balkans, which on his way to Russia he traversed on foot in order to record data about the terrain. Obradović wrote about Serbs through his own experiences. His approach is reminiscent of humanism, particularly in its evocation of classical values. It has been said of Obradović, who was at Hopovo monastery from 1757 until 1760, that he symbolizes the Serbian transition from an otherworldly to a secular outlook. It is interesting that Fruška gora, a community of Serbian monasteries of which Hopovo is one, is referred to by Obradović as "the Serbian Parnassus."[15] Those of a religious frame of mind had been accustomed to think of it primarily as a spiritual center, a "Serbian Mount Athos."[16]

From the time of Serbian conversion to Christianity, monasteries had played a predominant role in national, cultural, and political life. Monks had constituted both a social and intellectual elite. They were often related by blood to the Serbian ruling families, and some had once been political figures themselves. The monasteries molded the religious life of the Serbs. They also immortalized Serbian medieval heroes, preserving their remains as national relics. As centers of Serbian intellectual and cultural activity, the monasteries bore a distinct Byzantine imprint. But in the last two centuries before the Ottoman conquest, the art and literature produced in these monasteries had become unique and noted for quality and originality.

The defeat of Serbia changed all this. Some monasteries were ravaged by the conquerors. Others declined for lack of contributions and from the extinction of their Serbian ruling-class patrons. Orthodox Christian intellectual activity throughout the Balkans quickly deteriorated. Some monks fled abroad; when those who remained eventually died, their successors did not, or could not, sustain the tradition. The Greek

hierarchy, to whom the Turks had given supervision of Orthodox Balkan Christians, did not encourage learning. The local
Balkan clergy consequently lapsed into semi-literacy. To become a priest in those years, it was necessary only to be
able to read; but frequently even that requirement was disregarded. Church rites and liturgy were, more often than not,
simply transmitted orally from father to son, as certain families
became the priestly ones.[17] The monasteries of the Balkans,
formerly distinguished centers of learning, fell into disrepair
literally and intellectually. Few monks could read or write; few
felt it was important. This situation prevailed even on Mount
Athos, where little respect was shown for its libraries and
rich manuscript collections. Pages of old manuscripts, Runciman tells us, were casually used by monks to wrap their food.[18]

Serbian monasteries did not begin to revive until the sixteenth century. The establishment of a Serbian patriarchate at
Peć in 1557, making the Serbian Orthodox community autonomous (that is, free of the religious and political control of
the Greek patriarch), represents a kind of turning point.[19]
Though monks were having trouble preserving the walls of
monasteries, which Turks dismantled in order to build cara-
vansaries, the Serbian patriarchs began encouraging the reconstruction of existing monasteries and the establishment of
new ones. The patriarchs, however, could offer little more than
moral support to the monks, who needed to repair monastery
roofs and chapel walls and to replace church objects that had
been pillaged by the Turks. Ultimately, those who assisted
Serbian monks most were Orthodox Christians who had riches
and the inclination to donate them. Until 1711 help came from
the Romanian princes of Moldavia and Wallachia. But most of
all, the Serbs were aided by Russians.[20]

Serbian monks began traveling to Russia in the sixteenth
century with appeals to Moscow. Uspenski monastery in Belgrade was probably the first to send such envoys.[21] Papraća[22]
and Hilandar are known to have sent representatives as early
as 1551 and 1556 respectively; the Hilandar monks at that
time traveled with credentials from Ivan the Terrible.[23] Such

trips in the sixteenth century, however, were rare. Conditions in the Balkans, and in Russia as well, were probably still too unstable. After the mid-1620s, however, Balkan monks made frequent trips to the expanding Romanov state. These journeys continued until almost the end of the eighteenth century.[24]

The fate of these missions varied. Monks from the Balkans would travel to the frontier towns—Putivl', Sevš, Černigov, and later Kiev—where they would present their papers and their reasons for crossing the border. Their purpose would invariably be to reach Moscow in order to present an appeal to the czar. The monks then were required to wait at the frontier while their documents were sent to Moscow to be examined by Russian officials. This frequently took months, and the outcome was not always positive. Moscow often refused entry to the monks, directing the provincial administrators—most often in Putivl'—to give them alms and send them home. Monks certainly were not welcomed if they were suspected of coming to spy. Slavic monks had less difficulty in this regard than did Greeks, who were generally thought to be in the pay of the Turks.[25]

On the other hand, Moscow in the seventeenth century was sometimes eager for Balkan visitors; monks might bring useful (strategic?) information about conditions at home. We know that Papraća monks were turned away at Putivl' in 1630 because they had brought no "news" from their land.[26] Presumably those who did supply "news" were granted entry.

Church reformers were also interested in what Balkan monks might offer. Though monasteries in Southeastern Europe may have ceased to be intellectual centers, they continued to be repositories for valuable manuscripts that the Russians wanted to examine in order to authenticate their own religious tracts. During the period of Russian church reforms in the mid-seventeenth century, requests for manuscripts and books were frequently sent to Serbian monasteries. In 1655, for example, three Hilandar monks carried to Moscow eleven handwritten books (seven Slavic, four Greek), which had been specifically requested by the Russian Patriarch Arsenii Suk-hanov.[27] They were to be used, according to the official request, to correct Russian religious books. Similarly, monks from Mileševo were given Russian passports in 1668 in order to bring four books to Andrej Savvinov'.[28]

If Serbian monks were not expressly asked to bring manuscripts, they often brought them anyway. The monks undoubtedly believed that a gift, such as a book, a saint's relics, or wood carvings,[29] would dispose Moscow to welcome them. This did not always happen. Monks from Krušedol monastery at Fruška gora arrived in Putivl' in 1628 with the relics of three martyrs but were nevertheless turned back. Alms were given them at the border.[30] But then, in the case of monks bearing relics, the Russians had reason to be strict. Monks in the seventeenth century were not above offering false relics in order to get to Moscow.[31]

Among the monasteries that dispatched monks to the Russian frontier in the seventeenth and eighteenth centuries were several located at Fruška gora, a monastic community northwest of Belgrade, between the Sava and Danube rivers, about midway between Sremski Karlovci (Karlowitz) and Belgrade. Most of the twelve to fifteen monasteries established there have little record of their early history. Most very likely were founded in the fifteenth and early sixteenth centuries, though neither founders nor date of origin is verifiable in many cases.[32] The monasteries of Fruška gora were probably populated largely by monks fleeing northward from Turkish wars. After the 1690s, when the region of Srem was incorporated into the Hapsburg domain, some of the monks came to Fruška gora from Serbian communities to the north. But throughout the seventeenth and eighteenth centuries, its monasteries remained in need of financial assistance. Five of these monasteries consequently established ties with Russia and sent envoys to the East somewhat regularly. These were Hopovo, Remeta, Krušedol, Beočin, and Bešenovo.[33]

None of the five monasteries seems to have sent monks to Russia before 1622, though each sent representatives sometime during the 1620s and 1630s. They came to Putivl' with tales of Turkish onslaughts, of deteriorating monastery buildings, of church objects that had been pillaged and books that had been burned. All Fruška gora monks who traveled to Russia after the 1717–18 conflict between the Turks and the "Roman Emperor," as they referred to the Hapsburg ruler, lamented that, because of book burning and the destruction of church objects, they could not even perform their simplest daily services to God.[34] They waited at the frontier, as had other monks, for a response from Moscow to the provincial governor's dispatch. If the delegation was lucky (monks traveled in threes and fours, and frequently with servants), it would be permitted to travel to Moscow, where it hoped to obtain leave to beg for alms. At times the czar or the patriarch, or even the czarina, would present money, other valuables, or church objects to the Balkan mendicants. The gifts might be designated for a specific purpose, such as the repair of a church roof, or they might be given to individual monks. Sometimes monks would also receive permission to beg for alms among private individuals. Most coveted of all was an Imperial decree that would allow a monastery to send three or four monks to Russia every seven or eight years for the purpose of collecting alms.

The monks of Hopovo, Krušedol, and Remeta seem to have been more successful than other Fruška gora monks in their contacts with Moscow.[35] Some of the church objects—often described as made of silver, bejeweled, or gilded—and other goods and money donated to them are recorded in documents preserved in Russian archives.[36] Others are itemized in the 1753 inventory of Fruška gora monasteries, from which it is apparent that most monastery valuables were still primarily of Russian origin.[37] But whether or not Serbian monasteries benefited materially from their travels to Russia, their inhabitants were certainly exposed to intellectually broadening experiences. Over the years, from the 1620s to the mid-eighteenth century, the monks' journeys took them through many foreign lands such as Hungary, Lithuania, Little

Russia, and Poland; the itinerary depended upon the security of the region. They encountered Slavs and non-Slavs, Orthodox and Western Christians. One delegation brought along a former prisoner whom the monks had bought in Belgrade. He had been taken captive by Tatars and sold in Istanbul, and surely he had interesting tales to tell his escorts. Some monks themselves were robbed or apprehended by Tatars, Turks, or, in one case, by Arabs in North Africa.[38]

The journeys were long. Sometimes a year or more was spent on a particular mission. There was always a delay at the border and an opportunity to talk with new acquaintances. If permission was granted to go to Moscow, there would be a meeting with Russian rulers; and, of course, monks also came into contact with their own counterparts in Russian monasteries. Balkan monks were generally housed and fed by Russian monks. Bešenovo monks, for example, recorded that in 1721 they stopped for a time in Varlaam monastery in Smolensk.[39] Balkan monks sometimes also joined up with colleagues of other monasteries while traveling. Monks from Beočin, in 1629, joined with Romanian monks, who were carrying letters of introduction to the Russian patriarch from the Romanian metropolitan Grigori, the Kievan metropolitan Iov, and the metropolitan of Pečerski monastery, Peter Mogila.[40]

It is extremely important to keep in mind that, at the time Serbian monks were traveling to Russia, the Russian state and church were going through fundamental transformations. Russia was beginning to modernize and secularize, looking increasingly to the West for various kinds of expertise. The Balkan monks, as they came to rely on Russia for both material support and philosophical direction, were bound to be affected. The very frequency and duration of the contacts with Russia would render this inevitable. Moreover, there was no stigma attached to accepting ideas from Moscow (though there would have been aversion to similar interaction with Rome or even with the Greeks). Though it may seem paradoxical that Balkan monks had to go to Russia to absorb

Western concepts, it appears that this is, in fact, what happened. We know Balkan merchants had extensive contacts with the West and were opened to new perspectives through commercial exchange. The monks, on the other hand, interacted almost exclusively with Russians, or coreligionists. They, too, experienced an intellectual awakening. The actual process was all the more subtle for having flowed through Orthodox Russian channels.

In their contacts with Russia, Serbian monks were, among other things, witnesses to that state's becoming a secular absolute monarchy. The Serbs learned at first hand of the czar's determination to assert the principle of autocracy. Monks who arrived at the border with appeals in which the czar was not addressed as "autocrator" (*samodjeržec*), were sent away or, at the very least, duly reprimanded.[41] Most monks therefore learned to pay meticulous attention to addressing the emperor properly. The address became lengthy, the praise and flattery excessive.[42] The monks generally pledged daily prayers for the emperor and for the "glorious" Russian state.[43] In these matters and in appeals that the czar act as protector of Slavic Christians against Greeks and Turks who ravaged Serbian lands, one can discern the beginnings of a binding Serbian-Russian relationship.[44]

The Russian state during this time was also instituting religious reforms and through them asserting its authority over the church. The reforms were the result of decades of work and bore the imprint of Western cultural influences. Russians had consulted non-Russian scholars and religious documents extensively in their correction of religious texts. The Russian scholars themselves were often products of the Kievan Academy,[45] where Latin was a part of the curriculum and where humanistic influences were strong. There were many in Russia who would not accept the state-supported church reforms, but Balkan monks probably had little, if any, contact with the nonconformists. Serbian monks courted official Russia. They paid homage to the autocratic czar. It was, after all, at his pleasure that they might beg for alms. And, if they did not become educated in the reformed liturgy and the new church-state relationship while in Russia, the monks had ample opportunity to do so after returning to the Balkans. Among the gifts they carried back to their monasteries in substantial quantity were printed books—the products of official Russia's church reforms.

Whether Serbian monks traveling to Russia in the seventeenth century were particularly eager to obtain books is difficult to establish from documents in the Russian archives. We know only that Fruška gora delegations were definitely given liturgical texts. Beočin monks in 1622, Hopovo monks in 1641 and 1658, and Krušedol monks in 1650 brought back a variety of psalters, "apostols," prologues, evangels, numerous prayer books, and other religious reading materials.[46] A good many of these were presumably destroyed between 1716 and 1718, for Fruška gora monks who reached Russia thereafter all maintained that their books had been burned by Turks during recent warfare between the Hapsburg emperor and the Ottoman Empire.[47] On visits to Russia in the early eighteenth century, Serbian monks, therefore, made specific requests for more books.

That they received new supplies of Russian publications is evident from the 1753 inventory.[48] Virtually all of the printed books in the monastery collections (of rather respectable size),[49] or in the private possession of monks in 1753, had come from Russia. The inventory even specified whether the books were produced in Moscow, Kiev, or, on occasion, Lvov, and whether they had been acquired before or after 1733.[50] Unfortunately, the 1753 document does not indicate dates of publication, nor does it elaborate on author or contents of particular volumes.

We do know something more about the books at Fruška gora, however, from Ostojić, who in 1907 wrote about Dositej Obradović and his sojourn at Hopovo.[51] Ostojić examined Hopovo's library collection in order to determine how it might have influenced Obradović's intellectual development. Obradović read avidly in his three years at Fruška gora, often entering marginal notations in the volumes he read. Ostojić found that the Russian books at Fruška gora were overwhelmingly products of that intellectual awakening which took place in the seventeenth century in southwestern Russia, in those territories newly acquired from Poland and Lithuania. Books of the leading writers of the period—Gol'atovskij, Baranovič, Polotskij, Prokopovič, Javorskij, and others—were all to be found in one or more of the Fruška gora monasteries in 1753.[52] The writings themselves, Ostojić discovered, were not narrow or strictly religious; they demonstrated a wide range of interests, in spite of what the titles may have suggested.[53] The authors were men of the mid or late seventeenth century, who had introduced Greek and Latin learning into Russia. In their works they discussed astronomy and other scientific knowledge; they knew about ancient mythology, and they wrote histories.[54]

One can only conjecture about how many monks were influenced by these Russian books and in what way. Obradović, at Hopovo in the late 1750s, was clearly stimulated by them. In his *Life and Adventures*, he identifies some volumes that especially impressed him;[55] Ostojić discovered others by reading Obradović's marginal notes in Hopovo's library collection. Ostojić concluded that Obradović, between 1759 and 1766—that is, before he came directly under Western European intellectual influences—was still strongly motivated by what he had read at Hopovo. The outlook Obradović acquired at Hopovo was that of Russian scholasticism, as it had been established in the Polish territories from Western, Latin roots, says Ostojić, and it "was more than a small step toward a true Western view of the world."[56]

Though there is little other autobiographical literature to confirm it, many monks appear to have been similarly influenced by this Russian material. Balkan monks themselves began to write books for the first time in centuries. And though there was probably much religious veneer, what they wrote about was often of this world—the nation, its culture, its history. Sometimes, as in the case of Paisii, they included

entire passages from Russian-language books in their writings.[57] The Russian materials, one must repeat, were virtually the only ones available to these monks until the mid
eighteenth century.

Serbian monks were certainly not all national forefathers,
nor is it likely that even a majority of them were stimulated
directly by seventeenth-century Russian intellectual developments. Some would contend that the level of learning in Serbian monasteries was still extremely low in the mid eighteenth
century.[58] The monasteries of Fruška gora by this time, however, were no longer typically monastic. Worldy ways and
attitudes were evident even in the daily lives of the monks.
Isolation from the world, poverty, asceticism, meditation—
features commonly associated with monastic life—did not
predominate. The monasteries appear to have become a
kind of social and intellectual crossroads, a kind of hub of
activity for the Serbs. It may be difficult to determine to what
degree Russian learning precipitated and shaped this new life
style, but we can say that both Russian influences and a more
worldly orientation characterized Fruška gora monasteries by
the mid eighteenth century.

It is evident from the inventory made of the Fruška gora
monasteries in 1753 that its inhabitants had a wide variety of
background and experience. They came from far-flung regions
of the Balkans and from the central Danubian area. Most
were educated, but training varied in content and level of
competence. The inventory indicates just how well each monk
read, wrote, and sang. It also records the place where the
monk had been educated and who had been his mentor.
Again, the range of experience was quite broad. Most of the
monks traveled periodically, many had been married, and
some had children. If a monk had living relatives, this is
indicated in the monk's inventory profile. Relatives are also
located geographically and sometimes identified by profession. It is interesting that a monk might have sons or brothers
who were merchants living in nearby towns.[59]

A sketch of one of the monasteries, taken from information

in the 1753 inventory, illustrates this diversity in background. Krušedol in that year was inhabited by eighteen monks of various ranks (an archimandrite, ten hieromonachs, one hieromonach hegumen, two hierodeacons, and four regular monks).[60] The monastery also had three students and eight servants. These servants often accompanied monks on their travels and, according to the inventory, were being paid in *forints* for their labor. Five families, who, in the words of the survey, were "from Turkey" (presumably because they fled the Ottoman Empire in wartime) also lived on monastery land.[61]

Most of the eighteen monks at Krušedol had come from nearby areas. Three were actually born at the monastery; others came from the Banat, Bačka, and territory just to the north of Belgrade. One, however, came from Montenegro, one was from Hungary, and another was Wallachian.[62] With regard to the monks' places of origin, there was probably more homogeneity at Krušedol than at other Fruška gora monasteries. Remeta had a Greek, a Bulgarian, a Little Russian, and a monk from Arad.[63] At Kuverždin there were monks from Croatia, Bosnia, and Dalmatia.[64] At Hopovo, there was a monk from Osijek and a Greek from Turkey. Šišatovac listed a monk from the region of the Polish border. At Jazak there were women, two of whom had come from Bulgaria.[65]

Of the eighteen monks at Krušedol, only one seems to have been completely illiterate; his training had been as a soap-maker and blacksmith.[66] The others appear to have had a respectable amount of instruction. What is interesting about this education is that it, too, varied from one monk to another. About a third of Krušedol's monks in 1753 had been instructed by regular clergy, either at Krušedol or at nearby monasteries. Another third had been trained by secular clergy in towns to the south such as Peć or Zemun. The rest had been instructed by laymen, either tutors ("magisters") or schoolteachers. The tutors and schoolteachers were often located in growing commercial centers, among them Novi Sad and Karlowitz. Some Fruška gora monks had even studied at the Karlowitz Orthodox Latin School.[67]

At Fruška gora by the time of the 1753 visitation, monks no longer lived communally, a situation that Pavel Nenadović, the initiator of the inquiry, later sought to remedy.[68] Monks often worked plots that they owned privately, where they grew grapes and plums. Both the number of containers for wine and brandy and the number of vines or plum trees that each monk possessed are enumerated in the inventory.[69] Monks had other private possessions, such as icons, books, animals, or even money.[70] Monks, moreover, did not seem to be restricted in their movements or in their contacts. Regular visits to nearby towns were common,[71] and townspeople must have also frequented Fruška gora. The marginal remarks in a book at Hopovo, for example, indicate that it had been read by Lazar Isaković, a merchant from Novi Sad.[72]

Traditional monastic life was declining at Fruška gora in the eighteenth century. Some monks would assume prominence as intellectuals in the emerging secular, commercial society. Merchants would generally subsidize their writings. Other monks left the monastery, as would Obradović in 1760. At Krušedol, between 1740 and 1753, eight monks had died and ten had left, leaving only eighteen inhabitants for the inventory to list. Of the ten who had left, only three moved on to other monasteries (one of these resettled at Hilandar). Six ran away: one to Montenegro, one to Belgrade, one to Turkey; the destination of the others is not known. Of the six who fled, two were reported to have married. A tenth monk left for the Banat with the permission of the eparch. Once there, he abandoned Orthodoxy and converted to Roman Catholicism.[73] The old order, under the impact of new ideas, was clearly breaking down.

These observations about the nature of monastic society are intended to help explain conditions that favored an intellectual awakening among the Serbs. The milieu of the mid eighteenth century was clearly receptive to outside (that is, Russian) intellectual influences, and it encouraged native scholarly activity. In the previous century Serbian monks hardly seemed interested in examining their own manuscripts, much less in writing scholarly works. By the second decade of the eighteenth century, on their journeys to Russia they were requesting books; and by 1720 the Serbs had established their own Latin school. Although this essay has focused on the monks of Fruška gora, much of what is written here might apply to other Serbian monastic communities.

Certain aspects of the topics have not been examined. It seems most important here to emphasize that the monks' journeys were regular and had a certain continuity, particularly after 1620. The political and intellectual situation in Russia has been alluded to only briefly. It would be interesting to discover why certain czars, such as Michael (1613–45), Alexis (1645–76), or Peter (1696–1725) welcomed Balkan visitors and exactly how Russian patronage of Balkan areas evolved in this early period. Whether the Serbian monks were aware of the turbulence of Russian internal affairs or of Russia's fortunes in wars with the Ottoman Empire is hardly mentioned in sources used for this study.[74] The subject of Russian intellectual influences on the Balkans—particularly the nature of the influence and the means by which it was transmitted—also requires elaboration.

Another topic treated only peripherally here is the relationship of the Fruška gora monasteries to the Hapsburg Empire. The monasteries had come under Hungarian, that is, Hapsburg, jurisdiction in the last decade of the seventeenth century. Each of the monasteries was subsequently accorded an imperial decree assuring it of the ruler's protection. The earliest of the decrees was issued during the 1690s by Leopold I; most, however, date from the reign of Joseph I (1705–11).[75] The Hapsburgs guaranteed exiled Serbs, who had fled from the Turks with their patriarch in 1690, religious freedom and some administrative autonomy. And the Hapsburgs did not oppose Serbian scholarly activities. The earliest Serbian books in the modern period were, in fact, published in printing houses in southern Hungary or in Vienna.[76] Yet Serbs continued to go to Russia regularly in the eighteenth century and continued to look to the East for philosophical guidance. The Hapsburgs tolerated this until the mid 1770s.

Serbian intellectual development and the emergence of a modern Serbian national consciousness were also affected by the existence of an autonomous Serbian patriarchate. It had been reestablished under the Ottomans by a grand vezir of Bosnian Serb origins,[77] and it lasted from 1557 to 1766. The history of the patriarchate was stormy. Spokesmen for the Serbian church were forced to be assertive. The patriarchate came to regard itself as the leadership of "Serbia" (even the Porte referred to it as the "Serbian throne");[78] and it began to offer ethnic reasons for the existence of the nation. Given the absence of a Serbian state, of a Serbian ruling class, and the flight of the people from traditional Serbian territory, the ethnic justification of nationhood was the only one that might be used to explain the patriarch's position. Since Hadrovics has covered this subject thoroughly, it need not be discussed here.[79] It should be noted, however, that the Serbian patriarchate, like the monasteries, became dependent on Russia's patronage.

After 1690, the exiled Serbian church administration established itself in Karlowitz, not far from the monasteries of Fruška gora. Serbian commercial activity centered in Karlowitz and nearby towns, such as Zemun and Novi Sad. The Hapsburg Serbian community soon became an intellectual Piedmont for the Serbs, where thrived the secular and Western ideas that had been transmitted to it via Russia. This community at the turn of the century would supply Serbian rebels in the Ottoman Empire with financial assistance against the Turks, and it would provide intellectual justification for the national state that would emerge in the wake of the Napoleonic wars. Dositej Obradović, having left Fruška gora in 1760 to travel extensively in the West, was one of those who supported the rebellion that broke out in 1804 in the Pashalik of Belgrade. He left the Hapsburg state, where he had been living since the eighties, to become secretary to

Karageorge, leader of the insurgents. When the first stage of the rebellion against the Turks was over, Obradović was made superintendent of Serbian schools. As a former monk, Obradović had clearly translated what he had learned in Russian language books at Fruška gora into secular, nationalistic terms. This transition from an other-worldly to a secular Western-oriented outlook must have been repeated innumerable times among Serbian clergy and middle-class elements in the eighteenth century. One thing is clear: such developments did not augur well for the Ottoman Empire, which was trying to maintain its power on traditional religious foundations.

1. See L. S. Stavrianos, "Antecedents to the Balkan Revolutions of the Nineteenth Century," *Journal of Modern History* 29 (1957): 335–48. L. S. Stavrianos, *The Balkans since 1453*, (New York, 1963), chap. 9. L. S. Stavrianos, "The Influence of the West on the Balkans," *The Balkans in Transition*, ed. Charles and Barbara Jelavich, (Berkeley, Calif., 1963), pp. 184–226. Traian Stoianovich, "The Conquering Balkan Orthodox Merchant," *Journal of Economic History* 20 (1960): 234–313. Traian Stoianovich, "Land Tenure and Related Sectors of the Balkan Economy, 1600–1800," *Journal of Economic History* 13 (1953): 398–411.

2. Stoianovich, "The Conquering Balkan Orthodox Merchant," pp. 234–313.

3. Stoianovich, "Land Tenure," pp. 398–411.

4. Stoianovich, "The Conquering Balkan Orthodox Merchant," pp. 244–48

5. Among the Serbs, pig-raising became the chief occupation (ibid., pp. 282 83).

6. They moved in especially great numbers into Southern Hungary, the Voivodina, and Croatia-Slavonia (ibid., pp. 266–67).

7. Stavrianos, "The Influence of the West," pp. 184–96.

8. For a summary of the relationship of the Orthodox church to the Ottoman administration, see Steven Runciman, *The Great Church in Captivity*, (Cambridge, 1968), pp. 165–85.

9. Stavrianos, "The Influence of the West," p. 188.

10. See, for example, *Život i Priključenija Dimitrija Obradovića*, (Belgrade, 1833), where subscribers are listed at the back of the book and are identified by profession and the town in which they live.

11. *Opis srpskih fruškogorskih manastira od 1753 godine*, ed. D. Ruvarac (Sremski Karlovci, 1905), pp. 1-488 (cited hereafter as *Opis*). "Gradja za srpsku istoriju iz ruskih arhiva i biblioteka," ed. St. Dimitrejević, *Spomenik*, 53 (1922), 1 289 (cited hereafter as "Gradja").

12. Paissi, whose work was distributed in handwritten copies, found documentary material for his history at Hilandar and at Zografu, both monasteries on Mount Athos. He rendered Slaveno-Bulgarian history in humanistic terms, having been

familiar with the writing of Mavro Orbini (in Russian translation), from whose work Paissi appropriated parts for his own history. Orbini had been lavish in his praise of Slavs.

Paissi, it is interesting to note, was sent by Hilandar in 1761 to Karlowitz, near Fruška gora, a monastic community that will be discussed below. See "Nekoliko nepoznatih podataka o Paisiju Hilandarskom," *Hilandarski Zbornik* (Belgrade, 1966) 1: 171–81. Also see Dimitr Kossev, "Sur l'idéologie de Paisij de Chilendar," *Paisii Khilendarski i negovata epokha 1762-1962*) (Sofia, 1962), pp. 7–32; Emil Georgiew, "Paisij Hilendarski-Zwischen Renaissance und Aufklärung," *Paisii Khilendarski i negovata epokha (1762–1962)* (Sofia, 1962), pp. 253–84; and Hristo Hristov, "Paissi of Hilendar: Author of the Slav-Bulgarian History," *East European Quarterly* 8 (Summer 1974): 167–75.

13. See Keith Hitchins, "Samuel Clain and the Rumanian Enlightenment in Transylvania," *Slavic Review* 23 (1964): 660–75.

14. Miroslav Ravbar and Stanko Janež, *Pregled Jugoslovanskih Književnosti* (Maribor, 1960), p. 93.

15. Dositej Obradović, *The Life and Adventures of Dimitrije Obradović,* ed. and trans. George Rapall Noyes (Berkeley, Calif., 1953), p. 191.

16. Boško Strika, *Srpske Zadužbine: Fruškogorski Manastiri* (Zagreb, 1927), p. 52. The author, wiring in 1927, refers to Fruška gora as a "Serbian Athos."

17. Ladislas Hadrovics, *L'Eglise serbe sous la domination turque* (Paris, 1947), pp. 16–21. Although Hadrovics's study is about the Serbian church under the Ottomans, he extends his comments on the intellectual level of the Serbian clergy to the Bulgarian and Romanian churches as well. Citing *Acta Bulgariae,* pp. 69–70, 96, as his source, Hadrovics notes that among Bulgarian clergy who could read few understood the meaning of what was written. Discussing the Romanians, Hadrovics observes that the situation was even worse than among the Serbs and Bulgarians; for in the cases of the latter two, at least the Old Slavonic reading material bore some resemblance to the vernacular, whereas in the Romanian church it was virtually incomprehensible to the Romanian speaker. See also Runciman, op. cit., pp. 219, 224.

18. Runciman, op. cit., p. 224.

19. On the Peć patriarchate, see R. Grujić, "Pećska partijaršija (1346–1463, 1557–1766)," *Narodna Enciklopedija Srpsko-Hrvatsko-Slovenačka* (1928), 3:395–99. See also Hadrovics, op. cit., pp. 1–168.

20. R. Grujić, "Monaštvo i manastira kod pravoslavnih Srba," *Narodna Enciklopedija,* 3:1029–31.

21. Ibid., p. 1030.

22. "Gradja," p. 187.

23. Greek Documents 7131, no. 6; 7132, no. 6, cited in ibid., p. 116. In order to determine the year according to the Gregorian calendar 5508 must be subtracted from the Russian date; for example, 7132 – 5508 = 1624. 1624 was the year Czar Michael renewed Ivan the Terrible's decree, so that Hilandar monks might again travel to Russia.

24. *Letopis Matice Srpske,* 158 (1889), 27, cited in ibid., p. 199.

25. Peter the Great in 1708 ordered that all Greek clerics register with the authorities. He was determined to halt the spying and intrigues of Greek clerics in Russia. Greek Documents 1708, no. 2, cited in ibid., p. 134.

26. Greek Documents 7139, no. 2, cited in ibid., p. 187.

27. Ibid., p. 126. Dimitrejević indicates where each of the volumes is located in Russian libraries.

28. Greek Documents, 7176, no. 23, cited in ibid., p. 163.

29. Monks from Krušedol in 1684 brought with them two carved wooden crosses for the co-rulers of Russia, Ivan and Peter (ibid., p. 196).

30. Greek Documents 7137, no. 4, cited in ibid., p. 194.

31. Ibid., p. 134.

32. See Strika, op. cit., pp. 51–178, for a historical sketch of these monasteries.

33. "Gradja," pp. 189-211.

34. Greek Documents 1720, no. 11, cited in ibid., p. 194; also see pp. 197, 205, and Greek Documents 1721, no. 2, p. 211.

35. See ibid., pp. 189-206.

36. See, for example, Greek Documents 7174, nos. 54, 63, cited in ibid., p. 204.

37. *Opis*, pp. 240–49, 279–93, 328–43.

38. Greek Documents 7173, no. 30, cited in "Gradja," p. 204; *Opis*, pp. 261–62.

39. Ibid., p. 209. Some Serbian monks lived and studied in Russia (see ibid., pp. 174–75).

40. Greek Documents 7138, no. 3, cited in ibid., p. 206. In this case, Beočin monks were stopped at Putivl' where they were given alms and sent back to Fruška gora. Yet they must have gained insights from having traveled with the Romanians, who bore letters from distinguished clerics.

Peter Mogila was the son of the hospodar of Wallachia (1601–7) and of Moldavia (1607–9). Born in 1596, he was brought up in Poland and educated in foreign universities. He is known best for his establishment of a college at Kiev in 1632; it later became the Kievan Academy. At this institution Latin was, according to Treadgold, the *chief* language of instruction. Those affiliated with this school are credited with revolutionizing Russian intellectual development by exposing it to Western learning. Though Kiev itself was not a part of the Russian state until 1667, churchmen and scholars in Moscow were taking cues from the Mogila school by the early 1650s.

The Kievan metropolitan mentioned in the text was Iov Boretsky, probably an early patron of Mogila. See Donald Treadgold, *The West in Russia and China: Religious and Secular Thought in Modern Times* (Cambridge, 1973), vol. 1 (Russia, 1472–1917), pp. 57–60.

41. "Gradja," p. 190. A monk from Remeta in 1624 was reprimanded for addressing Michael as *knjaz* of all Russia. He explained that in his language the term *knjaz* had only the highest connotations, and that he meant no offense in not using *samodjeržec*. The Russians also questioned the Remeta monk's system of dating, which was reckoned according to the date of Christ's birth. Russians, who urged calendar reform later in the century, defended it on the grounds that Balkan coreligionists already used the proposed system.

42. For example, see how monks of Krušedol address Alexis Mikhajlovič in 1650: Greek Documents 7159, no. 3, cited in ibid., p. 195.

43. Ibid.

44. Ibid., p. 129. Monks from Hilandar seemed particularly anxious to be protected from the Greeks. This appeal was written in 1683, but in it the monks recited a whole history of abuses suffered at the hands of either the Greeks or the Turks.

45. The Kievan Academy was founded by Mogila in 1632.

46. Ibid., pp. 195, 201, 204, 206.

47. Ibid., pp. 197, 205, 209.

48. See, for example, how the books and manuscripts of Hopovo are listed: *Opis*, pp. 248–50.

49. Hopovo in 1753 had 113 books: 28 were in Serbian (26 manuscripts, 2 printed books); all the rest were printed Russian books (see Tihomir Ostojić, *Dositej Obradović u Hopovu* [Novi Sad, 1907], p. 341).

50. Inventories of the Fruška gora monasteries had been taken in 1733 and 1740, but neither is extant.

51. See note 49 above for bibliographical citation.

52. Ostojić, op. cit., p. 340. See Francis Dvornik, *The Slavs in European History and Civilization* (New Brunswick, N.J., 1962), pp. 510–20, and Treadgold, op. cit., pp. 54–115, for the contributions of these writers to Russian intellectual development.

53. Simeon Polotskij, who was interested in child-rearing, for example, included observations on the subject in his collected sermons (Ostojić, op. cit., pp. 346–48).

54. Ostojić (ibid., pp. 336–52) identifies and abstracts the Russian books housed in one or more of the Fruška gora monasteries by 1753. Among these were: Gol'atovskij's *Kljuc razum'enije* (4 copies), his *Mesija* (1 copy), Baranovič's *Meč duhovnii* (3 copies), Polotskij's *Objed duševnii* (2 copies), Javorskij's *Kamen' vjeri* (3 copies), Teofan's *Reglament' Duhovnii* (3 copies), Baronius's (a Jesuit, whose work was translated into Russian) history (4 copies), Maksimovič's *Bogomislije* (2 copies), Kopinskij's *Alfabit' duhovnii* (6 copies), the *Paterik pečerski* (1 copy), and Mogila's *Trebnik* (1 copy).

55. Obradović, op. cit., pp. 191–208.

56. Ostojić, op. cit., p. 367.

57. See footnote 12 above.

58. Obradović, op. cit., Noyes's introduction, pp. 6–7.

59. At Remeta monastery one of the monks had three sons who were merchants, and another had two merchant brothers; the first monk was a Greek, the second a Bulgarian (*Opis*, pp. 321–22).

60. Of the more than one dozen monasteries at Fruška gora, Krušedol was selected for this profile because it was one of the five that had regularly sent monks to Russia; the others were Hopovo, Beočin, Bešenovo, and Remeta. Hopovo was eliminated since Noyes has discussed it at some length in his introduction to *The Life and Adventures of Dimitrije Obradović*, as has Ostojić in *Dositej Obradović u Hopovu*.

61. *Opis*, pp. 278–79.

62. Ibid., pp. 261–73.

63. Ibid., pp. 318–21.

64. Ibid., pp. 172–73.

65. Ibid., pp. 232–33, 137, 98.

66. Ibid., p. 273.

67. Ibid., pp. 261–72. An Orthodox Latin school had been established in Sremski Karlovci (Karlowitz) in 1720 (see Peter Sugar and Ivo Lederer, *Nationalism in Eastern Europe* [Seattle, Wash., 1969], p. 402). Some of the Fruška gora monks had studied there. One Krušedol monk in 1753 reported that his brother was currently a student at the Latin school in Karlovci. The very idea of an "Orthodox" Latin

school suggests that the Serbs were emulating their Russian patrons in their own intellectual development.

68. Nenadović was the eparch of Sremski Karlovci and the Serbian Metropolitan (ibid., p. 1).

69. Obradović, living in Belgrade in 1808, was sent kegs of wine by a monk at Fruška gora (Obradović, op. cit., Noyes's introduction, p. 54).

70. See, for example, *Opis*, p. 274.

71. Obradović, op. cit., Noyes's introduction, p. 7.

72. Ostojić, op. cit., p. 377.

73. *Opis*, pp. 273–74.

74. On occasion, monks arriving at Putivl' might say that they had come to Russia because they had heard that the czar had recently made peace with the Turkish enemy; little else, however, seems to have been reported about current events ("Gradja," p. 204).

75. Most of the monastery libraries at Fruška gora possess a number of decrees from the eighteenth century, the initial decree giving to the monastery Hapsburg protection and the decrees of subsequent rulers renewing the pledge or modifying it; see, for example, *Opis*, pp. 301–2.

76. Ravbar and Janež, op. cit., p. 92.

77. Mehmet Sokolli (Sokolović) as grand vezir was instrumental in establishing an autonomous Serbian church. His brother Makarij, a monk at Hilandar, was made its head.

78. Hadrovics, op. cit., pp. 108–9.

79. Ibid., pp. 110–11.

William Spencer

Ottoman North Africa

North Africa, the Bilad al-Maghrib or western region of the Arab-Islamic world, held a special status in the Dar al-Islam long before the assumption of Islamic leadership by the Ottomans. This special status, assigned to the region by the Arabs but echoed by both previous and subsequent invaders, was derived from certain behavior patterns that in a later age would be considered essential components of nationalism. The reputation of North Africans for courage, resiliency, and treacherous behavior was attested to by none other than the Caliph 'Umar Ibn al-Khattab in his famous warning to 'Amr Ibn al-'As when the latter proposed to march on *Ifriqiya* (Little Africa—Tunisia and Libya): "It is by no means Ifriqiya, but rather *al-mufarriqa*, the land of treachery which misleads and betrays and which no one shall attack so long as the water of my pupils shall bathe my eyes."[1] The militant defense of their homeland, which produced such heroes as Jugurtha, Massinissa, Kusaila, Kahina, and more recently 'Abd al-Qadir, 'Abd al-Krim, and 'Umar Mukhtar, represents in retrospect a nationalist effort capable of obtaining the support of at least some segments of the North African population.

The absence of a collective national consciousness in the Maghrib limited the effectiveness of these figures to one of essentially local particularism. The Maghrib peoples were, and to some extent still are, supremely tribal. In common with other dispersed ethnic groups such as the Kurds and Basques, they have preserved a unique capacity to assimilate external forces without alteration to their basic cultural value system. The Arab warrior-missionaries carrying the Prophet's message westward, when they paused at sunset for the ritual evening prayer (*salat al-maghrib*), gave North Africa its first regional identification but also signaled their awareness that Islamization would require more subtle means than preaching or conquest by force of arms.

Nationalism in North Africa, therefore, springs from deeper wells of consciousness than the purely Islamic. It is derived from the configuration of the land, which forced populations to coexist in relatively small isolated units; from the Berber egalitarian tradition and the floating pattern of *soffs*, or expediency alliances, observed by many writers;[2] and from the ideological resistance to Arabism generated by the Kharijite heresy. The resentment of Maghribi Berber tribes to the exactions of the caliphs' governors and tax-collectors assumed the proportions, at times, of a class struggle.

The Arabs, although they had arrived by an overland route and were identified as cultural brothers, as well as possessors of a desirable religion, language, and social system, seemed to be imposing unjustified restraints on full participation by the Berbers in the development of the *umma*. Yet Maghribi nationalism lacked the essential ingredients of full social cohesion, profound religious vision, and supratribal leadership that might have enabled it to progress beyond the class struggle to genuine regional or ethnic unification. The grand design of the Almoravid amirs, and the even grander one of Ibn Tumart's al-Muwahhidun, inspired an ephemeral linking of the region under a single indigenous caliph, but each movement foundered in less than a century.[3] Opposition to their strict orthodoxy, the distances between urban centers, and the endemic rivalry of those same centers conspired to undermine central authority even as it was being established.

The formation of an acceptable, visible nationalism in North Africa outside of Morocco was in large measure the work of the Ottoman Turks. Ottoman rule was introduced by corsair captains supplemented by contingents of *Yenicheri* (Janissaries), and solidified through a state bureaucracy modeled on that existing elsewhere in the empire. The end product was three nation-states: Algiers, Tunis, and Tripoli, whose structure, institutions, external policies, and socioeconomic cohesion marked them as different from anything that had existed previously in the region. The durability of these states is shown not only by their capacity to dominate western Mediterranean affairs for three centuries, but also by the lengths to which European powers went to denigrate their legitimacy during the period of French (and in Tripoli's case, Italian) colonization.[4]

This chapter will concern itself primarily with the elements and growth of North African nationalism during the period of Ottoman rule. Since our objective in this book is to examine national development in a multinational state, it could be said that North African nationalism is neither Arab, nor Turkish, nor even non-Arab, but that it combines elements of all three. The Ottoman presence, however, provided the North Africans with more than a means of attachment to the highest Islamic authority and the establishment of legitimate governments. The attachment of the three states was *filial*—they were at all times *eyalat* (or sometimes referred to as *eyalat-i mümtaze*), "autonomous provinces" of the empire. The Ottoman leaven was considerable; it introduced administrative concepts, a bureaucratic establishment, customs, costumes, language, and many other cultural elements. The degree of filial obligation varied, and for long periods the eyalats pursued independent foreign policies, although these were always designed to maintain Ottoman interests. Ottoman North

Africa's relationship to the parent state is perhaps epitomized
by an inscription on the wall of the Mosque of the Chavush,
built by the soldiers of the Algiers garrison in the sixteenth
century. It reads: "This mosque has been built by the Sultan,
Süleyman, Religious Defender of the God of the Worlds,
Lord of the Two Seas . . . [and] our Master Khayr al-Din,
son of the famed Prince, Champion of the Faith, Abu Yusuf
Yakub the Turk. . . . "[5]

The Ottoman advance into North Africa was undertaken for
two reasons: to secure the region as an essential forward
base against the renewed militancy of Christian Europe (led
by Spain), and to reunite the divided Dar al-Islam under the
rule of the sultan-caliph. In accomplishing these objectives,
the Ottomans relied heavily on the *jihad* appeal to unem-
ployed, dispossessed, or adventurous sea captains and their
crews operating throughout the Mediterranean in defiance of
the commercial or treaty agreements governing relations between various Mediterranean city-states. Those engaging in
these extralegal activities were known as corsairs, members
of a trade practiced for centuries in the waters from Gibraltar
to Suez. It remained for the Ottomans to regularize the corsair "profession" as an instrument of state policy.[6] Corsairs
who elected to accept the invitation were enrolled as auxili-
aries in the Ottoman fleet, subsidized as well as remunerated
for exceptional exploits, and regardless of origin could aspire
to high rank in the imperial military establishment.[7]

In a corresponding manner, the sultans prudently permitted
a wide latitude of operations to the corsair squadrons. They
were expected to supply contingents of manpower and war-
ships upon request if the empire felt threatened by external
attack or engaged itself in major naval campaigns, as at
Lepanto. Notification to Istanbul of changes in leadership in
the three eyalats—an event that took place more frequently
in Algiers than in Tripoli or Tunis, owing to differing methods
of selection and greater factional conflict in the former—was
customary and was reciprocated by the sultans with dispatch
of the appropriate symbols of investiture.[8] Otherwise, the

corsairs were assumed to be operating under mandate from God, transmitted through a chain of command down from the sultan and delegated through his instruments of authority. They flew their own flags while at sea, and they formed in each eyalat a self-sufficient union or guild, the *taife reisi*. Although the *taife* at certain periods contributed to the factionalism of the ruling establishment in Ottoman North Africa, notably in Algiers,[9] in the main the corsairs' marine vocation and their polyglot backgrounds militated against political involvement.

Inasmuch as the three North African eyalats developed along distinctive lines, a brief description of the circumstances of their incorporation into the Ottoman Empire is in order. Algiers was the first province to be incorporated into the empire. An insignificant town with a mediocre anchorage formed by three islets (*jaza'ir*, the name given it by the Arabs), it developed a modest urban identity under a merchant oligarchy as a result of Islamic-Christian economic coexistence in the Mediterranean. The oligarchy's local autonomy was assured by the protection of the seminomadic Tha'liba tribe, which controlled the Algerine hinterland, under an agreement whereby the Tha'liba provided protection against all outside forces in return for tribute, trading privileges, and recognition of their paramount shaykh as commander-in-chief of the city.[10]

The Tha'liba, however, proved unequal to the task of resisting the Spanish occupation of Algiers. The oligarchy avoided a direct Spanish assault in 1511 only by agreeing to pay an annual tribute; the Spaniards installed a fortified post on one of the islands (the Peñon), whose guns assured Spanish authority over the port from a distance of several hundred yards. A change of rulers in Spain encouraged the Algerines to seek a Muslim protector to aid them in overcoming the Spanish garrison and ending the obnoxious tribute. Al-Tawmi, then paramount shaykh of the Tha'liba, sent an emissary to certain corsairs installed in a port some distance up the coast. The corsairs, well known to European history as the brothers Barbarossa, accepted the invitation, becoming, as events unfolded, the principal agents in the organization of Ottoman North Africa.[11]

The assumption of power in Algiers in 1516, which was made first by Aruj (Oruc) and subsequently transferred to his younger brother Khayr al-Din, was made on the basis of an agreement that specified that Algerine municipal sovereignty would be respected. Other provisions of the agreement were that no new taxes would be imposed, and that the corsairs and their Kabyle allies would depart as soon as the Spanish fortress on the Peñon had been reduced. However, the corsair cannon proved ineffective against the Spaniards. His lack of success caused Oruc to arrogate more and more of the functions of municipal authority to himself and his supporters. He drew on the public treasury to pay the three hundred Janissaries whom the Hafsid ruler of Tunis had lent him for the expedition to Algiers. Turkish officers were assigned to supervise such municipal responsibilities as customs receipts, proper use of weights and measures, and price scales in the principal markets. These actions not only violated the agreement but began to appear to the oligarchy as a trend toward military occupation by foreigners. A conspiracy was launched to assassinate Oruc with the cooperation of the Tha'liba shaykh, who had prudently withdrawn to the tribal encampment outside the city. Oruc learned of the conspiracy, invited the shaykh back to Algiers to discuss the terms of withdrawal, and is said to have strangled the Tha'liba leader while the latter was in the midst of ablutions for the noon prayer. Then the Janissaries and Kabyle horsemen, fully armed, conducted Oruc to the Great Mosque, where they saluted him as king of Algiers.[12]

Apart from the lack of effective internal opposition, Algerine acceptance of the transfer of power from a native North African chief to a Levantine corsair was assured when Oruc notified the sultan of his assumption of power in Algiers and requested the protection of the Ottoman Porte. The corsair also established the basic political organization of the state, with authority vested in the three-hundred-man Janis-

sary corps that had accompanied him from Tunis, the *Ocak*.[13]
It is doubtful, however, that Oruc intended the attachment to
be more than one of convenience as he attempted to expand
his personal power across North Africa. His death in an
ambush near Tlemcen left Khayr al-Din in command at
Algiers. Khayr al-Din, less motivated by similar ambitions
than by the grand design of extending Ottoman power against
its adversaries, sent an emissary to Istanbul to ask the sultan
for reinforcements. The campaign was described as one
inspired by the defense of Islam against its greatest foes,
the Spaniards. In response Sultan Selim I dispatched a
contingent of two thousand Janissaries. He also issued a
firman to the effect that volunteers for the African campaign
would be provided with free passage to Algiers and would
be enrolled on a regular wage basis in the Ocak. The firman
identified Algiers for the first time as an eyalat. The appointment ceremony set the pattern for future Ottoman-Algerine
relationships. Khayr al-Din was presented with a copy of the
firman by Ishaq Pasha, Selim's envoy, which he read aloud
before the citizens. It stated *inter alia* that the Padishah-i
Islam accepted the homage of the Algerines, agreed that they
could issue currency with his seal (*tughra*) and use his name
in the *hutbe* and *salavat*. Khayr al-Din was confirmed as his
lieutenant with the title of *Cezayiri Beylerbey*, and as supreme commander of the Ocak.[14]

The capture of the Peñon in 1530 and construction of a mole
to link it with the mainland ended the Spanish threat and
endowed Algiers with a safe artificial anchorage for the corsair squadrons. Khayr al-Din also returned to Algerine authority the territory east and west of the city, formerly subject
to his brother, so that Algiers became a *de facto* city-state.
The state-building process he had begun was sufficiently solid
to survive his departure to take command of the imperial
fleet in 1534 and the siege by the fleet of Charles V of
Spain seven years later.[15]

Khayr al-Din's successors continued his work, transform-
ing Algiers in the process into a state on the Ottoman model.

On land Algerine sovereignty was extended to limits corresponding to those of French Algeria, with the exception of the Sahara.[16] The districts around Bougie and Tlemcen, traditionally attached to Tunis and various Morocco-based Muslim dynasties respectively, were incorporated definitively into the new state, an important factor in the emergence of a composite Algerian territorial identity. The installation of Ottoman regimes in Tunis and Tripoli and recognition by the Ottoman sultans of the legitimacy of the Alawite sultans of Morocco defined the basis for the present quadripartite division of North Africa.

Algiers was "created" as an Ottoman eyalat, whereas in Tunis the Ottomans inherited a functioning state structure, which they transformed by institutional practice into an eyalat. In terms of national awareness, the Algerian peoples, although less socially cohesive than the Tunisians or Tripolitanians and less subject to the demands of a central authority, were first to adopt a distinctive nationalistic identity. Their nationalism derived from a number of factors more fully operative in Algiers than in the other eyalats. First, Algiers was the most remote of the three from the Ottoman center. Its remoteness and the difficulties of reinforcement enhanced the atmosphere of a self-reliant frontier community, defending the edges of Islam, brought to Algiers by the Barbarossas. Second, the ruling institution in Algiers was a clearly defined structure. Authority was vested in the Ocak, the military garrison based in the capital. Its members, although recruited from other parts of the empire through the normal *devshirme* process, were enrolled from the day of their arrival in Algiers in an elite corps with a controlling interest in Algerine affairs. They were made to feel that the state was their personal property; the more it prospered, the more they benefited.[17] The "meritocracy" of the Janissary order as it had evolved under the early sultans was preserved in Algiers. The *yeni yoldash* served three years in rank and then advanced to *eski yoldash*. In another three years he became *Bash yoldash*, or squad leader, of a unit of 16-20 men, the basic unit of the Ocak. Thereafter advancement came in three-year sequences in the ranks until the erstwhile yoldash reached the rank of sergeant major, *Chavush bashi.* There were in addition five officer ranks, up to *Agha.* The yoldash who reached this rank (which happened unless he was killed, retired for disability, or transferred) served for two months and was then pensioned off as *Mün'azil agha.*

A third factor in the emergence of Algerian national identity under Ottoman inspiration derived from the over-all system of administration and the social segregation practiced by the Turks. Recognizing the inherent factionalism of the Maghrib, the ruling institution encouraged recruitment of corsairs and auxiliary cavalry (*Sipahiyan*) from the indigenous Algerine population. The offspring of Janissaries who married local women, the *Kul oğlari,* were excluded from the Ocak but were eligible for appointment to various positions in the central and provincial administrations up to the rank of *bey* ("governor") in the three provinces (Constantine, Midiyah, and Titteri) of the state.[18] Once appointed, the beys were supreme in their own territories, although once annually a *mahalla* ("expedition") was sent to each province to collect tribute, distribute gifts, and receive the allegiance of the *makhzan* tribes (those who accepted Ottoman sovereignty in return for internal autonomy and remission from all taxes except the annual tithe). In the Algerine cities the *Kul oğlari,* being uninvolved in the factional rivalries of the Ocak that emerged at each change of leadership, became a separate class, like the Copts of Egypt, responsible for much of the day-to-day business of the bureaucracy. The abrupt departure of the garrison along with Dey Husayn after the French conquest, though it ended the Ottoman ruling institution in Algiers, did not materially affect the position of this class, which remained in a sense the link between the strong Algerine state of the past and the militant Algeria of today.

Ottoman management of Algiers was firmly rooted in a legal system that eliminated the destructive internal instability of the pre-Ottoman period. For practical purposes there were two legal systems, one based on Hanafi jurisprudence for Ottomans and another, drawn on Maliki prescripts, for the non-Ottoman Muslim population (including the *Kul oğlari*). The former was administered by a *kadi* in theory, but in practice the responsibility for law enforcement of the Ocak was vested in its *agha*. Only the *agha* could order punishment for an individual *yoldash*, and these punishments could be issued only for proved violations of the internal regulations of the Ocak. Otherwise the order was self-policing and exempt from civil suit or arrest.[19]

Maliki law was administered by a corps of *muftis* and *kadis*, one for each *kaidat* and provincial capital and one in Algiers. Other than the right of sanctuary in mosques or with marabouts, the law applied equally to all Muslim non-Ottomans.[20] Trials were swift and impartial, without the use of lawyers, although the litigants and defendants alike were allowed to call witnesses for verification of facts and as character references. Court reporters took down verbatim records of all trials and sentencing, with the punishment, in accordance with the charge, being rendered on the spot.[21]

Along with the impartiality and swiftness of justice, Ottoman methods of law enforcement ensured domestic order in the eyalat. The execution of justice was the responsibility of a body of officials known as *chavushan* (Arabic *sha'wush*). Their function under the beylerbeys, the first stage of Ottoman rule in Algiers, had been merely that of bodyguards, with the rank of sergeant. Under the triennial pashas (1568–1659) and the government by *aghas* of the Ocak (1659–71), they were simply messengers of state, but the deys (1671–1830) elevated them to the status of ministers of justice. Algiers had sixteen *chavushan*, one responsible for each district of the capital. They carried no weapons of any sort when they made their rounds, but their distinctive costume and identification with absolute Algerine Ottoman justice was such that their orders were instantly obeyed.[22]

The thoroughness of law enforcement, the principle of a

separate but equally just legal standard for the ruling institution, and the application of collective responsibility for criminal actions, together ensured the effectiveness of the legal system of the eyalet. Each urban quarter and rural district was held responsible for crimes committed within its limits. Night police patrols were a regular feature in Algerian cities as early as the seventeenth century. Also the trial and sentencing of members of the Ocak within the precincts of their barracks encouraged public confidence in the effectiveness of the dual system. The venality of traditional Maghribian governments was avoided in the Algerine state by the absence of a civil list with correspondingly high salaries for government officials. The Ocak received only its pay, plus a share in occasional land campaigns or in corsair profits for those of its members who had signed on for an expedition. As a result, Algiers was well-policed and orderly, and there were no internal uprisings throughout the period of Ottoman rule.

The eyalet of Tripoli underwent a somewhat different transformation process, although the circumstances of its founding were the same as those of Algiers. The nature of Libyan geography, comprised of two regions (Tripolitania and Cyrenaica) separated by desert, had from the period of earliest settlement precluded the growth of national unity or a core of national consciousness. The division was accentuated after the Islamic conquest when Cyrenaica, the eastern province, was attached to Egypt, and Tripolitania fell into the orbit of Islamic Tunisia and thus became part of Ifriqiya. The Aghlabid and Hafsid rulers of Tunisia encouraged the urban development of Tripoli as a useful, if distant, appendage of their state. Thus Tripoli was able to develop a marine vocation through its Tunisian connection, but Cyrenaica remained a region of self-governing pastoral tribes. The attachment to Egypt became noteworthy only when the Banu Hilal and Banu Sulaym, Arabian tribes expelled by the Fatimid Caliphs for misbehavior and used by them for revenge against their North African rivals, swept through the province and completed its Islamization.[23] These contrasting experiences account for the concentration of Libya's national identity for so long in the city and hinterland of Tripoli.

Tripoli acquired a separate civic status after its capture by Norman adventurers in 1146. Other than installing a garrison, the Normans did not interfere with local autonomy and recognized the authority of a council of ten Muslim notables. The practice was continued under the Almohad princes, who drove out the Normans. The city was recognized as a sovereign urban unit managed by an Assembly of Notables and its own grand Mufti.[24]

As in the case of Algiers, the conversion of a Tripoli-based urban identity to a broader national consciousness contained within defined territorial limits resulted from the Ottoman conquest. The Spaniards had taken Tripoli by storm in 1510, discovering to their surprise that the unarmed citizens, "who possessed not so much as table knives with which to defend themselves," were prepared to die before surrendering the city to the unbelievers.[25] The Spaniards, finding Tripoli difficult to provision and hard-pressed elsewhere, ceded it to the Order of the Knights of Saint John of Jerusalem in 1530, the order having been expelled from Rhodes by Sultan Süleyman I. Twenty-one years later, an Ottoman fleet commanded by the corsair Darghut restored Tripoli to Islamic control.

Unlike Algiers, Tripoli was acquired by forces operating under direct Ottoman authority. Murad Agha, commander of the Janissary force that had accompanied the fleet, was appointed as the first governor of the province. Subsequently the governorship passed to Darghut, who held it until 1565, when he led the Tripolitan corsair contingent in the attack on Malta.[26] During his governorship Ottoman authority was extended inland as far as Garian and eastward to Misurata.[27] The province also included Djerba, Sfax, the Tunisian Sahel, and Kairouan.

Direct Ottoman rule by *valis*, sent from Constantinople with the rank of pasha, continued through the sixteenth century. Each vali was accompanied by Janissary troop units sent to reinforce the Tripoli garrison, which suffered continual attrition because of tribal resistance to the *mahallas* seeking to impose tribute in return for local autonomy. About 1600 authority to appoint one of their number dey (alternately pasha-dey) of Tripoli was conferred on the senior officers of the Ocak, constituting a Divan, or Grand Council, on the Algerine model. From then until 1835 successive Ottoman sultans were content to accord vassal status to the appointee upon notification.

As was the case in Algiers, certain pasha-deys made significant contributions to the building of a Libyan state within the Ottoman-Islamic community. Sekizli Mehmed (1631–49) and Sekizli Osman (1649–72), in particular, extended Ottoman authority throughout Cyrenaica. However, the reverse of the ruling situation in Algiers occurred in Tripoli in the early years of the eighteenth century. Ahmed Karamanli, commander of the Tripolitanian *Sipahis*, put an end to a period of internal disturbances by leading his forces into the city and taking the entire divan as prisoners in 1711. All of the three hundred Turkish officers of the garrison were massacred, and Karamanli assured his triumph in a message to Sultan Ahmed III in which he pledged full loyalty to the sultan and advised him that henceforth Tripoli would require no further Janissary reinforcements.[28] The firman issued to acknowledge Ahmed's accession granted him investiture as pasha-dey for life, and in this fashion the Karamanli dynasty in Tripoli came into being.

The first Karamanli was of the *Kul oğlari*, and this fact plus the personal loyalty to Ahmed of the *Sipahis* ensured the domination of indigenous over ethnic Turkish forces in the political structure of the eyalat. Cyrenaica was attached to Tripoli by a *mahalla* that swept through the territory and secured the obedience of the tribes by force of arms. The same tactics were applied in Tripolitania. Ahmed's sons and younger members of the family were appointed as beys in the principal cities and towns. Tripoli, the seat of government, prospered under the first three Karamanlis as the dynastic principle and the caliber of the first three rulers (Ahmed, his son Mehmed, and his nephew Ali) ensured political stability.[29]

Karamanli autonomy ended in 1835 with the reimposition of direct Ottoman rule, once again prompted by external events. The French conquest of Algiers in 1830, contested by Mahmud II to the extent of sending an abortive mission to Dey Husayn that proceeded as far as Tunis, and by a flurry of diplomatic activity, signaled a change in Ottoman policy. Yusuf Karamanli, who had bowed to European dictates regarding corsair practice laid down at the Congress of Aix-la-Chapelle in 1816, and reduced Tripolitan state income by two-thirds as a result, abdicated in 1833. His successor, Ali, faced tribal hostility and a fratricidal uprising led by his cousins at the same time. The sultan, seizing the opportunity, dispatched a flotilla led by Necib Pasha to restore order in Tripoli. The last Karamanli was called aboard the Ottoman flagship, arrested, and deported with all members of his family to Istanbul.[30] From then until the Italian invasion of 1911–12 and the withdrawal of Ottoman forces, Tripolitania and Cyrenaica were administered as a single Ottoman *vilayet*, under a vali appointed from Istanbul. The *vilayet* was divided into four *sancaks*: Tripoli (including the capital), Homs, al-Jabal, and Cyrenaica.[31]

Ottoman rule in Tripolitania restored stability but contributed little directly to the growth of Libyan nationalism. The various valis, notably Izzet Pasha, Resim Pasha, and Recep Pasha, were chiefly concerned to forestall a French takeover and to obtain tribal recognition of Ottoman sovereignty. The death of Jum'a Ibn Khalifa, tribal chief in the Jabal, assured the second objective. The first, although conceivable after the establishment of a French protectorate over Tunisia, failed to materialize after the signing of a Franco-Italian agreement of 1902 affirmed Italy's recognition of French "rights" in Morocco and Tunisia in return for Italian "rights" in Tripolitania.[32]

Yet the Ottoman presence in Libya, though not assuming the status of a foreign occupation, indirectly brought about the formation of a purely Libyan nationalist movement, one destined in time to inspire creation of a sovereign Libyan state. The movement evolved out of two disparate factors—the demonstrated weakness of the Porte as an Islamic power in dealing with Europe, and the revived militancy of Islam propounded by such would-be reformers as al-Afghani. The two strands came together in Cyrenaica, finding fertile soil in a region whose tribal chiefs smarted under Ottoman authority.[33]

The founder of the movement, Muhammad Ibn 'Ali al-Sanusi, was a scholar and theologian of some reputation in Fez, Morocco. In the course of a year-long journey to Mecca to make the pilgrimage, he seems to have become aware of the divisions and weakness in the Islamic world, which he attributed to laxity among Muslims in observing the original doctrines of the Prophet. Receiving a sympathetic welcome among the Cyrenaicans, he founded a lodge (*zawiya*) at Baida in the Jabal Akhdar in 1843 on his return journey from the Holy City. In 1856 the *zawiya* was transferred to Jaghbub, an oasis 200 miles south in the desert and beyond effective Ottoman authority. Here the Sanusi order grew both in numbers and importance, acquiring equal status with the Ottomans as far as the European powers were concerned.[34]

When the Italians invaded Libya in 1911, Sultan Mehmed V issued a firman granting eyalat status to both Tripolitania and Cyrenaica, with the former occupied by Italian troops; the latter passed under *de facto* Sanusi government. The head of the order at the time, Sayyid Ahmad al-Sharif, styled himself *amir*, and all documents governing the administration of the territory were issued as emanating from *Hüküm-lük-i Senusiye*.

Apart from their replacement of the Ottomans, the Sanusiya through their doctrines and Islamic piety transformed Cyrenaica along lines similar to those established by the Wahhabis in Arabia. Zawiyas were organized in each of the habitable oases. The pastoral tribes were encouraged to practice sedentary agriculture in *Ikhwan* ("brotherhood") communities, and traditional Shariʻa law and rigid orthodox practice were reintroduced to peoples who, according to Sanusi precepts, had lapsed from both.[35]

In its emphasis on the dissemination of pre-Ottoman, Arabic-Islamic culture, the proclaimed descent of its leader from the Prophet's family, and the use of Arabic in place of Turkish, the order forged new links between Libya and the eastern Arab world. In this sense the Arab character of Libyan nationalism is dominant. Yet Sanusi expansion was accomplished among nomadic or semi-nomadic Berber tribes, following a North African tradition identifiable as far back as the eighth century and reminiscent of the tribal Almohad movement rather than any purely Arab effort toward Islamic unity. The Sanusiya emerged in the twentieth century barely touched either by European influence or by the urban, educated outlook of Arab nationalism as it evolved elsewhere in the empire.[36]

Italy's recognition in 1920 of the autonomy of Cyrenaica under Idris as hereditary amir symbolized the identification, for the Libyan people, of the Sanusiya as sole exponent of local nationalism, with the religious charisma of the Grand Sanusi simply transferred to the political sphere.[37]

Tunis, the most complex and intricately organized of all North African city-states, combined in its nationalistic structure elements of the other two eyalats. The assumption of power by corsairs and ascription of authority to the sultan-caliph followed almost the same pattern as had been the case in Algiers and Tripoli. Khayr al-Din, aided by dissension at the Hafsid court, invested Tunis with a combined Algerine-Ottoman fleet in 1534 and proclaimed the deposition of the Hafsids. Charles V, utilizing the dispossession of Moulay Hasan as his pretext, retook Tunis in the following year and restored Hasan to his position. Thereafter, the city passed back and forth between Muslim and Christian hands until 1574 when the Ottomans, commanded by Admiral Sinan Pasha and the corsair Uluch Ali, attached it definitely to the empire.[38]

The organization of Tunis by Sinan Pasha after the reconquest was analogous to that of Algiers with one important distinction. The province was administered by governors (pashas) appointed by the sultan for three-year terms, and accompanied by a corps of Janissaries recruited specifically for Tunisian service from Anatolian towns. A divan of officers similar to the one in Algiers advised the pasha on matters of state. Each 100-man section of the Ocak was headed by a dey, and a civil official, called a bey, was responsible for fiscal matters and for control of the dissident tribes of the interior. Control of these two vital levers of power enabled the beys gradually to appropriate authority from both the deys and the pashas. Bey Murad (1612–31) secured from the sultan the title of pasha along with the right to transmit the beylik to his son. In 1705 one Husayn Ibn 'Ali, the agha of the Ocak and a renegade Christian of Greek origin, utilized an Algerine attack on Tunis as a means of winning the unanimous support of the population for his election as Bey, replacing Murad III. After his successful repulse of the Algerines, he secured the approval of the Ottoman sultan for his elevation and abolished the titles of dey and pasha. The line of Tunisian authority was not fully established for some years, but as far as the Ottomans were concerned, the eyalat had been endowed with an effective hereditary vassal government.[39]

Despite the similarities in implantation and development of an Ottoman presence in the three North African provinces, Husaynid Tunisia appeared to both Europeans and to its nominal superiors in Istanbul as possessing the characteristics of national sovereignty to a much greater degree than either Tripoli or Algiers. In the Ottoman view, Tunis met the requirements of autonomous statehood, which were: exercise of effective authority by a central government, responsible leaders who understood their obligations toward their subjects, the support of the ulema, full observance of the millet system for non-Muslims, and acceptance of Ottoman authority in the tribal regions.[40]

The long-established urban traditions of the Tunis region

and the Sahel, exemplified by the cohesive Sahelian bour-
geoisie, supplied a solid base for Tunisian nationalism as
well as an alternative to the dependence on corsair campaigns necessary to the growth of economically deprived Algiers and Tripoli. In this sense the Husaynids capitalized on
an existing national system rather than inventing one in the
tradition of their Aghlabid, Almohad, and Hafsid predecessors.

Indigenous Tunisian nationalism in the eighteenth and
nineteenth centuries was revealed in two areas: the evolution
of governmental-popular relations and changes in the Tunis-
Istanbul relationship, particularly in the latter period. The
Husaynid administration, after the settlement of fratricidal
conflict in the 1740s, remained stable. Below the level of
supreme command, it mirrored the Algerine administration on
a smaller scale, having only three ministries (Treasury,
Foreign Affairs, and War). The beylical court was large because of the size of the Husaynid family and the numerous
Janissaries and mamlukes who constituted a privileged class
and whose exactions ultimately brought on the liberalization
of the regime. The duplicate legal system of Algiers did not
prevail in Tunis. The bey, as supreme judicial authority, held
public court four days a week at La Marsa, where he received petitions and rendered justice with the concurrence,
where legal opinions were required, of the ulema. Maliki
prescripts applied to all citizens, the only distinctions made
being in terms of punishments for particular ethnic groups.[41]
The uniformity of law was an important factor in the promo-
tion of national identity among Tunisians.

Yet the attainment of such an identity would have been
difficult had it not been for the influence of European representatives at the Tunisian court and the ultimate responsive-
ness of the beys to their pressures. The ancient right of Tunisian rulers to sign treaties with foreign powers, a practice
dating back to the thirteenth century,[42] enabled the beys to
wear the attributes of sovereignty even though their prerogatives ultimately rested on the consent of the sultan.

Aside from their military and naval forces (which were

contributed upon request to the defense of other parts of the empire), the beys maintained agents, although not formal diplomatic missions, in Paris, Malta, and the larger Mediterranean cities to look after their interests.[43] The principal European powers appointed either consuls or chargés d'affaires to Tunis. Intervention on behalf of their countrymen under the Capitulations (which were rigorously enforced in Tunis) by such consuls as Richard Wood of England and Matthieu de Lesseps, Alexandre Deval, and Léon Roches of France, was increasingly extended to Tunisian citizens employed in the consulates and ultimately to citizens of the millets. The Organic Law of 1857 and its successor the Tunisian Constitution of 1861 resulted from such pressures. The beys were, therefore, less disposed to emphasize their fidelity to the empire through adherence to the newly issued Tanzimat regulations than to demonstrate to Europe that in terms of basic-rights legislation they were as "modern" as any European nation.[44]

The Organic Law represents a significant stage in the development of nationalism in Tunisia. For the first time in North African Islamic history, the reciprocal rights and obligations of governors and governed were defined in non-Islamic terms. The law had eleven articles, of which the most important in a nationalistic context are: freedom of person and property under the law to all inhabitants of the beylik (art. 1), liability of all subjects to taxation assessed on a proportional basis (art. 2), equality before the law for Muslims and non-Muslims alike (art. 3), and abolition of special privileges granted to subjects of the beylik existing before the effective date of the Law (art. 8).[45]

As a further example of the Tunisian intent to formulate distinctive national values rather than taking its cue from Ottoman reforming practice, the Organic Law contained two articles relevant to foreigners. They were allowed to establish trades and commercial businesses (art. 10), a continuation of existing practice, and they were given the right to buy and own land (art. 11).

A by-product of the Organic Law was the decree of 1858

establishing a Municipal Council for the city of Tunis, another administrative measure urged upon the reluctant Muhammad Bey by the European consuls.[46] The council, composed of fifteen members chosen from notables, marked a further step in Tunisian nationalism since all its members were indigenous. Its responsibilities were to police the streets, establish the municipal budget, and maintain all public works and facilities; and most important, its jurisdiction extended over the entire city.[47]

The Constitution of 1861 carried nationalism a step further. In addition to incorporating the eleven articles of the Organic Law, the Constitution further codified administrative practice and responsibility. In chapter 2, "Rights and Duties of the Head of State," the bey was required to take an oath of office and give an oral commitment before the ulema to support the Organic Law (art. 9).

A similar oath was mandatory for civil and military officials (art. 10). A further safeguard was contained in the requirement that the bey, as head of state, was nevertheless responsible for all his actions to a Supreme Council (art. 11). However, this council, composed of sixty members appointed by the bey for five-year terms, was in no real sense representative of the Tunisian people, especially as membership was drawn from the baladi class and the Turco-Circassian elite.[48]

The sequence of complex events by which Tunisia became a protectorate of France are outside the scope of this chapter and need not be detailed here. However, certain aspects of the scenario are relevant to Tunisian nationalism. First, the process of change in the beylical state in the nineteenth century produced a genuine government-to-people relationship. However ill-intentioned the beys' reasons for conforming to Ottoman practice by promulgation of their own constitutional documents, these documents represented a compact with the people and were so interpreted by Khayr al-Din when he became prime minister. Second, the governmental exactions inspired a popular insurrection in 1864 that united tribal and urban groups in opposition to the "feudal regime" of al-Sadiq Bey and his autocratic minister, Mustafa Khaznadar.[49]

The failure of this effort, although resulting in impoverishment of the country, the reimposition of autocratic rule, and a crushing financial burden that led indirectly to the protectorate, symbolized the capacity for collective action of the Tunisian people that would be amply demonstrated seventy-odd years later with the advent of the Neo-Destour.

CONCLUSION

In conclusion it appears from the evidence that three centuries of Ottoman administration in North Africa produced, rather than three Ottoman states, three separate entities whose sense of national identity varied according to local circumstances. The Algiers *Ocak* because of distance from the Porte and the attractive possibilities of large-scale corsair activity in the defense of Islam, remained throughout its tenure an elite military establishment. Tripoli, not merely because of its relative accessibility, but also because of the unassimilable nature of urban and pastoral communities, achieved an accommodation of sorts only through the Sanusiya. Tunis, more exposed to external forces and dependent upon peaceful commerce, attained the highest degree of national identity, yet in doing so it raised leadership to a level of autocracy reminiscent of the early caliphs rather than the late Ottoman sultans. If there is a common thread of *North African* nationalism visible in the experiences of the three eyalats, it is one of the emergence of certain urban entities (Algiers, Tunis, Tripoli) as symbols of an enduring national awareness that is neither Ottoman nor Arab, but that partakes of elements of both.

1. An alternative phrasing is "no one shall attack so long as I live." See Ibn Khaldun, *Histoire des berbères* trans. by M. de Slane, 4 vols. (Paris, 1874), vol. 1, appendix 1, p. 304.

2. See article by David M. Hart in *Arabs and Berbers*, ed. by C. Micaud and E. Gellner, (Lexington, Mass., 1972); E. Gellner, *Saints of the Atlas* (Chicago, 1969); E. Hermassi, *Leadership and National Development in North Africa*, (Berkeley, Calif., 1972), especially chap. 1; J. Berque, *Structures sociales du Haut-Atlas*, (Paris, 1955); plus the important early works of R. Montagne, *La Vie sociale et la vie politique des berbères*, (Paris, 1931).

3. According to al-Baidaq (Abu Bakr Ibn 'Ali al-Sanhaji) in *Futuh al-Muwahhidun* [Conquests of the Almohads], trans. by E. Lévi-Provençal as *Histoire des Almohades* (Paris, 1928), p. 75. 'Abd al-Mu'min, secular chief of the movement, assumed the title of Khalifa Ibn Tumart, just as Abu Bakr had styled himself Khalifa Muhammad.

4. Y. Lacoste, A. Nouschi, and A. Prenant, *L'Algérie passé et présent*, (Paris, 1960); M. Emerit, *L'Algérie à l'époque d'Abdelkader*, (Paris, 1931); the various volumes issued in the Centenaire de l'Algérie Française, 1831-1931, and so on. For Libya see R. Graziani (Marshal) *Pace Romana in Libia*, (Milan, 1937); N. Placida, *La Riconquista della Tripolitania*, (Tripoli, 1928); Gabbelli, *La Tripolitania della fine della guerra mondiale all'avvento del Fascismo*, 2 vols. (Intra, 1939).

5. E. Watbled, "Etablissement de la domination turque en Algérie," *Revue Africaine* 100 (July-August 1873): 298.

6. Few authors treat the corsairs as an institutionalized profession. The standard English source is G. Fisher, *Barbary Legend* (Oxford, 1957). S. Bono, *I Corsari Barbareschi* (Turin, 1964), consists of biographical sketches of famous corsairs such as the Barbarossas, Darghut, and Rais Hamida. Gravière, *Les Corsaires barbaresques*, (Paris, 1887), borrows heavily from earlier, primary sources such as Haedo and Père Dan. R. Playfair, *The Scourge of Christendom*, (London, 1884), is concerned solely with Anglo-Algerine relations prior to the conquest. Works such as Père Dan, *Histoire de Barbarie et de ses corsaires*, (Paris, 1637), deal with the corsairs in passing as a faction within the social structure.

7. The elevation of Khayr al-Din has been recounted in *Ghazawat Aruj wa Khayr al-Din*, trans. by S. Rang and F. Denis as *Fondation de la régence d'Alger: histoire des Barbarossas*, 2 vols. (Paris, 1837). Other corsairs granted the honor were Salah Rais, Huseyin Mezamorta, and Hasan Veneziano.

8. The firman of investiture of Dey Ibrahim Hoca, sent to Algiers by Mahmud I in 1746, characteristically noted that "the nomination and despatch of the Deys of Algiers being done ordinarily by Our Sublime Porte, as the Chiefs of Algiers in their general petition, and Ibrahim Hoca in a private request have made supplication as a Mark of Our . . . Imperial favor We graciously deign to confer on the aforesaid Ibrahim Hoca the appointment of Governor and Dey of the Province." See E. Plantet, *Correspondance des deys d'Alger avec la cour de France, 1597-1833*. 2 vols. (Paris, 1898), vol. 2. As late as 1871 the Porte was using similar language to describe the relationship, viz., the firman of investiture of Muhammad al-Sadiq as Bey of Tunis. See A. M. Broadley, *Tunis Past and Present*, (London, 1882), Appendix, pp. 356-59.

9. During the period of rule by the aghas of the Ocak (1659-71), the taife reisi clashed constantly with the garrison until, in 1671, they elevated a reis to the position of dey, a title subsequently made over to the Ocak as the taife withdrew from internal political activity.

10. The standard references for these events are D. de Haedo, *Topographia e historia general de Argel* and *Epitome de los reyes de Argel* (Valladolid, 1612). Ottoman sources for the conquest and its antecedents, notably S. Ilter, *Shimali Afrika'da Türkler* [North Africa under the Turks], 2 vols. (Istanbul, 1937), draw heavily on Haedo and Père Dan, as do all European sources.

11. For the career of the brothers, in addition to *Ghazawat Aruj wa Khayr al-Din*, see Fuad Carim, *Cezayir'de Türkler* (Istanbul, 1962); E. Bradford, *The Sultan's Admiral* (New York, 1968).

12. Ibid.

13. The name was also applied to the garrisons sent from Algiers to accompany the provincial governors (beys) to their posts, but these garrisons were drawn from the one in Algiers, remaining responsible to its agha.

14. The term *Cezayiri beylerbeyisi* remained in use in dispatches from Istanbul to Algiers through the eyalat's existence. This and other firmans may be found in the *Mühimme defterleri* (defterler-i Ahkami Mühimme-i Divan-i Hümayun), "Register of Important Decrees of the Imperial Divan," classified by century.

15. The Spanish expedition has been well documented on the Spanish side and poorly from the Ottoman point of view. In addition to Haedo (q.v.), the *Descripcion generale de Affrica* of L. Marmol-Carvajal, 3 vols. (Granada, 1573–99), describes the siege and the attack on Tunis in 1556. Two other Spanish sources are R. Altimira, *Historia de Espana*, (Barcelona, 1900–1911), and Diego Galan, *Cautiverio y trabajos de Diego Galan*, (Madrid, 1913).

16. Oran remained a Spanish presidio until 1708, was abandoned during the Wars of the Spanish Successions, retaken in 1732, and finally ceded to the dey in 1791–92.

17. There were no restrictions on the Janissaries while they were in garrison. The men were at liberty to take up a trade, sign on for corsair expeditions, or open a shop. Dey Baba Muhammad Ibn Osman (1766–90) was a cobbler, as was Bey Hasan of Tunis.

18. In addition to the beyliks, there were four kaidats: Blida, Sebwa, al-Kala, and Sudan, each governed by a kaid appointed by the dey and responsible directly to the central government. Algiers had its own mayor (*hakim*) and council in continuation of a pact with the Barbarossas.

19. All cases involving Janissaries were held *in camera* in the Ocak barracks, giving rise to the belief among Algerine citizens that the organization would curb any excesses by its members.

20. Christians and Jews were subjected to their own magistrates or, in the latter case, rabbinic authorities, since the millet system was strictly observed. As shown in the Sfez incident, which led to the Organic Law in Tunis (see below, note 44), non-Muslims were subject to Maliki law in cases clearly seen to involve Muslims as litigants.

21. For observations on the penal system, see M. Russell, *History of the Barbary States*, 2 vols. (Edinburgh, 1814); T. Shaw, *Travels in Barbary* (Oxford, 1738); W. Shaler, *Sketches of Algiers* (Boston, 1826); G. Losada, *Escuela de Trabajos*, 4 vols. (Madrid, 1670), esp. vol. 2, "Noticias y govierno de Argel."

22. Their "uniform" consisted of an ankle-length green robe with wide cuffs, belted with a crimson sash, a double-printed cap of white calfskin, and iron-shod red leather boots.

23. On the Banu Sulaym's role in Libya, see M. Murabet, *A Brief History of Tripolitania* (Tripoli, 1965), pp. 25–27. F. Golino, "Patterns of Libyan National Identity", *Middle East Journal* 24 (Summer 1970): 338–52, also deals with this aspect of Libyan history as a positive factor in inducing Islamic nationalism rather than Ottomanism among the people.

24. J. N. Abun-Nasr, *A History of the Maghrib*, (Cambridge, 1971), pp. 189–91.

25. Murabet, op. cit., pp. 32–33. See also E. Rossi, *Il Dominio degli Spagni e dei Cavalieri di Malta a Tripoli* (Intra, 1937).

26. Darghut was killed during the siege; his body was brought back to Tripoli and buried there in the cemetery of the Darghut Cami, the mosque he had had constructed to mark the restoration of Islamic rule.

27. Murabet, op. cit., pp. 32–33. Darghut was unsuccessful, however, in securing the allegiance of the Banu Sulaym.

28. Abun-Nasr, op. cit., pp. 194–96.

29. Commented on in Murabet, op. cit., p. 39. Additional data on the Karamanlis is in R. Micacci, *La Tripolitania sotto il dominio dei Caramanli* (Intra, 1936).

30. C. Feraud, *Annales Tripolitaines* (Paris and Tunis, 1927), p. 373. On the French attempt to annex Fezzan, which motivated the Ottoman action, see P. Rouard de Card, *La France et Turquie dans la Méditerranée Occidentale* (Paris, 1910).

31. In conformity with the Vilayet Law of 1864, these were subdivided into *nahiyes* and *kazas* as per Ottoman administrative practice elsewhere. After 1879 Cyrenaica became a separate sancak administered from Istanbul.

32. Feraud, op. cit., p. 396, comments that a special tax levied on all subjects of the empire at the outbreak of the Russo-Turkish War of 1877–78 caused great resentment among the tribes who had hitherto been exempt from all forms of taxation in return for their allegiance to the Porte.

33. See J. Castelli, *Tunisi e Tripoli* (Turin, 1911).

34. On the Sanusiya there are numerous sources, including E. E. Evans-Pritchard, *The Sanusi of Cyrenaica* (London, 1949); N. Ziadeh, *Sanusiyya: A Study of a Revivalist Movement in Islam* (Leiden, 1958); also H. Duveyrier, *La Confrérie musulmane de Sidi Mohammed Ben Ali Senoussi* (Paris, 1884).

35. Noted in A. Pelt, *Libyan Independence and the United Nations* (New Haven, Conn., 1970). Additional comment is supplied in M. Khadduri, *Modern Libya: A Study in Political Development*, (Baltimore, 1963), pp. 8 ff.

36. Professor Khadduri, in *The Islamic Law of Nations: Shaybani's Siyar* (Baltimore, 1965), argues that according to Shaybani modern Islamic nations such as Libya evolved naturally in the course of evolution of the universal God-created Islamic state.

37. See M. Khalidi, *The Constitutional Development of Libya* (Beirut, 1956), for the diplomatic ramifications of the Libyan "question." Despite conflicting evidence as to the legal status and legitimacy of Tripolitania in the early years of the Italian occupation, it appears that urban Tripolitanian nationalists were ready to accept Idris's leadership. See also P. Grandchamp, *Études d'histoire tunisienne* (Paris, 1966), "Notes Tripolitaines," pp. 180–82, for the career of the principal Tripolitanian nationalist leader, Sulayman (Sliman) al-Baruni.

38. Accounts are in C. Monchicourt, *Documents historiques sur la Tunisie* (Paris, 1929); P. Cambon, *Histoire de la régence de Tunis* (Paris, 1948); A. Pellegrin, *Histoire de Tunisie* (Paris, 1948), and the standard work by C.-A. Julien, *Histoire de l'Afrique du Nord* (Paris, 1952), translated into English as *History of North Africa* (New York, 1970).

39. J. Ganiage, *Les Origines de le protectorat français en Tunisie* (Paris, 1959), pp. 11–13. N. Faucon, *La Tunisie avant et depuis l'occupation française*, 2 vols. (Paris, 1893), notes (p. 179) that in 1821 the Porte to confirm its sovereign rights in Tunis and Algiers enjoined the two eyalats to cease from a state of hostilities that had lasted intermittently for sixty years. An envoy was sent specifically from Istanbul for this purpose and on 14 March a peace treaty was signed between the two.

40. J. Serres, *La Politique turque en Afrique du Nord sous la Monarchie de Juillet* (Paris, 1925), p. 143.

41. H. Dunant, *Notice sur la régence de Tunis* (Geneva, 1858), pp. 46 ff.

42. Ganiage, op. cit., p. 12. The first such treaty was with Aragon in 1270; altogether by 1881 Tunis had signed 114 treaties with foreign powers, none ratified by the sultan.

43. Faucon, op. cit., p. 193. Tunis sent a naval squadron to join the Ottoman fleet at Navarino in 1827, and Ahmed Bey provided 6,000 soldiers for the Ottoman armies engaged in the Crimean War.

44. However, when issued, the Organic Law "proved to be almost a literal copy of the Hatt-i Sherif of Gulhane, which Ahmed Bey had previously refused to put into effect in his territory" (E. Fitoussi and A. Benazet, *L'Etat tunisien et le protectorat français* [Paris, 1931], p. 63). The Sfez incident (in which a Jew named Samuel Sfez knocked down a Muslim child with his cart and, upon being surrounded by an angry Muslim crowd blasphemed Islam, whereupon he was dragged before the Shari'a court and sentenced to death by having molten lead poured down his throat) was the main cause of promulgation of the Organic Law. The foreign consuls in Tunis not only protested the act but pointed out to the bey that it constituted failure on his part to extend to his subjects the same basic rights granted to Ottoman subjects by the Porte, regardless of religion, race, or nationality (Ganiage, op. cit., p. 73).

45. Text in Fitoussi and Benazet, op. cit., Appendix, p. V.

46. See the unpublished paper "The Municipal Council of Tunis, 1858–1870: A Study in Urban Institutional Change," by W. L. Cleveland, presented at the seventh annual meeting of the Middle East Studies Association, Milwaukee, Wisconsin, November 1973. The question is considered in detail in A. Raymond, "La France, la Grande-Bretagne et le problème de reform à Tunis (1855–1857)," in *Etudes maghrebines: Mélanges Charles-André Julien* (Paris 1964), pp. 137–64.

47. As Cleveland (op. cit., nn. 18–19) has observed, other urban councils of the period held jurisdiction only over European sectors, as in Constantinople (Pera) and Alexandria.

48. Text in Fitoussi and Benazet, op. cit., appendix I.

49. The most detailed study of the insurrection is B. Slama, *L'Insurrection de 1864 en Tunisie* (Tunis, 1967), especially pp. 160–61.

William Ochsenwald

The Financial Basis of Ottoman Rule in the Hijaz, 1840–1877

If nineteenth-century Middle Eastern history is seen solely as a prelude to the growth of twentieth-century nationalisms, the positive aspects of the Ottoman Empire may be ignored. In the central Arab lands, Ottoman provincial administration endured for four centuries despite decentralization, depopulation, and economic decay. Despite the attacks by nationalists and Western critics, Ottoman rule must have had supporters and provided some benefits. The other side of the coin of modern nationalism is the history of the successful functioning of Ottoman institutions. To understand either the final collapse of the empire or its long existence necessitates analyses of each of the areas of the empire with attention both to the failings and successes of Ottoman rule.

Although the Hijaz was both the birthplace of Arab political independence and the religious center of the Muslim world and the Ottoman Empire, its political history in the nineteenth and twentieth centuries is nearly unknown. Trying to reconstruct the history of the Hijaz brings to mind the fable of the blind seers and the elephant: each perceives a different kind of being depending on the source of information. The rare Christian traveler who managed to evade local authorities saw the Holy Cities during the pilgrimage as religious centers; European consuls, restricted to Jidda, knew that part of the merchant community which was engaged in international trade; chroniclers, later Arab nationalists, and the only full-scale history now available[1] all concentrated on the amirs of Mecca and their internal struggles and eventual leadership of the Arab revolt. If the role of the Hijaz in the modern period and its relationship to Arab nationalism are to be properly understood, these facets should be combined and one key missing ingredient added: the Ottoman part in Hijazi history. It is, however, easier to prescribe such an approach than to follow it. Ottoman records were not compiled with the purposes of the historian in mind. However, the slow piecing together of information from Ottoman sources, even when tentative and incomplete can add new clues toward the solution of the puzzle of modern Hijazi history.

Money, as always, was a major concern of the government. The financial relations of the Ottomans with the Hijaz were central to the actual existence of the people of the area as well as their attitude toward their rulers. Subsidies from the central government to Mecca and Madina provided the chief rationale for the presence of the Ottomans in the Hijaz. The Ottoman Empire was the defender and economic support of the chief religious sites of Islam for the four centuries following the conquest of the Arab lands in the beginning of the sixteenth century. The Ottomans sent food for the subsistence of the Hijazis and the thousands of pilgrims who came to the Hijaz every year. In return the Ottoman sultan gained religious prestige.

Mehmed Ali of Egypt had threatened the sultan's claim to be the protector of the Holy Places. Egypt administered the Hijaz for almost thirty years until 1840, when Ottoman administration directly linked to Istanbul was restored. The middle of the nineteenth century from 1840 to 1877 constituted a discrete block of time in the Hijaz ending with the accession of Sultan Abdülhamid II in Istanbul and the death of Amir 'Abd Allah in the Hijaz. The period 1840 to 1877 falls into three politically defined sections in the Hijaz: (1) 1840–51, the continuation of the reign of the Amir Muhammad b. 'Awn; (2) 1852–58, political turbulence with riots and massacres, first under 'Abd al-Muttalib and then the restored Muhammad b. 'Awn as amirs; (3) 1859–1877, political stability under Amir 'Abd Allah. There were then only three amirs from the family of the Prophet Muhammad who governed in Mecca beside the Ottoman governor and administration during the thirty-seven years under discussion. In the same time there were nineteen Ottoman *valis*, or provincial governors.

Before we turn to any one particular aspect of the financial relations between the central government and the province, it will be useful to establish a picture of the total cash budget and the changes in it from 1257/1840–41 to 1294/1877–78. Each category of revenue and expenditure may then be compared with the totals in a more meaningful way.

There are three especially important aspects of Ottoman-Hijazi relations that may be deduced from the cash totals (see table 1). First, there were the perpetual deficits. The average of the twelve available deficits is about 30,000 purses.[2] Local revenues were always inadequate to cover local expenditures. Usually the deficits were two-thirds of the total expenditures of the province. Even with the strictest economies, the Hijaz was necessarily dependent upon external subsidies to maintain its government. Second, the total sums involved were relatively small. In the year of greatest expenditure, 1279/1862–63, only about 47,300 purses, or keses, were spent on all aspects of government excluding the pilgrimage but including the military and gifts to local Bedouin leaders. Local revenue averaged around 11,000 purses. By comparison, Egypt's tribute payment to the Ottoman central government in Istanbul up to 1866 was 80,000 purses; after that it was 150,000. The revenue of Cyprus, perhaps more comparable in number of inhabitants, was 42,274 purses in

1868–69.[3] Finally, the fluctuations in all categories show no over-all patterns or are inconclusive. Changes are usually explainable in terms of short-term accounting decisions made within the provincial administration rather than a long-range plan to alter the amounts of revenues or expenditures. An example is the income from the customs collected at the Red Sea ports. Major changes in total customs revenues resulted from the inclusion or exclusion of the Red Sea ports of Ottoman Yemen and the cession of Suakin and Massawa on the African coast of the Red Sea to the administration of Egypt.

TABLE 1

TOTAL REVENUE AND EXPENDITURE FOR THE HIJAZ

Year	Local Revenue	Expenditure	Deficit
1257/1841–42	10,743	34,361	−23,618
1261/1845	12,991	(28,190)	−15,199
1263/1846–47	(7,000)	(37,926)	−30,926
1267/1850–51	13,418	45,509	−32,091
1268/1851–52	6,669	45,629	−38,960
1269/1852–53	7,389	41,880	−34,491
1270/1853–54	(6,263)	(36,506)	−30,243
1276/1859–60	17,203	. . . . .	. . . .
1278/1861–62	(8,513)	(38,490)	−29,977
1279/1862–63	13,607	47,306	−33,699
1280/1863–64	14,346	(47,306)	−32,960
1281/1864–65	(14,346)	(42,420)	−28,074
1282/1865–66	(16,646)	(41,772)	−25,126
1289/1872–73	. . . . .	(41,140)	. . . .

Note: All figures have been rounded to the nearest purse of 500 Ottoman kurush. Parentheses indicate estimates by the sources; audited amounts have no parentheses. Sources are as follows: Turkey. Bashbakanlik Arshivi (B.B.A.). Meclis-i Vâlâ (M.V.) 504 and Dahiliye (D.) 3548; M.V. 4889; M.V. 2948; M.V. 6334; D. 17876; Meclis-i Mahsus (M.M.) 1; Misir Defteri 592 Enclosure 26; M.V. 18661; M.M. 1120 and M.V. 24702; M.V. 22429 Enclosure 22; D. 37893; D. 45412. The figures for 1278, which originally covered a twenty-one month period, have been prorated for the year.

REVENUES

The sources of revenue available to the Ottoman government of the Hijaz were limited by the peculiar religious, political, and economic position the province occupied in the empire. Because of its religious role, it was the recipient of gifts from the central government rather than a source of revenue for Istanbul. But even if the central government had wanted to collect large amounts of taxes, it would have been difficult to do so. The Hijaz was too poor, too distant, and too accustomed to near-autonomy to submit to taxation. Hijazis basically did not pay taxes except in the disguised form of higher prices for goods taxed on entry to the Hijaz by sea. These customs revenues were outweighed by external sources of money: direct subsidies to the local government from Istanbul, gifts to individuals and religious groups (the *surra*), and food sent by Cairo and Istanbul. Despite these sources, money frequently had to be borrowed locally to tide the government over until the annual subsidies actually arrived in Mecca.

Every year the vali faced the problem of securing the money needed to balance his expenditures. When the changeover to Ottoman administration occurred in 1257/1841–42, the financial and grain contributions of Egypt to the Hijaz once again became an issue. Mehmed Ali of Egypt had annually sent 10,000 purses or their equivalent in grain as a gift in addition to his expenditures for military expenses in the Hijaz. He had, however, suppressed at least some of the waqf income from Egypt for the Holy Cities. In 1257/1841–42 he withheld a small part of the 10,000 purses despite protests from Vali Osman Pasha. Osman estimated that the Jidda customs would yield under 9,000 purses;[4] he thought he should receive another 8,000 from urban rents and agricultural property income from Egyptian waqfs. If Egypt provided its full 10,000 purses in gifts, the deficit would then be only about 3,000 purses.[5] Osman's estimates were over optimistic: he drastically underestimated expenditures. A complete list of revenues sent by the chief clerk of the Jidda local treasury to Istanbul showed actual receipts for 1257 as the following: (1) Jidda customs, 10,496 purses; (2) other local sources, 247; (3) Istanbul Treasury, 4,510; (4) Egypt had promised 8,000 in grain and cash but had delivered only 5,693; (5) grain already on hand in the Hijaz from Egypt, 2,856. The total of 23,802 purses, even if Egypt's missing contribution could be expected soon, was still far short of total expenditures. Short-term one-time measures were taken to raise about 7,000 purses. The remaining 3,500 purses of the deficit had to be sent from Istanbul. When 2,000 purses finally arrived, they were used to pay the troops in Madina and merchants in Jidda who were owed money by the local government.[6] The burden of the deficit fell on those groups, who frequently had to wait years to receive the money that was due them.

The next year that provides sufficient information for analysis of revenues was 1261/1845. The tangled web of the financial records of the Hijaz for this year was not finally settled by the Ottoman accountants until five years after the completion of the year itself. In April 1849 a detailed examination of the books of the province showed that 13,326 purses had come from Istanbul directly or by drafts on Egypt. The proportion of the money from Egypt is not known, although three years before in 1258/1842-43 Egypt had been expected to pay 13,000 purses. Local revenues accounted for almost as much as the subsidies from Cairo and Istanbul in 1845.

After a long dispute between two valis was adjudicated by the Istanbul treasury auditors, a relatively small deficit of about 1,800 purses remained to be paid for 1261. This money and 5,000 purses that had been borrowed from Jidda merchants to help cover the expenses of 1261 and 1262 were paid through Egypt. The banker of the vali of Egypt paid the vali of Jidda, and then Egypt was reimbursed by Istanbul.

In the period of unstable Hijazi political history from 1268/1851-52 to 1275/1858-59, detailed information on finances is possible only for the years 1268 to 1270/1853-54.

In 1268 Egypt paid the Hijaz on behalf of the Ottomans 19,623 purses for basic civilian expenditures. In addition to this there was a special 9,107-purse gift. Local revenues of almost 6,700 purses were a second source. The balance of the 45,000 purses—about 10,000—came from the central treasury to the Hijaz in cash. It was planned that nearly the same allocation would take place in 1269/1852-53. However, in both years actual payments ran behind the promised amounts.

Egypt paid for the Ottomans less than the customary 20,000 purses: only 16,859 in 1268 and 9,437 in 1269. On the other hand, audited accounts of expenditures showed that they also were lower than official estimates.[7] In 1270/1853–54 Egypt once again sent at least 20,000 purses from its total tribute owed to the imperial government.

The complete records of the local revenues for 1269/1852–53 show the results of separating the Yemen ports' customs from Hijazi administration. This year, as in 1263/1845–46 and 1268/1851–52, a severe drop in revenue naturally resulted. Of the 7,389 purses left, over five-sevenths came from the customs of Jidda (2,919) and Suakin and Massawa (2,344). Another important source of local revenue was the tribute of 460 purses paid by Najd to the Hijaz in recognition of nominal Ottoman sovereignty.[8] Zakat (taxes for alms) receipts were only 206 purses. Initially, the projected deficit, based on 1268 figures, was 27,532. Another 7,000 purses had to come from Istanbul after the separation of the Yemen customs.[9] The Istanbul treasury also paid Egypt for the shipment in 1268 of 4,144 tons of wheat, 9,279 of barley, and 2,089 of *ful* (Egyptian beans) to the Hijaz. In the two years 1269 and 1270/1853–54 the Nizamiye treasury supplied 20,140 purses, Egypt 20,000, and the imperial treasury 3,276 for grain to the Hijaz.[10]

The need for cash led the valis to borrow money from local merchants. Even when the income from Istanbul permitted them to pay for expenditures, it was difficult to transfer the alloted funds from Istanbul to Mecca. Payments were months and sometimes years in arrears, with the threat of an audit awaiting the vali who manipulated his accounts. The *defterdar*, or treasurer, of the provincial administration seems, at least in some instances, to have possessed independence of action and a separate channel of communication with Istanbul.

The risky business of providing credit could be undertaken only by the largest of merchants with a capital such that delays in payment would not ruin his other businesses. Even more preferable was a consortium of lenders who could share the risks and also apply more pressure on the vali in the event of a dispute than could one man. Faraj Yusr, an Indian Muslim, was the chief merchant of Jidda in the 1850s. His capital was estimated at between 24,000 and 30,000 purses.[11] He became the chief banker for the Hijaz. Yusr and another local merchant, Salim Sultan, lent the provincial government 1,600 purses in 1270. In 1271 Yusr advanced 4,300 purses to the Hijaz for the payment of soldiers and military expenses. He was to be repaid by drafts on Istanbul. The imperial treasury was ordered to pay Yusr's agent in Istanbul the total of both debts.[12] These loans plus others, unrecorded in their details, totalled 9,900 purses for 1270 and 1271. In 1272/1855–56 Faraj Yusr was asked for the large sum of 14,501 purses. Since payments in Jidda were actually made in riyals (Maria Theresa dollars), the rate of exchange between the *kurush*, treasury sight drafts, and the silver dollar was crucial to his undertaking such a large transaction. His agent at Istanbul demanded that the rate of exchange be fixed at thirty kurush per riyal rather than twenty-three; this would also make a difference of 2,000 purses in the payment of past debts that were due him. In 1273/1856–57 once again, Yusr paid for a large proportion of the grain imported into the Hijaz. In order to share the risk of these large sums, he formed syndicates.[13]

Yusuf Banaja was one of those who also lent the Ottomans money. Banaja provided 2,982 purses in 1268 and 1269. His loan illustrated the slowness of the Ottoman bureaucracy. Although he was supposed to be reimbursed shortly after making the loan, his agents in Cairo and Istanbul did not receive the money; and in 1272 the case still had not been settled.[14]

When Faraj Yusr was discharged as the treasury's chief agent in Jidda in 1276/1860, Ahmad Mashat and Salim Sultan became the province's chief bankers. The stated reasons for the change were the excessive profits Yusr was thought to be receiving, his slowness in supplying the money, and the rate of thirty-two kurush per riyal he wanted to use while the current rate was twenty-nine or twenty-nine and one-half.[15] Yusr's profit on exchange was estimated at eighteen percent. On the loan of 4,000 purses to the amir for military operations, which caused lively discussion in Istanbul, Yusr wanted a two percent commission plus the rate of thirty-two kurush per riyal. A competitor offered to make the same loan for the same commission but at twenty-nine per riyal. This would have given the amir more than 6,000 extra riyals, but the proposal was turned down in Istanbul. Yusr's agent there allegedly bribed the minister of the treasury to achieve this. Unfortunately there is insufficient evidence now available to determine whether the reasons for Yusr's eventual downfall were valid or a mere pretext for political or personal motives. Similarly, the profitability of most of the loans is not yet known; a five percent profit seems to have been the minimum expected.[16]

The reign of the amir 'Abd Allah, which constituted the third period for analysis, witnessed no major changes from the preceding two segments. The year 1279/1862–63 may be taken as an example. Local revenue came chiefly from the Jidda customs, which yielded a profit of 6,000 purses, and those of Yemen, which also provided 6,000. The customs of Massawa and Suakin declined to only 133 purses. Although the Najd's tribute of 600 purses was listed as a source of money, it was not paid that year.[17]

Egypt continued to be the chief source of payments. Every year, 20,000 purses from the Egyptian tribute to Istanbul had been used at the direction of the central government for the purchase of grain. When the decision was taken to send grain from Iraq rather than Egypt, part of the now-freed money was sent to Jidda for the operating expenses of the Hijaz and part was used to repay Ottoman debts to the Egyptian treasury for preceding years' expenditures in the Hijaz.[18]

Local merchants continued to provide money pending payments from Istanbul. Mashat had provided over 27,000 purses in 1277–78, and he remained a large lender in 1279 with almost 8,000 purses. Yet Mashat's own capital was reported to be insufficient to cover payments if Istanbul was late in reimbursing him.[19] Surprisingly enough, Faraj Yusr is also mentioned as providing 8,000 and being paid back by drafts on the treasury. Other merchants loaned 6,800. They and Mashat were repaid when Egypt sent 15,000 purses to Jidda for the account of the imperial treasury. There remained, however, debts of 36,000 purses from 1277–78 still unpaid. The imperial treasury sent 10,000 purses in cash to the Hijaz, so that 1279 expenditures were balanced even though the backlog from previous years remained. The surra in 1279 amounted to 6,179 purses and stayed at about the same amount in the following years.

EXPENDITURES

In the initial period of the restoration of Ottoman control, detailed information on expenditures is available only for the year 1257/1841–42. There were three major categories into which the local government's spending was divided. The largest was food. Grain and other items in storehouses cost 10,404 purses. This plus food for the military and the cost of transport of the grain was an additional 7,265 purses. Together they accounted for one-half of total expenditures. Most of the food went to recipients of pensions, government employees, the military, and the Bedouin. The second area of government spending was cash salaries to government employees, pensions to religious people, and money for the amir and the Bedouin. The bureaucracy took 4,075 purses and the other groups 3,853. *Bashibozuks*, or the irregular army, were paid 8,767 purses, or about one-quarter of the budget.[20]

In the second period of political instability, different categories were used in financial accounts. Allocations for the military in 1268/1851–52 included the cost of food. Total military costs rose to 26,588 purses, or well over one-half of all spending. Second that year were the salaries paid to government workers and the pensions to sharifs, the Bedouin, and those who prayed in the Holy Cities. The final fifth of the budget was used for imperial gifts and miscellaneous categories.[21]

Cash expenditures for 1269/1852–53 show the same preponderance of military spending as in 1268 but also demonstrate the duality of the Ottoman army in the Hijaz. Civil salaries and purchase of grain for civilians cost only 16,853 purses; the army consumed 25,027. However, this 25,000 was divided into two parts: the regular cavalry and infanty on the one hand and the *Nizamiye* infantry and artillery on the other. Judging by the total amounts spent, the regulars were more numerous, or at least more expensive, than the Nizamiye. The regulars' provisions were presumably paid for by the central government directly, whereas the cost of supplying the Nizamiye came from the Hijaz budget. In itself the cost for the Nizamiye that year and in others was deceptive because the first regiment of the Hijaz Division was permanently stationed in Istanbul. The 4,000 purses this regiment cost should be deducted every year from the formal expenditures of the Hijaz in order to ascertain the actual cost to the empire of militarily defending the province.[22]

The amount of grain sent by the Istanbul government to the Hijaz was substantial given the expense and distances involved. In the early and middle periods, it seems to have been sent from Egypt alone, although later it came from Iraq. Over 14,000 tons were sent to the Hijaz in 1269/1852–53. To take only barley as an example, the 9,125 tons of it that were sent to the Hijaz were divided as follows: 4,867 tons went to the military; 473 to the civil government; and 3,785 were presumably reserved for civilian and pilgrim use.[23]

The next year the commanding proportion of the army was increased. Although the actual amount spent decreased to 24,283 purses, other non-military spending declined even more. About two-thirds of all expenditures went to the military. Government salaries were only 6,446 purses, and pensions were an almost insignificant 2,818.[24]

A closer look at the kinds of expenditures in 1270 reveals

the diverse types of activities that involved the Hijaz provincial government. The safeguarding of the pilgrimage and
the carrying out of its ritual requirements were among the
major undertakings of the vali. Moving grain to Mecca and
Madina for the pilgrims and their military escorts cost 400
purses. The troops stationed in the Hijaz who were used to
help protect the pilgrimage themselves cost the government
about 2,300 purses. Amir 'Abd al-Muttalib received 540 purses
just for his expenses relating to the pilgrimage.[25] Some money
allocated specifically for the reconstruction of holy buildings
in Madina was diverted to other purposes. It was used for
salaries of the vali, the amir, the defterdar, the keeper of
the keys to the Ka'ba, and for a number of other religious
and political officials. None of the money seems to have been
spent on buildings in Madina.[26]

A long-standing system used in paying government employees, and probably soldiers as well, permitted some high
officials of the Ottoman government to make money at the
expense of their poorer colleagues. Pay warrants were issued
instead of cash. These warrants were always subject to
discount because it was only rarely that the recipient himself
could go directly to the treasury that had issued them in
order to cash them. Even when he could do so, the treasury
might refuse payment, at least temporarily, pending bribes.
Up to 1857, pay warrants in the Hijaz had been worth only
50-70 percent of their face value. Starting that year, it became
harder to cash the warrants with the vilayet treasurer for
cash; only too frequently the bearer had to settle for 40 percent of the real value.[27]

Ten years later, in 1279/1862-63, there is the only complete account of the provincial budget by cities (see table 2).
The Ottomans clearly attached greater importance to Mecca,
for they spent twice as much there as in Madina. Mecca was
larger, the seat of the amirate, and the more important of the
two in religious terms. In the only two categories where
spending in Madina was considerably greater than that in
Mecca, the transport of grain and payments to Bedouins,

special circumstances were present. Madina was physically farther from the Red Sea coast, and the camel caravans carrying grain had to traverse land in the hands of nearly independent Bedouin tribes. Particularly in administration Mecca was more important as the residence, *de facto*, of the vali, although he nominally was based in Jidda.

TABLE 2

EXPENDITURES OF THE JIDDA EYALET IN 1279/1862–63

Category	In Madina	In Mecca
The amir, the sharifs, and others	16	5,376
Servants of the haram	. . . . .	78
Neighbors of God and the Prophet	782	617
Civil servants	506	4,208
Nizamiye	4,437	9,774
Regular army	5,411	6,404
Military supplies	268	594
Navy	. . . . .	190
Grain and transport*	2,426	260
Living expenses	507	1,216
Travel expenses, mail, etc.	276	799
Bedouin	152	. . . . .
Subtotal	14,781	29,516
Miscellaneous	400	2,600
Total	15,181	32,116
Grand total	47,297	

Note: All figures have been rounded to the nearest purse of 500 Ottoman kurush. Source: B.B.A. M.V. 22429 Enclosure 14.

* Also see table 3.

Well over half of the money in 1279 was spent on the armed forces. Food consumption from officially provided storehouses reflected the same financial priority (see table 3). Of 3,683 tons of barley, 1,527 went to cavalry based in Madina and 1,326 to military forces in Mecca. Civil servants were paid both in cash and in food. Grain was also given to religious persons in Mecca ("neighbors of God") and Madina ("neighbors of the Prophet"). Because of existing stores in warehouses in Yanbu', Rabigh, and Jidda, the actual amount of grain to be purchased and laboriously transported to the Holy Cities was only 3,650 tons that year.

A list of the individuals who received money and food in Madina and Yanbu' in 1280/1863–64 provides the first opportunity to see the reality of individuals behind the collective terms used in most records. The importance of this may

TABLE 3

FOOD TO BE PURCHASED BY THE JIDDA EYALET in 1279/1862–63

Category	Ful	Barley	Wheat
In Mecca			
The amir, other sharifs, and sayyids	103	282	137
Servants of the haram and neighbors of God	1	26	120
Civil servants	4	53	6
Military	503	1,326	1,060
Total	611	1,687	1,323
In Madina			
Sharifs	53	35	58
Servants of the haram	2	42	27
Neighbors of the Prophet	5	11	16
Bedouin	48	27	426
Civil servants	. . .	41	13
Syrian pilgrimage	66	32	20
Military	109	1,593	601
Total	283	1,781	1,161
Grand total	894	3,468	2,484

Note: All figures have been converted to tons. Minor categories have been omitted, as have the amounts of coffee, sugar, etc. Totals, therefore, are larger than the sums listed here would indicate. Source: B.B.A. M.M. 1120 Enclosure 35.

be illustrated in the first category of table 4, sharifs and sayyids. The gross figures are, in themselves, only of importance when seen in comparison with other categories, i.e., a good deal more was spent on these descendants of the Prophet than on the servants of the Madina haram, who numbered at least twenty. If, however, the total money given the sharifs and sayyids is divided by thirty-eight, the number of recipients, they become more meaningful. On the average each sharif or sayyid received about 3,080 pounds of wheat, 1,805 pounds of barley, and 1,590 pounds of ful. The head of the Madina haram received 21,600 pounds per year of wheat.

Presumably he maintained a large household and entertained many guests, so that much of the grain was used; but he might also have been able to sell a good part of it. An official might get most of his pay in cash and some in grain.

TABLE 4

CONDENSED STATEMENT OF THE
1280/1863–64 EXPENDITURES FOR MADINA AND YANBU'

Category	Money	Ful	Barley	Wheat
Sharifs and sayyids	17	30	34	59
Servants of the Madina haram	. . . . .	1	39	27
Neighbors of the Prophet	53	3	16	23
Civil servants, servants, etc.	521	1	3	1
Storehouses of Madina, special occasions, some Bedouin	154	. . . .	. . . . .	4
Nizamiye army and artillery Salary	2,756	. . .	. . . . .	. . . . .
Supplies	4,487	178	105	447
Cavalry and guards for roads	8,060	. . .	1,892	526
Bedouin	. . . . .	63	62	522
Pilgrimage, including grain bought for pilgrims	5,676	196	175	171
Administration of Yanbu'	226	. . .	. . . . .	. . . . .
Total	21,950	472	2,326	1,780

Note: All figures have been rounded to the nearest purse and the nearest ton. Some minor categories have been omitted. Totals, therefore, are larger than the sums listed here would indicate. Source: B.B.A. M.M. 1223 Enclosure 32.

Pensions were given not only to retired civil servants but also to their children. In addition, payments of other sorts were also inheritable. The money originally given to the leader of a Bedouin tribe might be divided and redivided over the years. By 1280, for example, thirteen people were dividing 1,400 pounds of wheat and two hundred pounds of barley originally given to one person. Even spies were listed on the roster, though not by name.

The pilgrimage from Syria, which brought part of the yearly influx of money needed so desperately in the Hijaz, also entailed expenditures by the provincial government. Official receptions and ceremonies in and near Madina marked the arrival and departure of the caravans; they cost 161 purses. Ottoman troops and officials rented camels from the Bedouins for 428 purses. The Bedouins who lived in the vicinity of the hajj route received 14,000 pounds of wheat, 424,000 of barley, and 280,000 of ful. Ottoman official hospitality to their Bedouin guests extended to 1,320 pounds of sugar to sweeten the coffee of their guests. Grain that was transported to Madina and Yanbu' for the pilgrims and their protectors was perhaps partially paid for by money from the surra.

Yanbu', the port of Madina, was a *qaimmaqamate* under the jurisdiction of Madina. With probably fewer than 5,000 people, Yanbu' nevertheless had a harbor that was filled with ships from Qussayr and Suez on the Egyptian coast and, during the pilgrimage season, was frequented also by ships from all the Muslim world. Its administration in 1280 cost 226 purses. Half of this consisted of the salary of the *qaimmaqam*, Khalil Pasha. Ten soldiers in the local garrison were paid three purses each per year.

Payments to the Bedouin were divided into two sections corresponding to the tribal confederations of the Harb and the Juhayna. The Harb controlled the crucial passes from the Red Sea coast to Madina and some of the routes between Mecca and Madina. They received ten times more food than did the Juhayna.[28]

Differences in the categories used make it difficult to compare with precision Madina's expenditures in 1280 with those of 1279. Two major changes seem to have taken place: (1) the pilgrimage is included in 1280 but not in 1279; (2) the expenses of all branches of the military went up by about 5,000 purses in 1280. The increase in military spending may have been caused by disputes with the Bedouin of Rabigh and Yanbu'. A few months after the report on 1280/1863–64 was written, the Yanbu'-Madina and Madina-Mecca roads were cut by the Harb Bedouin.[29]

In the years following 1280, only scattered information on

expenditures is available, with the exception of the salary schedule of 1288/1871–72. Most documents deal with grain shipments to the Hijaz. From the taxes of Varna in the European section of the empire came 12,322 purses used for the purchase and shipment of food to the Hijaz in 1287/1870–71. In 1288/1871–72 Varna and other sancaks contributed 5,380 purses for grain and 2,130 for transportation. At least 4,474 purses were spent on the same items in 1291/1874–75.[30]

The Ottoman central government went bankrupt in the 1870s because of excessive borrowing from Europe, the disastrous wars of that period, and the inability of the state to raise the level of the economy. In an initial attempt to cut expenditures, a careful investigation was made of the civil employees of the Hijaz in order to reduce their number and expense. In 1288/1871–72 total salaries were 15,737 purses. By eliminating some posts entirely, combining others, and cutting the salaries of some of those remaining, it was proposed to save 1,536 purses. The chief victims of the cuts were to be the vali, who would lose two-thirds of his 1,440-purses salary; the chief clerk, whose salary was cut by one-half and whose assistant was dismissed; and the Jidda qaim-maqam, whose post was to be abolished. It was suggested that the salary of the qaimmaqam of Mecca be raised from 120 to 180 purses per year and that he be responsible for the administration of Jidda rather than simply act as an aide to the vali. The reforms may have been implemented in part, but the Jidda qaimmaqamate was retained.

The total number of employees of the Hijaz Ottoman government, from the vali to the coffee-maker in Madina (but excluding the police), was about 170. They shared 7,828 purses in 1288 but with a wide gap between the amir, with 2,160, and a water-carrier, who was paid under 2 purses annually. Intermediate ranks included clerks who received between 10 and 20 purses, a translator with 12, and teachers in Mecca who were paid 30 purses each. Religious-legal figures such as the deputy judges of Mecca and Madina had only 30 purses per year in salary. The Hanafi mufti of Mecca

TABLE 5

Condensed Statement of the Salaries of the
Hijaz Vilayet in 1288/1871–72

Hijaz Mutasarriflik

Interior	
Amir of Mecca	2,160
Vali	1,440
Qaimmaqam of Mecca	120
Chief clerk	120
Zaptiye police	7,909
Subtotal	12,076
Treasury	
Defterdar	216
Assistant	144
Subtotal	746
Total	12,822

Mecca Sancak

Interior	285
Treasury	47
Legal	103
Education	216
Commerce	120
Public utilities	13
Total	782

Jidda Sancak

Interior	
Qaimmaqam of Jidda	200
Governor of Taif	12
Governor of Rabigh	19
Shaykh of Rabigh	6
Muhafiz of Qunfuda	18
Subtotal	490
Treasury	120
Commerce	403
Subtotal	523
Total	1,013

Madina Sancak

Interior	
Shaykh al-Haram	336
Muhafiz of Madina	200
Qaimmaqam of Yanbuʻ	88
Subtotal	713
Treasury	155
Legal	112
Commerce	140
Subtotal	407
Total	1,120

Grand total 15,737

Note: All figures have been rounded to the nearest purse of 500 Ottoman kurush. Some categories have been omitted. Totals, therefore, are larger than the sums listed here would indicate.
Source: B.B.A. D. 44765.

was paid the surprisingly low sum of 6 purses. Health officials got more: doctors in Jidda and Madina were paid 36 and 130 respectively, though quarantine officials received far less.

The sole public utility in all the Hijaz that received government support was the spring that supplied water for Mecca.[31]

CONCLUSION

To obtain a complete idea of the scope and cost of government in the Ottoman Hijaz it would be necessary to obtain information on all the thirty-seven years involved rather than the fragmentary data now available. It would also be advisable to complete the survey of the history of the Hijaz to the end of the empire there in 1919, as well as obtaining comparable data on the other provinces of the region, before drawing definitive conclusions about the nature of Ottoman-Arab relations. The amirs of Mecca, who played such an important part in the Arab rebellion and subsequent Arab nationalism, enjoyed authority and power under the Ottomans. Their own financial history is nearly unknown, although it seems that the money they received from Istanbul remained stable throughout the nineteenth century at about 2,000 purses.[32] This was, however, by no means the only source of revenue available to them.

Granting that the financial evidence is both incomplete and perhaps in part misleading, it does help establish the major concerns of the Ottoman government in the Hijaz and the dependence of the area upon external sources of money and food. Most importantly, the primary role of the military is made clear. Although consuming the largest part of most years' budgets, the army managed to maintain order only in the main towns; the countryside, mostly desert, was outside its control. Because of the danger of first Egyptian and then European expansionism, the riots and rebellions of 'Abd al-Muttalib, and the continual menace of the Bedouin, it was impossible to reduce the level of spending for the military.

In the central lands of the empire, 1840–77 was the period of the Tanzimat, the Crimean War, and military and administrative reform. These changes were apparently not felt in the Hijaz. Civil government was limited to record-keeping, the courts, minimal health precautions, and, most important, the buying, storage, and distribution of food purchased by Istanbul for the people and the pilgrims.

The people of the Hijaz lived by means of religion. Pilgrims to Mecca and Madina provided probably the greatest source of income, but the gifts and subventions from the central Ottoman Empire and Egypt were certainly next in importance. Other than customs fees there were practically no taxable resources; the area was too poor to pay its own way. Yet at the same time there was a strong tradition of autonomy among the tribes and near-autonomy among the amirs of Mecca. There were, therefore, strong reasons both for loyalty to the Ottoman sultan and suspicion of any centralizing measures adopted by Istanbul. On balance Ottoman sovereignty in the Hijaz provided financial benefits for all groups that outweighed resentment caused by the limited degree of political interference. Arab nationalism did not exist in the Hijaz of 1840–77 but neither did strong Ottoman loyalty.

The opportunity to do the research for this article was provided by grants from the American Research Institute in Turkey and the Faculty Research Abroad program of the Department of Health, Education, and Welfare.

1. Gerald de Gaury, *Rulers of Mecca* (London, 1951).

2. A purse, or kese, is equal to 500 Ottoman kurush. All Ottoman money as well as foreign currency has been converted to purses, which have been rounded to the nearest whole number.

3. Harry Luke, *Cyprus under the Turks, 1571–1878* (London, 1969), pp. 239–47.

4. The Jidda customs in 1814 during the first years of Mehmed Ali's administration were estimated at 8,000 purses (J. L. Burckhardt, *Travels in Arabia* [London, 1829], p. 49). In 1829 it was said to be about 6,000 purses (Boislecomte [Alexandria] to French Foreign Minister, 3 July 1833, printed in Georges Douin, ed., *La Mission du Baron de Boislecomte* [Cairo, 1927], p. 126).

5. Turkey. Bashbakanlik Arshivi (B.B.A.). Meclis-i Vâlâ (M.V.) 504.

6. B.B.A. Dahiliye (D.) 3548.

7. B.B.A. D. 17876 Enclosure 8.

8. R. B. Winder, *Saudi Arabia in the Nineteenth Century* (New York, 1965), pp. 179–82, says that the payment of Maria Theresa $10,000 (about 460 purses) by the Saudis to the Hijaz was not made in 1846, leading to the campaign of the Amir in Najd that year. Muhammed b. 'Awn then secured the money, but there were again at least partial defaults in 1850 and 1854–55.

9. B.B.A. Meclis-i Mahsus (M.M.) I Enclosure 28.

10. B.B.A. D. 14696; D. 24863

11. Richard Burton, *Personal Narrative of a Pilgrimage to El-Medinah and Meccah* (London, 1855–56), 1:47; Great Britain. Foreign Office (F.O.) 195/375 Qaimmaqam of Jidda to Page, 4 November 1856; Charles Didier, *Séjour chez le Grand-Chérif de la Mekke* (Paris, 1857), pp. 160–161.

12. B.B.A. M.V. 12723; M.V. 13320; D. 20141.

13. B.B.A. M.V. 15507; M.V. 15511; M.V. 16307; M.V. 19627.

14. B.B.A. M.V. 15540.

15. B.B.A. M.M. 736.

16. Ahmed Cevdet Pasha, *Tezâkir* (Nos. 13–20, edited by Cavid Baysun; Ankara, 1960), 2:93–95.

17. B.B.A. M.V. 22429 Enclosure 22.

18. B.B.A. M.V. 22429, Enclosures 52 and 29.

19. F.O. 195/681 Stanley (Jidda) to Bulwer, 22 February 1861.

20. B.B.A. D.3548.

21. B.B.A. D. 17876 Enclosure 8.

22. B.B.A. M.M. I Enclosure 28.

23. B.B.A. M.M. I Enclosure 28.

24. B.B.A. Misir Defteri 592 Enclosure 26.

25. B.B.A. Misir Defteri 592.

26. B.B.A. Misir Defteri 592.

27. F.O. 195/375 S. Page (Jidda) to Stratford de Redcliffe, 20 October 1857.

28. B.B.A. M.M. 1223 Enclosure 32.

29. French consul at Jidda to Ministry, 5 February 1864, and 10 August 1864, in René Tresse, *Le Pèlerinage syrien aux villes saintes de l'Islam* (Paris, 1937), p. 54; Adolphe d'Avril, *L'Arabie contemporaine avec la description du pèlerinage de la Mecque* (Paris, 1868), pp. 84–85.

30. B.B.A. D. 45149; D. 50455; D. 49474.

31. B.B.A. D. 44765.

32. The subsidy to the sharifs was said to be 1,920 purses in the 1810s; see Burckhardt, op. cit., p. 225. By 1267/1850–51 it was about 2,160 purses with 228 tons of barley and other goods whose value was estimated for 1271/1854–55 at 285 purses per year; see B.B.A. D. 14524 and D. 21257.

Caesar Farah

Censorship and Freedom of Expression in Ottoman Syria and Egypt

Censorship of printed material had an earlier start in the Syro-Lebanese region of the Ottoman Empire than in Egypt and intensified gradually in direct proportion to the increase in criticism of the established order and the custodians thereof. Besieged by internal and external pressures aimed at disrupting what unity was left in the Ottoman Empire and threatening now to disrupt the social balance of its core, the Arabo-Muslim heartland, Ottoman rulers and their administrative representatives hoped to head off further disintegration by tightening the reins of control so as to prevent what was construed as political sedition and dishonor to established institutions. But writers who championed freedom of expression were convinced that they were speaking up as loyal citizens motivated by sincere desires to reform the system and to eliminate measures ensuing from policies of suppression and misrule. As one writer put it,

Ottomans like myself are not in the vanguard of civilized nations nor in their trail, nor even in a state of negligence because in spite of all suppressive efforts they have still taken an important step forward in the world and in civilization.[1]

Salim Sarkis, the boldest protagonist of free expression, summed up the sentiment of fellow writers in an open letter dated 25 April 1896, and addressed to Sultan Abdülhamid, which he dispatched to Istanbul from his safe haven in Cairo while enjoying the immunity provided him by an official of the British embassy there. The letter and examples illustrating his complaints were later published in a monograph entitled *'Aja'ib al-Maktubji* [Rarities of the Censor], and was ironically dedicated to Sultan Abdülhamid by his critic.[2] The work represented a formal appeal to the sultan calling on him to remove the impediments barring the achievement of full and unrestricted freedom of expression, which had had a negative impact on all areas of writing. He reflected the sentiment of other journalists, who stressed the fact that in entering this their plea they were acting as proud Ottomans and loyal subjects seriously disturbed by the ill-effects of misrule and general mismangagement of the affairs of the empire in the provinces and the impact thereof on the Ottoman society's potential for survival, modernization, and growth. "The cause of all our misfortunes", stated Sarkis, "is the attempt by officials to smother our minds as they would our lives."[3]

During this critical period in Ottoman-Arab relations, when the survival of their commonly shared values was at stake, writers had become a restless lot. After enduring centuries of intellectual stagnation, they burst upon the scene with renewed vigor, stimulated by new knowledge and ideas made available to them through fresh experiences derived from immediate contacts with progressive European nations and their enlightened ideals. Such contacts made them aware of their own society's state of over-all stagnation. They now believed they knew how to awaken it and instill new life into it, fully confident of their milieu's potential for intellectual, social, and political growth. Such were the men who were identified with the "Arab renaissance," and who in spite of all handicaps placed in their path did indeed succeed ultimately in flooding their audiences with modern and progressive ideas. They placed their mark on the literary revival movement, to the inception of which they contributed substantially if they did not sire it in the first instance.

EVOLUTION OF THE PRESS

The attitude of censorship was determined to a large extent by the orientation and content of publications, mainly newspapers and journals. It behooves us therefore to highlight the course of their evolution, both in Syria and in Egypt. With Napoleon's expedition to Egypt, we witness the introduction of the earliest publications: *Décade Egyptienne* and *Courrier d'Egypte*, both short-lived, terminating with the end of the expedition. The subsequent development of a national press covers four periods: (1) formative years during the reign of Mehmed Ali, (2) from Mehmed Ali to the reign of Khedive Isma'il, (3) from Isma'il to the British occupation, and (4) the period of the British occupation. It was during the latter two periods that the era of censorship commenced in Egypt. The intervening reigns of 'Abbas and Sa'id, prior to Isma'il's, discouraged journalistic activities. No newspapers or journals appeared in Egypt during these years (1849–63). The shift meanwhile was to Syria, where the key elements in the rise of educational and cultural activities, foreign missionaries and their establishments, took the lead in fostering the introduction of presses and publications. There, in 1851, Eli Smith published the first journal, yearly at first and then trimestrally thereafter till the end of its short-lived existence in 1855.[4]

From its inception the Arabic press in Syria developed a strong political orientation owing to the disturbed situation there, with the Crimean War and the events culminating in the bloody internecine strifes of 1858–60 leaving their scars on the inhabitants and the arbiters of their affairs. Intense foreign involvements in the domestic affairs of these Ottoman provinces and the over-all exigencies of the so-called Eastern Question had an impact on both the content and tone of the nascent press in Syria.

The first non-official political publication was *Mir'at al-Ahwal* of Rizq Allah Hassun of Aleppo in 1854. It lasted little over a year owing to its bitter attacks on the Turks and the government. When an order for the arrest of the owner was issued by the authorities, Rizq Allah fled to Russia.[5] In 1858 Khalil al-Khuri published for the first time his *Hadiqat al-Akhbar*, and in 1860 Fu'ad Pasha, the Ottoman foreign minister who at that time had come to Syria to deal with the aftermath of the 1860 incidents, proposed to him that he convert his newspaper into a semiofficial publication and arranged for him a monthly stipend until the official publication *Suriya* came out. It resumed an official status during the governorship of Franco Pasha in Lebanon, 1869–73. For a short period he remade *Hadiqat al-Akhbar* into the official organ of the country.[6]

Other newspapers pioneered by Syrians during this early period in and out of their homeland include *'Atarid* and *Birjis Baris* in 1858, published respectively in Marseilles and Paris, the latter by Count Rashid Dahdah until taken over in its fifth year by Sulayman al-Jaza'iri al-Tunisi; *al-Jawa'ib* of Ahmad Faris al-Shidyaq, 1860 in Istanbul until 1884, subsidized by the Ottoman government, in whose bureau of translations the owner-editor served on occasion and whose newspaper had a strong impact on literary circles and men of authority both at the capital and in the Arabic-speaking regions of the empire; *Nafir Suriya* of Butrus al-Bustani in 1860, right after the incidents of that year but short-lived in duration; and *al-Ra'id al-Tunisi* in 1861. Among the publications directly induced or sponsored officially by the Ottoman district governors can be listed *Suriya* at Damascus in 1865; *al-Furat* at Halab in 1867 through the recommendation of Cevdet Pasha; *Lubnan* at Beirut, put out by Da'ud Pasha, the first *Mutasarrif* of Mount Lebanon in 1867; and *al-Zawra'* by Midhat Pasha at Baghdad in 1869. Interestingly enough, it was during this period that the term *jaridah* came to be employed formally to describe the newspaper; hitherto it had gone by the appellations *al-nashra*, *al-waraqa al-khabariya*, or *al-waqa'i'* and the like.[7] Official publications in Egypt at this time include *al-Waqa'i' al-Misriya*, introduced by Mehmed Ali in 1828, first in both Arabic and Turkish and later in Arabic only. But the first nonofficial publication was the biweekly *Wadi al-Nil* of Abu al-Sa'ud in 1866, at Cairo, which terminated with the death of its owner in 1879.

The over-all assessment of the early Syrian press by those who studied it is that it was not on a par with later publications in Egypt, Tunis, Europe, and Istanbul. This is attributed to the pressures of censorship, which appeared in Syria quite early. Almost from the start the American Mission's press ran into difficulty with Ottoman authorities in Beirut on account of certain publications of undetermined origins. In his letter to the governor dated 31 March 1849, Eli Smith wrote:

> Since its establishment fourteen years ago, our press has printed circulars for the government, the customs office and merchants in addition to various books on general knowledge and Christianity. We have never been told, before now, that there was anything in all this product contrary to the noble *shar'* or the wishes of the high authorities in the guarded *mahrusah* Ottoman dominions. The press has been following similar lines as all the numerous Christian presses in this country.[8]

Ottoman authorities were highly sensitized to the wedding of politics and religion in the squabbles of feudal and sectarian parties in the Syrian region, so ripe with the spirit of partisanship. Since the return of the Syrian provinces to direct Ottoman control with the aid of the major European powers in 1841, there was almost no end to the impact of foreign intervention in the administration of this area through the manipulation of protégés steeped in petty rivalries ensuing often from selfish personal ambitions.[9] It was quite natural that

Ottoman administrators should wish to curb writings heavy with the aroma of political and religious sedition. The zeal of the Protestant missions of the Church Mission Society of England and the American Board of Commissioners for Foreign Missions of Boston in making converts from the traditional Near Eastern Greek and Roman sects coupled with the disdain of the native Muslim inhabitants for their activities intensified hostile feelings on both sides. The situation reached such a point in 1864 that the Jesuit fathers pressed Uniate Christians and Ottoman authorities to curb Protestant publication activities. It is believed such pressures were directly responsible for inducing Ottoman authorities the following year to institute rigid censorship for the purpose of silencing the American press, though the Catholic press of the Jesuits ran the risk of being subjected to the same type of restrictions.[10]

Thus the first press rules introduced by the Ottomans in Syria came into force in January 1865 with the specific object of curbing what could be construed as political sedition. They called for the inspection of newly printed books, pamphlets, and newspapers.[11] Although the rules did not discriminate between Muslim and Christian publications, it was Christian publishers and writers who bore the brunt of censorship since very few Muslims were engaged in publishing during this formative period.[12]

The impact of the earliest form of censorship was felt in Beirut, the center of literary activity in Syria, and revolved around both political and religious subjects. As noted earlier, it was the Syrian press that had carried the banner of resistance to what it dubbed "Ottoman misrule" and first called for the assertion of an Arab identity. It had progressed from a state of simply printing news items, official decrees, commercial tidbits, and bureaucratic decisions to one of strong editorialization on prevailing political and social conditions.[13] The languages employed at first were Arabic and Turkish, then Arabic and French. Though semi-colloquial and weak, the Arabic of the press was eventually upgraded by the efforts of two erudite watchdogs and litterateurs in their own right, Ibrahim al-

Yaziji and Ahmad Faris al-Shidyaq, who resented colloquialization and the wholesale imbibing of foreign expressions by writers ignorant of their own language's wealth of expressions.

Ottoman censorship restricted the efflorescence of the press in Syria and stultified its growth in the decade and a half following its coming into being, the case of 'Abd al-Rahman al-Kawakibi being a good one in point.[14] He was an example of those who not only severely criticized bureaucratic practices in his home city of Aleppo but also preached freedom of the press, suffering persecution and having his publications confiscated or suspended one after the other. In justifying publication of *al-Shahba'*, al-Kawakibi explained his motif: "to fulfill all obligations incumbent upon popular newspapers: publicize 'the niceties of events' and the evil deeds of officials, expose the needs of the country to those in charge, and publish all that which is decreed by teaching good manners and widening the circle of knowledge, both educational and political."[15]

The Syrian press continued to hammer away at the issue of freedom and unity. During his brief ascendancy in the councils of the central government and his appointment in Syria, the liberal and reformist attitude of Midhat Pasha contributed considerably to the trend toward freedom.[16] The expansion of educational facilities and the establishment of constitutional rule aroused Syrian writers to demand liberty to criticize prevailing ills.[17] Authorities, meanwhile, ostensibly condoned critical writings, but seized every opportunity to redirect the strength of the press in support of the government. Newspaper owners were flattered with rank and medals, and the recalcitrant had "their pencils broken," i.e., were prevented from writing, and were either imprisoned or forced into exile. This insidious two-pronged approach was continued by British authorities following the occupation of Egypt. Both knew how to combine fear and encouragement, the granting or withholding of support from newspaper editors, and permitting proliferation in newspaper publications so as to create confusion in the contradictory stances many of them represented, all for the sake of watering down the opposition spearheaded by the nationalist press.

Sultan Abdülhamid tolerated only a few of the Syrian publications, namely, those that gave in to him, e.g., the *Jawa'ib* of al-Shidyaq. Among the newspapers and journals that appeared in the early 1870s and managed to stand up for a while during the reign of his predecessor, Abdülaziz, were *al-Zahra* of Yusuf al-Shalfun, *al-Bashir* of the Jesuit fathers, *al-Janna* and *al-Jinan* of Butrus al-Bustani, and *al-Nahla* of the Reverend Luwis al-Sabunji, with its strong tones and hostile argumentations. They all contributed materially in one form or another to the generation of the renaissance trend with its lasting social, political, and literary impact on awakening Arabic society.

Intolerable conditions fostered by Abdülhamid's authoritarian rule and the arbitrariness of his officials in Syria had much to do with the emigration in the late seventies of intellectuals and writers who would not be intimidated. From the point of view of Ottoman authorities, writers were not particularly prudent either in their choice of topics or in the manner of commenting and criticism. Hassun's *Mir'at al-Ahwal*, the first newspaper in the Arabic language, was suspended within a year following its appearance, but its publisher was not to be deterred. Emigrating to London, he reinstituted the newspaper there in 1876 and continued the battle. In 1879 he converted it into a political journal with the twofold aim of resolving both the "Egyptian" and the "Eastern" questions.[18]

Articles of unknown authorship attributed to Ibrahim al-Yaziji attacked both authorities and men of the cloth, the former in the call for an Arab awakening with strong nationalist and separatist appeals, and the latter in likening clerics unto devils disguised in priestly robes.[19]

Faris al-Shidyaq's brother As'ad was the first victim of priestly intolerance when the Maronite hierarchy would not tolerate seeing a brilliant young communicant convert to Protestantism in the late 1820s while in the service of the newly arrived mission in Beirut. Faris himself was forced to leave his country under related pressures.[20] Butrus al-Bustani, also a Maronite, appeared to advance in some of his writings a sort of ideal natural religion to unite men divided by warring dogmas and ended up hiding in an American missionary's house to escape the wrath of his patriarch.[21]

Another good example of religious skepticism and indifferentism coupled with anticlericalism is the case of Adib Ishaq, a brilliant young writer of Greek Catholic background from Damascus. He was educated in its Lazarist school but compelled to emigrate to Alexandria in 1876 in search of freedom of expression. Armed with a letter of introduction, he went to Jamal al-Din al-Afghani in Cairo the following year and immediately became one of his most ardent disciples. Al-Afghani's ideals and preachings were presented in the pages of Ishaq's newspaper *Misr*, which he established with another émigré from Syria, Salim al-Naqqash.[22] Although forced into exile for his outspoken frankness, Ishaq continued his battle against the establishment and its archaic institutions from Paris until his failing health compelled him to return to Syria and reside in Beirut. There he was attracted to Freemasonry, since the secrecy of the organization was particularly conducive to its quiet fostering of progressive and social humanitarian ideals. He, like other religious skeptics, undertook to defend Freemasonry and was locked in a polemical duel with the Jesuit fathers and the editors of their chief publications, *al-Mashriq* and *al-Bashir*.[23] Shaykhu, then editor of *al-Mashriq*, wrote later that the Masonic chapter in Beirut was abolished in consequence of its members' attack on established religions, their strong criticism of government, and their partisanship.[24]

Another subject that occasioned reaction from custodians of religion and the authorities was Darwinism. Before being transplanted to Egypt, *al-Muqtataf* of Ya'qub Sarruf and Faris Nimr was formally rebuked by the *vali* for espousing both Darwinism and anticlericalism. The editors were told that some of their articles had exceeded the limits of propriety and that to continue to publish in such veins was perturbing to both public opinion and the general good. *Al-Bashir*, which had been drawn into the feud with the Darwinists and anti-clerics, also suffered rebuke for its polemics and personal attacks. It was told following publication of an article condemning Voltaire that it had cited "among others a seditious sentence the publication of which was forbidden."[25]

Shibli Shumayyil, perhaps the leading Arab Darwinist of his time, also emigrated to Egypt in search of freedom to continue defense of his views. While there he was one of the earliest specifically to address himself to the question of freedom of the press in an article so entitled that Adib Ishaq published in his *Misr al-Fatat*.[26] Men like Ishaq, Sarruf, Shumayyil, and numerous other writers influenced by Western thought and ideals had been compelled to carry on their struggle outside their home country when the relative freedom of the seventies vanished with the tightening of controls under Abdülhamid.

The sultan soon realized, however, that it was not advantageous for him to permit recalcitrant critics to continue their criticisms from distant European capitals. By a variety of inducements, including bribery with money and decorations, he succeeded in winning over some of his opponents. Ibrahim al-Muwaylihi was induced to cease publishing his *al-Khilafa*, which had been coming out in Italy since 1867 in Arabic and Turkish, and also his *al-Ittihad*, *al-Anba'* and *al-Raja'*, which he had been publishing in France. Al-Muwaylihi was a devoted Muslim and loyal citizen who felt that the Ottoman sultans were betraying the Muslim cause in selling their country to foreign powers, specifically to England and Russia. He questioned their fitness to fulfill their roles as caliphs when Muslims "were falling prey to the snakes" and their lands were being assailed by outsiders.[27] He called for concerted action by Muslims everywhere to preserve the integrity of their lands and heritage and assailed in the process Muslim rulers for being opportunistic in the pursuit of self-interests and sultans for being derelict in the discharge of their

caliphal role.[28] He relayed a news item from the English newspaper the *Standard*, which had published decisions made in
Istanbul by authorities prohibiting Ottoman newspapers from
discussing current politics, news of which had become the
subject of ridicule in the Parisian press.[29] Through money
and flattery, Abdülhamid finally succeeded in getting al-
Muwaylihi to retreat to Istanbul in 1886, where the two subsequently became friends. With the Sultan's encouragement
al-Muwaylihi instituted in Egypt another publication, *Misbah
al-Sharq*, which he dedicated to the service of Abdülhamid
and collected handsome rewards from him for his efforts.[30]

Ahmad Faris al-Shidyaq was one of those who endorsed
British policies in the East and advanced their interests until the Ottoman government applied pressure against him.
His *al-Jawa'ib* was soon converted to the support of the Ottoman caliphate, khedival rule in Egypt, and the bey of Tunis;
and for staying on the right side of the authorities, he was
subsidized to the tune of five hundred pounds sterling a year
by the sultan-caliph.[31] But other newspaper publishers like
Khalil Ghanim refused to be lured back by money and decorations to the side of the sultan. Ghanim married a French-
woman and remained in Paris. Luwis Sabunji was one of the
ardent supporters of British policies who continued to serve
their interests in Egypt during the occupation period. He
published *al-Nakhla* in London, commencing in 1877, in both
Arabic and English, and also *al-Ittihad al-'Arabi* and *al-
Khilafa*. The latter was financed by the British with a capital
expenditure of ten thousand pounds. In it Sabunji attacked
the Ottoman caliphate and spoke unkindly of Islam and of
Sultan Abdülhamid and his ministers. His *al-Khilafa* was
translated into Turkish, Persian, and Hindu and circulated
widely by courtesy of the British. But Abdülhamid managed
in the end to lure Sabunji back to Istanbul in 1890, and
henceforth he worked for the sultan's interests.[32]

Owing to the spirit of freedom that prevailed immediately
after the deposition of Sultan Abdülaziz and in the second
half of Khedive Isma'il's reign, Syrian writers and intellec-

tuals flocked to Egypt. There they started numerous publications, which were tolerated as long as they did not criticize the person of the khedive. The oldest such publications were launched in Alexandria, namely the short-lived *al-Kawkab al-Sharqi* of Salim Pasha al-Hamawi in 1873, followed by *al-Ahram* of Salim and Bishara Taqla in 1875, which moved to Cairo the following year and still publishes as perhaps the leading Arabic newspaper in the Arab world today. Then came *al-Mahrusa* of Adib Ishaq and Salim al-Naqqash in 1879.

The press in Egypt at this time enjoyed full freedom. It flourished through government encouragement, namely because of the enlightened policies of Riyad Pasha, who was particularly well disposed and helpful, both culturally and financially.[33] That the Syrian émigrés, mostly Christians, should take the initiative in the advancement of journalistic publications was logical in view of their having had greater educational opportunities in their home country and thus being better equipped for it. They also came with a purpose: continue the struggle to redress the ills of Ottoman society as they saw them.

But prudence was not their motto in Egypt any more than it had been in Syria for some of them. Extremists, remaining the standard-bearers of attack on the Ottoman system and its custodians, called for an Arab caliphate and Arab unity. In their extremism they allowed themselves to become the tools of foreign interests whose policies aimed at disrupting Ottoman political hegemony in the most crucial provinces of the empire. Yet up till the British occupation, most newspapers of whatever predisposition were concerned primarily with the welfare of Egypt and that which promoted it. There was little concern with other countries, except for *al-Ahram*, which was quite clearly a partisan of France and a promoter of French interests.

It was the occupation that finally precipitated the rise of partisanship in the press. New issues became constant topics of concern: the occupation itself and the demand for evacuation, the so-called Egyptian question, and the Ottoman question—all now considered serious problems worthy of attention. Besides Sabunji's in England some newspapers became distinctly pro-British, others sided with France against Britain, to wit, *Kawkab al-Mashriq* (*L'Astre d'Orient*), a weekly published in Paris with the lead article discussed under the heading of "La France en Orient."[34]

In Egypt the first clearly pro-British publication was *al-Zaman* of 'Alkasan Sarafian, the first daily newspaper. When shut down by the government, its owner went to Cyprus and there published in 1889 the also short-lived newspaper *Dik al-Sharq*. In that year, at the urgings of the British occupation authorities, Faris Nimr introduced *al-Muqattam*, which lasted until 1952 and became one of the most important publications in Egypt since it was looked upon as the organ of the British, through whose aegis it enjoyed for a while the widest circulation in the country.

Such partisanship in turn precipitated the rise of the nationalist press, with al-Afghani taking the lead in urging it into being. He incited such publications and supervised a number of them, calling for freedom of Muslim lands from imperialist control. Among his disciples who responded were Ishaq and Naqqash, founders of *Misr* and *al-Tijara*; 'Abd al-Rahman al-Kawakibi, institutor of *al-Shahba'* in 1877 and *al-I'tidal* in 1879; and Ya'qub Sannu', who introduced for the first time the elements of satire and caricature to resist both the British and Khedive Isma'il. Exiled to France, Sannu' founded in Paris his *Abu Naddara* using the spoken language to reach a broader segment of Arabic readers. He attacked the British occupation with the slogan "Egypt for the Egyptians." He also supported French cultural influence. Ending up also in France, al-Afghani and Muhammad 'Abduh published their *al-'Urwa al-Wuthqa* in Paris, the first issue dated 13 March 1884. It was a bold newspaper that advocated Islamic unity and destruction of British influence both in Egypt and in India. Altogether only eighteen issues appeared, and the British tried hard to keep the publication out of the reach of both Indians and Egyptians.[35]

But the standard-bearer of the nationalist press was 'Ali Yusuf's *al-Mu'ayyad*, established the year following the appearance of *al-Muqattam*, no doubt in angry response to it. *Al-Mu'ayyad* came to play a great role in championing the nationalist and Islamic cause.[36]

Egypt had now become the home of the Arabic press, and in observing its fate, three distinct periods can be discerned. (1) 1892–1900, when about one hundred and fifty newspapers appeared, more than in the previous sixty-three years, owing to the relatively free rein granted the press. Rules governing such publications were relaxed in practice and the posting of financial bonds in advance was not insisted on. The orientation of the press during this time was predominantly cultural and educational. (2) 1900–1910, which was characterized by intense political and nationalist activities and in which polemics against the occupation intensified. During this period the Ottoman throne and the Islamic caliphate seriously preoccupied nationalists. Mustafa Kamil and the organ of his party *al-Liwa'* spearheaded nationalist activities. (3) 1910–1914, during which time Gorst replaced Cromer as resident and consul general (1883–1907) and adopted a more relaxed attitude toward the press until the assassination of Foreign Minister Butrus Ghali in 1910. Kitchener (1911–1914), Gorst's successor, felt compelled to restrict once again the activities of the press because of the intense nationalist spirit supposedly fostered by the unrestricted press. As a consequence *al-Liwa'*, *al-'Alam*, *Misr al-Fatat*, and other newspapers similarly oriented were shut down. Thenceforth it was much more difficult to obtain a license to start a newspaper, and only a few of the bigger ones managed to survive.[37]

As for the over-all orientation of publications during this year, two trends are discernible: (1) the nationalist press, shielded by parties, enjoyed popular backing and the guidance of free leaders, and (2) the neutralist press, which went along with those in authority and supported the sultan and ruling classes be they khedival or colonial. The nationalist press expectedly fell by the wayside. Newspapers suffered confiscation and shutdowns, and proprietors and editors, trial and imprisonment. It survived after a fashion through its many ups and downs, while the neutralist press managed to grow and gain readership because its leaders knew how to circumvent adversity with skill, blend in with divergent trends, steer a medial course by supporting the views of the middle-of-the-roaders, and avoid the pitfalls into which the nationalist press stumbled time and again.

EVOLUTION OF CENSORSHIP

Censorship, then, was a key factor in influencing the fortunes of the press, and it behooves us at this point to detail the course of its evolution, how it operated as well as the range of its impact. Press supervision in the Arab world could be dated to Napoleon's legislation of 14 January 1799 with six provisions completed by 'Abd Allah Menou[38] and embodied in his decree of 26 November 1800 as publicized in *l'Avertissement*. In 1819 Mehmed Ali founded the Bulaq Press, but since it was an official establishment publishing works on science and school texts,[39] it required no formal controls. Its supervisor, Nicola Masabiki, indiscreetly printed a poem entitled "Religion of the Easterners" by the Italian Bilotti, then an instructor in the School of Arts. In it he belittled Islam and Muslims. The attention of the pasha was drawn to the poem by the British consul Solt, who was then feuding with Bilotti, thus occasioning the first act of censorship in Egypt. Masabiki's life was spared through the intercession of someone close to the pasha. On 13 July 1823/4 Zilkade 1238, Mehmed Ali issued a decree forbidding thenceforth the publication of any work at Bulaq before specific clearance was obtained from the pasha himself.[40] The decree applied to both natives and foreigners.[41] He himself supervised *al-Waqa'i' al-Misriya* from its first appearance in 1828, as did his son, Ibrahim, *al-Jarida al-'Askariya*. first published around 1833.

Two laws governing publications were promulgated in the reign of Sa'id. They were much broader in scope than the preceding one, relating separately to Egyptians and foreigners. Specifically, no item could be contracted or prepared for publication before a copy thereof was reviewed by the Ministry of the Interior to ascertain that it did not contain information harmful to religion and the state, to foreign states and the public; no journals, newspapers, or notices were to be printed without a license from the council of the ministry; books and tracts harmful to religion, the political system, norms of etiquette, and good manners were subject to confiscation by the police and the propagator or owner was to be treated as a thief liable to criminal prosecution. The slightest violation of these conditions by a printer exposed his press to closure and himself to punishment in accordance with the law, and he who sought to make a living out of publishing had to commit himself beforehand to honor the conditions detailed in these laws.[42]

By and large, Sa'id (1854–63) remained friendly to foreign publications in Egypt; and as a consequence of his tolerance, five French and Italian newspapers were launched during his reign. However, because of their rival and conflicting views and in order to ensure against attacks on the country, the government instituted censorship, granting license to publish only on the condition that there would be no violation of the laws of the state or derogatory statements made against the ruler.[43] Nevertheless, some infractions were committed, and Sa'id's government was obliged to remind foreign consuls of the circular governing foreign publications issued in Istanbul on 6 January 1857.[44]

In the laws issued that year for the purpose of regulating the relations of the Sublime Porte with nationals of foreign powers residing in the Ottoman Empire, there is a special section relating to the press, and this too was reproduced for the consuls to pass onto their nationals in Egypt. The salient features of this section stressed the following prohibitions: no criticism whatever of the government's affairs;

no focus on matters that were not of immediate concern to the sultanate but that could upset good relations between nations; provincial news editors must confine themselves to stating the facts and not commenting on them or on the actions of officials; correspondence should not be published without clearance first from the bureau of the press; if time did not permit draft copies to be reviewed by censors, then the opening article was to be orally discussed with the supervisor of the bureau and the editor must agree to follow his recommendations; the advice of the bureau was to be taken seriously in order to avoid the publicizing of false news; newspapers must belie and correct articles published in Europe if the bureau so decreed; every violation of the foregoing was to be punished first by a warning and following three such warnings by the temporary or permanent suspension of the publication; and, if such crime was repeated when no exceptions applied, the punishment would be twofold; finally, whosoever established without license a printing press, denigrated in writing the government, an official of the Sublime Porte, or any state subject to Ottoman jurisdiction was to have his publication liable to suspension or confiscation and he himself to punishment with fines ranging between five and fifty Mejidi pounds depending on the nature of the offense committed.[45]

Copies of the law were circulated among consular representatives of foreign powers with instructions to their nationals who were already engaged in publishing to apply for formal licenses or cease publication within a month's time. They were also informed of the establishment in the foreign ministry of a press bureau with authority to enforce this law.[46] To counter libelous articles, this bureau did not hesitate to provide Ottoman editors with appropriate information and data.[47] It was also common for authorities to observe a double standard in dealing with foreign and native publishers. Foreign editors often had the advantage of enjoying the immunity of consular protection, and officials found it difficult to take action against violators among them.[48] Hence, it was the native editor who tended to bear the brunt of repression. For such and similar reasons, they realized there could be no freedom of expression as long as the government arbitrarily reserved for itself the right to decide what should or should not be printed.

It was not till January 1865 that the central government of the sultan enacted the law of publications applicable to all citizens, even though the *sadriazam* did not officially promulgate it before 13 March 1867. In substance it departed but little from the law of 1857. Altogether it contained thirty-five provisions. The most significant items were those that stressed the need for newspaper operators to be Ottoman nationals not less than thirty years of age, with no record of violation, and for editors to submit a copy of the publication draft to the minister of education for review before a final copy could be printed and circulated. Clause three permitted foreigners to publish provided they abided by the same laws governing native citizens and agreed in advance to submit to the Ottoman judicial process, not consular courts, for the adjudication of violations. The government specifically reserved for itself the right to withhold or grant licenses without explanation.[49]

The relaxation of controls in the 1870s came about as a result of the imperial rescript of 11 December 1870. It announced formally freedom of the press in the entire Ottoman realm but without officially abrogating all existing prior laws, decrees, and ordinances providing for the abolition of foreign publications if administrative considerations warranted such action.[50] In Egypt, Khedive Isma'il (1863–79) was particularly interested in cultivating the press, and in the process he allowed it such freedoms as prevailing laws often militated against. To be sure, the ultimate power of control rested with him, and for that reason perhaps he chose to be lenient. Over seventy newspapers and journals came into being during his reign, or were permitted to publish, even though not all were favorably disposed toward him and his policies. In this period even the bureau of the press was more carefully and meticulously administered.[51]

On 26 October 1866 Isma'il Raghib, official in charge of foreign affairs, informed the Sublime Porte that the khedive's government would comply with the imperial rescript's provision for the institution of a press bureau in the foreign ministry for the purpose of enforcing laws governing publications.[52] A khedival order to that effect was not issued until 28 April 1869, when the bureau was formally constituted, consisting of three foreign and two native members and presided over by Goudard Bey, who at the same time was heading the European bureau. The two Egyptians reviewed the Arabic and Turkish press and the three Europeans the foreign language press. The bureau remained operative until the end of the khedive's reign, with one important modification in 1878: on 1 December the khedive ordered surveillance of the native press, which he placed in the Ministry of the Interior under the directorship of *al-Waqa'i' al-Misriya's* supervisor.[53]

Thenceforth, for all practical purposes, the foreign press began to slip out of surveillance with a commensurate rise of a chorus of strong protestations from native publishers, who felt, and rightly so, that they were being discriminated against.[54] The foreign ministry bureau issued licenses to foreign nationals on petitions submitted through their respective consuls following the approval of the khedive himself.[55] The would-be publisher had to commit himself in advance to abide by all pertinent laws, and to not sell or transfer management of the licensed publication unless the new owner first petitioned for a license in his own name through proper channels.[56] The same procedure applied if the manager of a publishing newspaper or journal sought to expand the scope of his publication beyond what was spelled out in the original petition as approved by the bureau and the khedive.[57] The khedive on occasion turned down such requests.[58] Unlike foreign publishers, native owners did not have to go through an intermediary to secure their licenses. They could petition directly to the bureau by means of an *'ardhal.*[59]

The new situation persisted until the enactment of the law of publications of 29 November 1881, when the process of surveillance for both the native and foreign press was united in the Ministry of the Interior. This law might be termed the most significant legislation of its kind enacted in Egypt,[60] coinciding as it did with the beginnings of Tawfiq's khedivate (1880–92) and events surrounding the 'Urabi uprising that culminated immediately in the British occupation. The 'Urabi revolt had served to galvanize the partisanship trend already manifest in the multiplicity of journalistic publications, and the ensuing occupation simply added fuel to the fire of separatism and nationalism.

There was nothing particularly new in this law. In twenty-three provisions existing rules were more carefully spelled out and ambiguities occasioning complaints from publishers in the past clarified. The first ten provisions specified conditions for starting a publication, matters of licensing, posting bonds, fines and punishment, all essentially as before. The next six provisions stressed the need for permits and the non-transferability thereof, the bond posted to be equal in value to one week's circulation of the proposed publication, a fine of between five and twenty pounds for continuing to publish after a cease publication order had been issued if deemed to be disturbing to morals, religion, or public order, or if the publisher attempted to smuggle into the country material under a ban. Provision nineteen spelled out rules for circulating publications, and provision twenty-two abrogated all former decrees or rules contradicting terms of this new law.[61] Because of the hardships it engendered, the provision on posting cash bonds was relaxed in a supplementary decree dated 17 January 1883, permitting instead the substitution of personal guarantees.[62]

The law of 1881 remained operative until World War I, revised periodically in part. The provision on punishment was rewritten on 14 February 1904 to plug loopholes in the supplementary law on the same of 13 November 1883. Complaints from editors alleging loose and arbitrary interpretations by censors of what constituted items disturbing to public order, religion, and morals led to further revisions in the enactment of 16 June 1911. Thenceforth what were deemed criminal acts by newspaper publishers became subject to litigation in criminal courts.[63] The whole aim appeared to be one of intimidating the press by eliminating its recourse to preliminary appeal stages. In further emendations subsequently introduced, the right of appeal was barred altogether, allegedly to prevent jeopordizing public security.[64]

To editors and publishers laws on publication constituted acts of tyranny. Shibli Shumayyil was among the first to address himself directly to this issue in an article that he entitled "Hurriyat al-tiba'a wa qanun al-matbu'at" [Freedom of publishing and the law of publications].[65] The target of his attack was Borelli,[66] whom he described as "a capable foreigner to whom the government delegated [the task of] laying down the substance of this law (1881) which, in the absence of other models, was based on a French prototype." In a letter to Borelli accompanying a copy of the article, Shumayyil asks: "How could you participate in a scheme to stifle freedom when you yourself were deprived of yours in your own home country?"[67]

From his account it is clear, however, that khedival authorities made little effort to enforce the provisions of the 1881 law. Apparently only one newspaper (*al-Ahram*), leaning heavily on a foreign power (France), was suspended for a while with the government compelled in the end to apologize to its owners and to indemnify them for their losses. Not until after 1888 was the law rigorously enforced, and Shumayyil takes the blame for the hardening of official attitudes toward the press. Thereafter editors were hauled into court, and some were jailed, sometimes the innocent along with the deserving, merely for assailing the khedival family or speaking unkindly of the British occupation.[68]

The hardening of official attitudes seemed inevitable given

the proclaimed aim of zealous publishers. In the first issue of his *Misr al-Qahira* (24 December 1879), Adib Ishaq stated that his aim in publishing was "to excite the ardor of the East, stir the virtue of Arab blood, lift deceit from the eyes of simpletons, and revive zeal in the hearts of those who know." "Let my people know," he wrote, "that they have a right that has been plundered, which they should restore, and stolen possessions they should retrieve, and let them exit the path of frivolity." With the tone of his publication thus set, Ishaq proceeded to assail the policies of Riyad Pasha, the prime minister under the newly installed Khedive Tawfiq, who quickly earned the enmity of all nationalists. Riyad suspended Ishaq's newspaper, as he had done to the other two critical ones, *Misr* and *Tijara*.[69] Ishaq also lashed out against foreign powers whom he accused of having designs on Egypt and was forced to leave the country, seeking refuge in Paris.

Other ideological correspondents of Ishaq ended up in Paris. Al-Afghani and Sannu' continued the battle from Paris. Tawfiq had placed great faith in al-Afghani, whom he told on one occasion, "You are the repository of my hope in Egypt."[70] In the khedival decree sentencing him to exile, al-Afghani was accused of being one of the instigators and of heading a secret organization bent on corrupting religion and spreading dissension in the world. No newspaper other than *Mir'at al-Sharq* dared publish news of his sentence; and because it spoke of al-Afghani with high esteem, the khedive ordered the publication closed for five months.[71]

The period of the occupation (1882–1914) following on the heels of the 'Urabi uprising (1879–82) was not, in the long run, particularly favorable to the press. To be sure, Cromer exercised a measure of tolerance toward the press. He believed that freedom would provide a safety valve for zealous writers, which explains the relaxation of official attitudes toward the press in the first five years of the occupation and the multiplication of publications that resulted. But there were numerous opportunists in the new crop of so-called journalists, many with personal axes to grind. It soon became evident that the aim of publishing for them was to carry on vendettas on the pages of their publications against both individuals and groups. Men in sensitive positions and those of means were often maligned and threatened, and their assailants would be silenced more often than not with payoffs. Publishing for them was a good business and a form of potential enrichment. Large gains were made by some at the expense of exploiting the embarrassments and scandalous affairs of others. On the positive side of the ledger, this momentary respite for the press resulted in nearly every faction or ideological group acquiring for itself a spokesman in some publication.[72]

During the 'Urabi revolt 'Abd Allah Nadim became the standard-bearer of the opposition, publishing *al-Ta'if* to express its ideals, applauding 'Urabi, and denouncing Britain and the khedive. But with the defeat of 'Urabi, the nationalist press almost ceased to exist for a number of years. Its tone was far from bearable. One might define it as arrogant and defiant, attacking all forms of foreign interference in Egypt, the highhandedness of the khedive's policies and ministers doing the bidding of imperialists, and, in equally vociferous language, the alleged repression of Sultan Abdülhamid's domestic policies. This segment of the press called for constitutional government and representative bodies elected by the rank and file; for freedom, free institutions, and public welfare through bodies appropriately organized to promote it; for the broadening of the circle of education; and for the enlightenment of public opinion without censorship.

Quite clearly, granting publishers the kind of freedom they asked for in the light of their proclaimed aims would not redound with benefit to the establishment. If anything, the lines became more clearly drawn during the occupation, as can be seen in the orientation of important journals and newspapers. *Al-Liwa'*, for example, embodied the bold nationalist sentiment; *al-Jarida*, a sectarian newspaper, the moderate attitude, pursuing sobriety and speaking kindly of those in authority; *al-Muqattam* unabashedly promoted British interests and for all practical purposes was the organ of the occupation; *al-Mu'ayyad* promoted khedival interests; and *al-Ahram* waved the *tricolore* in the name of freedom and all freedom-seekers. Returning to the arena of publication after its brief suspension, *al-Ahram* proceeded in its first resumed issue (29 September 1882) to attack 'Urabi, praise the occupation, particularly General Wolsely, subduer of the 'Urabists, and the ministers who went along with it. But in 1884 it turned on the British because of a shift in French policy over maneuverings in the Sudan, and *al-Ahram* suddenly found itself aligned with the nationalists headed by Mustafa Kamil. France was giving refuge to those incurring the wrath of the occupation; indeed, it had become the nursemaid of all liberation movements and freedom-seekers. It was little wonder that al-Afghani, 'Abduh, Ishaq, Sannu', and numerous other uprooted intellectuals could publish in France, and that Mustafa Kamil's most vehement polemics against British imperialism should be publicized widely, courtesy of the French. Paris served also as the first home of the earliest Arab conference, staged there in 1913–14. The periodical *al-Ustadh* of 'Abd Allah Nadim, spiritual mentor of Mustafa Kamil, was shut down by Cromer nine months after its first appearance (13 June 1893) for its strong attacks on British imperialism and opposition to the occupation authorities.

When Gorst replaced Cromer as resident and consul general (1907–11), the press entered a more critical stage, one characterized by some as "the stage of sectarian strife,"[73] which the British allegedly kindled in the name of the "Christian press." The Coptic newspapers *al-Watan* and *Misr*, founded in 1877 and 1895 respectively, spearheaded the Christian sectarian trend. Gorst's period marked an intensification of resistance to the nationalist movement, with an increasing number of its publications being confiscated or shut down until eventually only those that "carried incense burners before men in authority" could continue to publish. Relations between

Christians and Muslims were aggravated by *al-Watan*, which on occasion went so far as to call on Britain to exercise full political sway over Egypt, and in its extremeness even suggested that the Copts give up their own nationality. Salih Hamdi Salih best stated the situation in a lecture delivered before the Egyptian conference (9 April–4 May 1913) when he declared: The Coptic press on the one hand and the Muslim on the other were most instrumental in cultivating the separatist spirit. Copts attack Muslims in strong language and besmirch their reputation in fostering intrigues against them, and Muslims retaliate with equal vigor while defending the interests and prestige of the majority inhabitants.[74]

The situation was already tense in 1901 when Shumayyil called attention to an additional complicating factor: an increasing number of Ottoman spies were cultivating a segment of the press to vilify the enemies of the sultan without restraint from censorship. A point was reached where newspaper publishers themselves demanded enforcement of the law on publications in order to do away with the chaotic situation that had come to prevail. This was the situation that induced him to write his article "Fawda al-matbu'at" [Chaos of Publications] in the hope of bringing about evenhandedness in the treatment of publications.[75] Publishers had banded together in a general association (al-Jam'iya al-'Umumiya) to demand an end to yellow journalism and the irresponsiblity of some journalists by insisting that supervision on the part of the government be made more strict.[76] He also claimed that it was the ambivalence of the government over the years and the inconsistency of its supervision policies, alternating between extreme harshness and laxity, that contributed to the state of confusion prevailing in the publication industry in his days.[77]

Gorst responded by pressuring Butrus Ghali, head of the council of ministers at that time, to enforce the provisions of the 1881 law, which were reviewed and restated in stronger terms on 25 March 1909. Thereafter only those who favored the occupation were issued licenses to publish, and the posting of substantial financial bonds was strictly enforced. The

Young Turk revolt of the year before had brought about a temporary respite from censorship in the Syrian provinces, but the opposite was occurring in Egypt.

Its fluctuating fortunes notwithstanding, the press in Egypt has been credited with the formalization of political parties, the creation of a national university, bringing on the second constitutional attempt, and acceptance of the principle of social amelioration and administrative reforms. It persistently supported liberation for women and for Egypt from British control. World War I brought about a moderation of attitudes on both sides.

In Syria the Young Turk movement had been endorsed by the press, which was allowed in consequence of its support a measure of freedom. But this proved very short-lived, as members of the ruling triumverate began to impose restrictions often harsher than those experienced under Abdül-hamid's rule. World War I put an end to self-rule in Lebanon, schools were closed, and censorship was reimposed on the Syrian press. A number of publications ceased to function altogether, and others were confiscated with increasing frequency.[78] The Catholic press became the special target of the government's wrath, and even its equipment was confiscated. The printing press at Zahlé, known as *al-Matba'a al-Sharqiya* [The Oriental Press], was transferred to al-Hijaz by Ottoman authorities. The owners of another, *Matba'at al-Arz* [The Cedars Press], the brothers Filib and Farid al-Khazin, were arrested, tried, and executed for treason. Quite expectedly, the Ottoman government, at war against France and Britain on the side of Germany, would take such steps against the Syrian supporters of French policies and permit only government-owned or directly supervised presses to function in these the twilight years of Ottoman hegemony.[79]

THE EXAMPLE OF SALIM SARKIS

Salim Sarkis's career is a good example of journalistic restlessness, impatience in the face of restraint, and the type of crusading zeal manifested by those who continuously hammered away at the freedom of expression issue.

He was born in Beirut (1867) into a publishing family, learning Arabic at home and English at the British School for Girls where his aunt was teaching, then later at a school sponsored by the Scottish church, and ending his secondary studies at 'Ayn Zhalta in Lebanon. It was there at the age of sixteen that he launched his journalistic career by publishing a weekly newspaper that he entitled *al-Arz* [The Cedars]. Shortly thereafter he joined his uncle Khalil, who had founded in 1875 the oldest continuously publishing newspaper, *Lisan al-Hal*, and eventually took over its editorship. It was in this capacity that he was first exposed to the workings of censorship, and for his defiance was driven out of Lebanon in 1892.

He went to Paris and there with another Lebanese, Amin Arslan, founded *Kashf al-Niqab* [Lifting the Veil] to promote the ideals of the budding Young Turk movement. Next he went to London, and there he established *Raj' al-Sada* [Return of the Echo]. Compelled to leave again because of strong Ottoman embassy pressures, he went to Egypt in 1894 and there set up his weekly *al-Mushir* [The Counselor], in which he lashed out against his Ottoman persecutors. For this he was condemned to death *in absentia*, so he fled to the United States, where he sojourned for five years, shuttling between the Boston area and New York. In Boston and nearby Lawrence he founded *al-Rawi* [The Recounter] and *al-Bustan* [The Garden], both short-lived as were his other newspapers based in Europe. He returned to Egypt in 1905 and there instituted perhaps his most popular publication of all, *Majallat Sarkis* [Sarkis's Journal], in which he pioneered the humorous vein of writing. He continued to publish it until his death in 1926.

By the time he died, Sarkis had carved out quite a career for himself as newspaperman, author, and agitator, or, as some preferred to describe it, stimulator of the intellect. Altogether he instituted nine newspapers in five different countries

(Lebanon, Egypt, France, England, and America) and on four continents (Asia, Africa, Europe, and North America), as he liked to remind his readers. He personally edited at one time or another five of the nine, corresponded with ten other newspapers, edited for a while *al-Mu'ayyad* and served on the editorial staff of *al-Ahram*, translated a dozen major and a hundred minor plays from English and French into Arabic, and wrote or edited ten separate books. He was a leading champion of women's rights, evidenced in his dedicating his periodical *Mir'at al-Hasna'* [Mirror of the Belle] to the opposite sex.

Among his important accomplishments mention should be made of his organizing a bureau for copying and translating to serve other journalists in Cairo, and another, which he called Maktab al-Isti'lamat al-Suri [The Syrian Bureau of Information] for the purpose of keeping Syrian émigrés residing in Egypt informed about happenings in their homeland in order to excite their nationalist ardor against Ottoman repression, which was part of the vendetta he aimed to keep alive. He was also the principal organizer of the Nadi al-Ittihad al-Suri [The Syrian Union Club] where between 1908 and 1913 some of the leading personalities in Arabic letters used to congregate and exchange views.[80] To encourage new trends in poetry, Sarkis sponsored contests and awarded cash prizes to the winners, in keeping with his self-conceived role as literary innovator and stimulator of the intellect in others. Indeed, he was known for his unconventional, energetic style, wittiness, and boldness of expression.

His abrasiveness did not endear him to a number of people. He went to prison twice for his outspoken denouncement of men in authority, the first time in Ba'lbak (Lebanon) and the second in Cairo, on the very day of his wedding. Even Lord Cromer eventually gave up on extending him effective protection, for the roster of his personal enemies had become quite formidable. It listed among others the sultan, who had Sarkis condemned to death for his alleged inside information on the conditions of deposed Sultan Murad's prison treatment and other facts of his deposition personally implicating Abdülhamid; the khedive, who to strike back at Sarkis chose the latter's wedding day to send him to prison; and then there were Kaiser Wilhelm II, the *shaykh* of the Azhar, and Sarkis's own bishop, who had him excommunicated for his alleged Protestant leanings and espousal of Freemasonry.[81]

It is his early career in Syria prior to his emigration in search of freedom that interests us, specifically, when he edited *Lisan al-Hal* for his uncle Khalil. According to Salim's reckoning, it was actually in 1877, when the Ottoman governor appointed a native Syrian, Khalil al-Khuri, owner and editor of the prestigious *Hadiqat al-Akhbar*, as supervisor of publications in Syria, that censorship began in earnest. Up until then it was the secretary of the governor who oversaw, and rather loosely at that, the nascent publication industry. But the press still managed to enjoy for a while longer the type of freedom it had experienced earlier. Writers at home and abroad still tackled unpleasant current events and managed to voice their discontent with little fear of repression. Even the inflammatory articles of Adib Ishaq from Paris and his appeal for freedom of expression were sometimes reprinted in Syrian journals.[82]

But the picture changed rapidly in the 1880s, and no area of printing or type of publication seemed to escape the attention of the *maktubji* (Turkish *mektupchu*), by which title the supervisor was known. This official's main function until now was secretary in charge of the bureau of recording in a given governmental department. In the earlier days of the Ottoman system, he was known invariably as *Mektub-i Sadr-i Ali* or *Divan Ffendisi*. Over the years there had evolved gradations of maktubjis, ranging from those attached to the *Sadaret* and various *nizarets* to the general *müdürlüks* and *vilayets*. The chief secretary in each bureau was known as *Mektub-i Qalemi*. Until he acquired the function of publications supervisor, the maktubji's primary task was to record, polish, and make available in print the transactions of the principal functionaries of the department, be they the grand vezir's or the provincial governor's. Needless to say, this additional function was acquired when the Ministry of Education in Istanbul began to enact laws to circumscribe freedom of the press and the circulation of printed material, "one of the chief factors," according to Shaykhu, "which led ultimately to the Young Turks' revolution."[83]

Bookshops, cultural societies, printing presses, and publications of all sorts became eventually equal targets of surveillance. In Syria before 1880 there were only three to four bookshops; after 1880 the number increased to twenty or more with energetic owners purchasing books from countries as distant as France and India. About 1880 a recently established cultural society made the wrong turn in politics, and its newly educated nondenominational membership soon raised placards in the principal cities of Syria demanding in immodest terms that Arabic be made the language of government, freedom from censorship, and, worse yet, autonomous rule for the whole of Syria.[84]

New printing presses had come into being, both in Beirut and in the Mountain, after the temporary relaxation of licensing rules in 1885.[85] But the radical tone of their publications, bordering on sedition in the eyes of local authorities, soon brought back stricter enforcement of surveillance. Not only did the censor bear down on those who spoke irreverantly of the sultan's policies, but even scholarly works were confiscated on mere suspicion. Quite indiscriminately bookshops were prevented from importing such seditious works as *al-'Iqd al-Farid* of Ibn 'Abd Rabbihi and *al-Ta'rikh* of Abu al-Fida'. Commenting on the ludicrousness of the new situation, Shaykhu wrote: "We witnessed such wonders and rarities by way of surveillance from officials that were we to enumerate them all they would be counted among the fables of the ancients and the tales of barbaric nations."[86]

The hardening of official attitudes toward the press was precipitated by such frivolities as the announcement, for example, in *Lisan al-Hal* of the arrival of Ra'if Pasha in 1885 to take over the governorship of Syria only for it to be discovered to the consternation of the editor that Ra'uf Pasha was the one who arrived. Ra'if was a former minister of utilities known for his fair-mindedness and justice; Ra'uf was the former governor of Jerusalem, known for his uncompromising and tough attitude. Although Sarkis managed to explain away his error in humble apologetic tones, word soon came from Istanbul that a six-month holiday had been decreed for his newspaper.

The new governor wasted no time in dispatching his dragoman Michel Eddé to summon all publishers into his presence and serve notice on them that henceforth no item would be published before it was cleared in advance by Eddé. The latter was a native Christian (of the Iddi family) who knew Arabic; but soon he was replaced by Cemal Bey, a Turk, who knew no Arabic. When the bey's language handicap developed into a serious stumbling block for the proper discharge of a maktubji's functions, he was replaced by Jabi Zadé Sa'adatli Hasan Fa'iz from a respectable Damascene family who at one time had been a close associate of Midhat Pasha. But either through accident or design, his knowledge of Arabic proved to be also limited in range.

THE MECHANICS OF SURVEILLANCE IN SYRIA

The mechanics of surveying publications operated in this manner: an editor would prepare an article for publication, set the type, make all necessary adjustments and corrections, then run off two copies for the review of the censor and hopefully his approval. These were submitted to him usually at ten in the morning; and if matters were expedited, the publisher might receive a copy back by four in the afternoon. In the meanwhile everything and everyone at the press establishment were at a standstill. What went on at the maktubji's establishment is best left to Sarkis to describe; he writes:

The present *maktubji* knows as much Arabic as I know of Adam's language; so he turns the copies over to 'Abd al-

Rahman al-Hut,[87] who is truly a *hut* [whale]; and since no defined procedure governs the process of censorship, al-Hut
proceeds to cut out anything suspect in his eyes with black
ink. If he is not sure of a certain expression, he places a red
mark opposite it. At the end of the process there are more
black and red marks than can be tallied. He then initials the
drafts and returns them to the *maktubji*. The latter does not
know Arabic. Upon seeing all these red marks the *maktubji*
says to himself: if there is no room for doubt, al-Hut would
not have inked them. He then crosses them out permanently.[88]

The net result of the entire process was that often half of the
items or more in any single edition could be sacrificed on the
altar of the maktubji's ignorance before the editor could expect the magical imprimatur *görülmüshtür* ("seen") and the
censor's signature of approval.

To fill in space frequently created by the *maktubji's* merci-
less axings, new material had to be introduced that also had
to be cleared by the same process all over again before the
newspaper could go to press. Further axings and delays were
unavoidable. If and when the edition was finally printed,
three copies were dispatched to the maktubji's office; one was
for comparison with the censored draft he kept in his files,
and the other two for dispatch to Istanbul, where the Encu-
men-i Maarif kept them for future reference—or recrimination
if developments should warrant it.

Sadly enough, the eagle-eyed surveillance of the maktubji
was not infallible, nor did it necessarily protect the newspaper against a cease-publication order, particularly if Istanbul should discover later that something unprintable had
slipped by him. And since no set rules governed censorship,
publishers were often hard pressed to second-guess the maktubji. When his arbitrariness grew too intolerable for them to
endure, they delegated to one of their number, the highly regarded 'Abd al-Qadir al-Qabbani, manager of *Thamarat al-
Funun*,[89] the task of trying to learn from the maktubji what
rules he wished them to observe. When queried, however,

by al-Qabbani, all the maktubji did was to point to his own head —that apparently was where the rules reposed.

It is interesting to note in this connection the exchange that took place between a French editor, "whose articles were cut to ribbons so often" that he finally sought out Rif'at Bey, the maktubji of Salonika, and asked him what might he speak of. He received the following reply:

> You may speak of everything. . . . Absolutely of everything except, you understand, of crowned heads, of foreign governments, of nihilism, of socialism, of revolution, of strikes, of anarchy, of liberty, of foreign policy, of domestic policy, of religion, of churches, of mosques, of Muhammad, of Jesus, of Moses, of the prophets, of atheism, of free thought, of the authorities, of feminism, of the harem, of the fatherland, of nation, of nationalism, of internationalism, of republic, of deputies, of senators, of constitution, of plots, of bombs, of Midhat Pasha,[90] of Kemal Bey, of Sultan Murad, of the crescent, of the cross, of Macedonia,[91] of Armenia,[92] of reforms, of grasshoppers, of the month of August,[93] and of a few other subjects corresponding more or less to these.[94]

What remains then to speak about, asked the bewildered editor, and he received another "specific" reply:

> Everything, the rain, good weather, provided you do not mention rain in August or the light of the moon. You may speak of the dogs in the streets, provided it is not to demand their extermination. You may speak of the authorities so long as you do not point out abuses. You may speak of his imperial Majesty to sing his praises. In short you have full and entire liberty to speak of whatever seems good to you.[95]

In spite of the humorous vein of the exchange, the list of prohibitions appeared to run true to form in all parts of the empire given the touchy nature of the subjects Abdülhamid inveighed against.[96]

If any one principle can be deduced from the above, it is this: the Ottoman system, its custodians, *modus operandi*, and friends must not suffer insult or humiliation in whatever form and from whatever quarter. Much of the motivation underlying censorship was unquestionably political. In the latter part of his reign, Abdülhamid's suspicions and fears bordered on paranoia. Prohibitions due to religious sensitivities and perennial fear of plots against his reign, not to mention radical political notions that could only undermine further what semblance of unity the Ottoman Empire still retained, were the direct result of his conviction that intellectuals and publishers were the leaders of sedition. Such convictions underlie the nature and extent of censorship throughout the Ottoman provinces.

The arbitrary and discriminatory application of censorship, however, had a devastating effect not only on "seditious" writings but also on all aspects of literary production. As can be seen from the sample illustrations below, poetry, translations, texts, plays, novels, newspapers, periodicals, publishing houses, and all aspects of freedom of expression endured severe setbacks at the hands of the maktubji.

RARE DOINGS OF THE CENSOR

The following examples, selected at random from Sarkis's *'Aja'ib al-Maktubji*, serve to illustrate the wide-ranging impact of censorship and the entertaining side of it all.

The American Mission's press in Beirut published a map for school use. On learning about it, the maktubji called in the director (As'ad Wakid) and demanded to know why Egypt was colored red while the rest of the Ottoman Empire was shaded in white. When the director answered it was done in conformity with the rules of cartography, he was promptly accused of committing treason in treating Egypt apart from the Ottoman Empire. To avoid pending disaster, all maps were recalled and new ones drawn showing everything that had ever been part of the Empire in one color.

Amir Sa'id Arslan, whose appointment to the bureau of the maktubji was short-lived, was taken to task one day for permitting the Catholic publication *Jaridat al-Bashir* to publish an article that had appeared earlier in the Egyptian press containing the expression *nayl al-murad* ("attaining the desire"), which was construed as a subtle attempt to bring the deposed Sultan Murad and the Nile together under the auspices of the British occupation. Efforts to explain what the expression meant failed, and the whole article was struck out.

Ignorance of the language had its hilarious moments. One advertisement appeared in print after it had been censored reading as follows: "The house of *Emperor* Muhammad 'Ali al-Trabulsi is for rent" in lieu of the original, "A house, property (*mulk*) of. . . ." The explanation given was that *mulk* (mistaken for *rule*) is the prerogative of the sultan only.

When President Carnot of France was assassinated in Lyon, the maktubji ordered the word *assassinated* deleted and *death* substituted for it, with the simple explanation that the term disturbs the sultan. At the end of the day, the boys who had been selling copies of the newspaper on the streets of Beirut did not report to the manager. In tracing their steps, Sarkis was led to the local jail, where he found them and had to bail them out. It seems they had been going around announcing "the death of the president of the (French) *republic*" and it was decreed illegal to use the term *republic*.

On the death of Yusuf Mutran, a Syrian emigrant residing in Egypt, the Cairo newspapers published an elegy that was reprinted in the newspapers of Beirut. It contained the following verse:

la budda min faqdin wa min faqidin
    falaysa bayna al-nasi min khalidin

The maktubji ordered the word *khalidin* (immortal) removed since it was the governor's first name and it did not seem proper to him that it should be associated with death. There appeared instead the word *ta'id* (soaring), which the maktubji insisted meant *thabit* (enduring). "No one can outdo our maktubji at deriving new Arabic words," wrote the newspaper editor later.

When the Maronite bishop, Ilyas Hawik, returned to Beirut

from a visit to Rome, *Lisan al-Hal* wrote three columns on the warm welcome accorded the dignitary upon his landing while saying little about the *serasker*, 'Uthman Nuri, who was departing that same day for Istanbul. Worse yet, Sarkis stated that a *nafar* of troops had been on hand to salute him. "Why do you say *nafar*," snorted the maktubji, "when a whole detachment was present?" "But *nafar* does not mean one soldier," replied the frightened editor; "it means many!" "Then why don't you use language I can understand," retorted the maktubji; "surely you can't expect me to carry a dictionary around with me!"

The language specialist Yusuf Harfush published a book of proverbs in Arabic and French. One proverb read: "*al-haraka fiha baraka*" [there is blessing in *activity*]. The word *haraka* was ordered cut on the grounds it implied *thawra* (revolution).

When Henry Jessup sought to publish in the weekly issue of the American Mission's newsletter a picture of Queen Victoria with the caption "Queen of England and Empress of India," the maktubji crossed out "Empress" for the simple reason that the inhabitants of India are Muslim and no Christian queen is permitted to rule Muslims! It was printed in its original form.

The maktubji circulated at last a list of titles by which dignitaries were to be addressed in print: *jalala* ("majesty") and *'azama* ("grandeur") were reserved strictly for the sultan; *hishmatlu* ("possessing dignity") was for other kings and emperors; but when Sarkis addressed the queen of England with *hishmatlaha* (his conception of the feminine form) the riled maktubji demanded he address her with *hadrat* ("presence") instead. The shah of Iran's title was to be *shahamatlu* ("possessing respectability"), but no "sultan" for the sultan of Zanzibar, since there is no other sultan beside Abdül-hamid; Zanzibar's ruler henceforth was to be retitled *hakim* ("ruler"). Similarly no "empress" for the queen of England, only *malaka*.

While journeying in Europe, Nasib Shibli sent to Beirut's

newspaper editors a description of Italy. He wrote among other things that Italians eat much macaroni, and because of it are dubbed "the macaroni nation." The maktubji was very upset; he feared the use of such an appelative might be construed as an insult to the Italian people with all its attendant diplomatic repercussions. "As if the Syrian press can be likened unto the London *Times* or the *Daily News*: everyone reads it," mumbled Sarkis audibly as he left the maktubji's office.

Lisan al-Hal used to publish translations of romance novels, but had to desist because the maktubji deemed such stories dangerous in that they taught readers *'ishq* ("passionate love").

In order to encourage local writers to emulate the ways of the Western press, Amin Arslan announced a prize of eighty francs for the one who could best recast a European poem into an Arabic mold. Sarkis decided to enter the contest, and he chose de Mossier's "Souviens toi!" [Remember!] for recasting after giving it the appropriate Arabic title "Tadhakkari!" After readying the French text and the Arabic adaptation for printing in four full columns, he took it to the maktubji for review. First he ordered him to delete the French text on grounds the newspaper was licensed to publish in Arabic only. Next he looked at the terminology employed. What, for example, did the author mean by *tadhakkari*? Unsatisfied with the answer received, he deleted it with the notation "hadhihi maghmuzat" [*sic*], meaning *aghmad*, or "these are ambiguities." He was disturbed also over the use of *hawajis* ("apprehensions") in the verse:

idha zaluma al-naharu wa ja'a al-laylu bi-*hawajisihi* [when day turns to dark and the night with its apprehensions appears].

To him the term implied "plotting," that is, "by night!" It too was struck out with the notation "hawajis yoktur" ("no *'hawajis'* "). By the time he finished cutting up the translation, the poem likewise was finished. In tears Sarkis rushed over to see Khalid Bey, the governor, imploring him to come to his rescue. Khalid laughed with amusement over the revisions introduced by the maktubji; and though upholding the latter's decision on not printing the French version, he did allow Sarkis to proceed with the Arabic adaptation. But fearing the consequences attending a newspaperman by an overruled maktubji, Sarkis decided to drop out of the contest and not to publish the poem at all. The whole episode became known as the "Hawajis Affair" and, by Sarkis's account, received publicity in London, Paris, and Beirut.

One day a translated report from the foreign press stated that "the health of French troops in Dahomey is not good." The maktubji ordered publishers to print "it *is* good!"

One newspaperman decided to print an article written by a woman. The maktubji, undaunted by the nascent feminist movement, persuaded the editor not to print it because it would put more wrong ideas than were already tolerable in women's minds. Besides, "it is not the concern of women to become involved in writing," argued the maktubji.

One report mentioned that a certain party had visited Madras (a city in India). The maktubji mistook the word for *madrasa* ("school") and ordered the term *maktab* substituted for it. So the traveler visited an elementary school instead.

A visitor to the Spanish pavilion at the Chicago Exposition sent back a description of what he saw to a Beirut newspaper. One observation referred to "the sword and shield of Columbus, the discoverer of America." The maktubji proceeded to take the editor apart in some of the strongest language yet employed against his victims for insulting his own people and Islam. "Luckily I don't understand Turkish," the editor later stated, but "I did understand *qalil al-adab* [short on manners]." "Don't you realize that it was the Arabs who discovered America?", screamed the maktubji! "We reached a compromise," the editor wrote afterward, "by agreeing to print that foreigners claim Columbus discovered America when actually it was the Arabs who first discovered it."

The widely heralded performing troop of Iskandar Sayqali from Alexandria was invited by the governor and notables of the vilayet to give a performance of *Aida* in Beirut. It was scheduled to run for three nights. The maktubji along with other dignitaries were present at the opening performance. Everything went well until the pharoah's army marched onto the stage carrying a banner upon which was inscribed "fathun min Allah wa nasrun qaribun" [Victory from God and triumph soon]. The appearance of this banner literally brought down the curtain. The performance was terminated abruptly, and so ended its three-night engagement. The cause of such indignation was the utilization of a Qur'anic verse in public display, and worse yet to describe the accomplishments of a pagan tyrant. It had been ruled earlier by the maktubji that no verse from the Qur'an or quotation from the Hadith could be printed in newspapers because these might be torn and cast to the ground, thus becoming subject to unintended desecration.

One last sample illustrating the tug-of-war between the maktubji and writers: when *Jaridat al-Ahwal* referred to Ilyas Bey al-*Basha* in one of its columns, Ilyas lost his surname on the grounds that he might be mistaken for a real "pasha." But then, it was a small price to pay when one considers that the pope lost his successorship (*khilafa*) to the See of Peter on the premise that there can be no *khilafa* outside the sultan's! The Catholic publication employing such terminology was abolished in the process.

Briefly, it is quite evident from the Salonika maktubji's encounter with the French editor and Sarkis's with his counterpart at Beirut that there was some consistency in what censorship inveighed against. Ottoman censors were enjoined to uphold the dignity and honor of *din ve devlet* ("religion and state"). Proper respect was insisted upon for the custodians of both, for dignitaries and officials both Ottoman and foreign. Ethics and morality as traditionally observed were not to be questioned or flaunted irreverently; the prerogatives of authority and rule were not to be challenged or defied; and no new idea or behavior upsetting to inherited norms were to be tolerated lest they lead to sedition.

No doubt liberal writers spearheaded by journalists had made themselves suspect for their lack of circumspection, and some like Sarkis were accused of disloyalty and condemned for treason. Culturally they had tended toward alienation and identification with those European societies whose imperial designs on Ottoman territory threatened its survival. It mattered little that a person like Sarkis could elicit years later a statement in writing from one of the toughest of all maktubjis (Jabi Zadè) attesting his sincerity and loyalty to the Ottoman state.

When all is said and reflected upon, we might describe the bouts between censor and writer as irritants more than systematic attempts to suppress all forms of free expression. Not so much maliciousness as ignorance underscored the maktubji's naïve conduct. But the impatient budding crop of half-baked intellectuals could scarcely be expected to be patient, let alone use prudence, in their restless desire to awaken overnight a society that had fallen into a lethargic state through a millenium of benevolent neglect. The Ottoman leaders were tired old men who understandably would not suffer the serenity of their quiet convictions and time-honored ways to be disturbed by impulsive youngsters peddling indigested radical ideas and ways of dubious morality and relevance for their own milieus. Liberal authors of this period were in certain respects the "hippies" of their generation, rebelling against excessive parental supervision and outmoded restrictions. They persisted in their audacity to defy their mentors with unchaste notions and to express their defiance in a multitude of newly discovered or rediscovered embarrassing devices: newspapers, journals, books, and even the theater.

1.   Salim Sarkis, *'Aja'ib al-Maktubji* (Cairo, 1896), p. 6.
2.   The original autographed copy was seen by this writer in the Belediye Kütüphanesi in Istanbul.

3. Op. cit., p. 7.

4. Filib Tarrazi, *Ta'rikh al-Sahafa al-'Arabiya* (Beirut, 1913), 1:53.

5. Jurji Zaydan, *Ta'rikh Adab al-Lugha al-'Arabiya*, vol. 4, ed. Shawqi Dayf (Cairo, n.d.), p. 53.

6. The newspaper continued to publish until the death of the owner-editor in 1907; for details see Tarrazi, op. cit., pp. 55–60.

7. Zaydan, op. cit., p. 54.

8. Cited by A. L. Tibawi, *American Interests in Syria, 1800–1901* (Oxford, 1966), pp. 126–27.

9. Details in my "Problems of the Ottoman Administration in the Lebanon," Ph.D. diss., Princeton University, 1957.

10. See *Missionary Herald* 60 (1864): 141.

11. In Ibid. 61 (1865): 104.

12. The first Muslim journal in Syria was *Thamarat al-Funun* in 1885, organ of the Society of Arts (Jam'iyat al-Funun) under the presidency of Sa'd al-Din Hamada; it was managed and directed by 'Abd al-Qadir al-Qabbani and continued publication until 1908. For more see Tarrazi, op. cit., 2:25–27. In Iraq, besides *al-Zawra'*, to which the leading poets al-Zahawi and al-Rusafi contributed their editorial talents, official publications appeared eventually at Mosul and Basra. Altogether there were only three newspapers in Iraq until the Young Turk revolt and the proclamation of the constitution on 23 July 1908. See Anwar al-Jundi, *al-Sahafa al-Siyasiya* (Cairo, 1962), pp. 13–14.

13. Al-Jundi, op. cit., p. 12.

14. See chapters "On Freedom" and "Struggle with the Ottomans" in Muhammad 'Amara, *al-'Amal al-Kamila li-'Abd al-Rahman al-Kawakibi* (Cairo, 1970).

15. Al-Jundi, op. cit., p. 47.

16. Zaydan, op. cit., p. 57.

17. For more see Muhammad Kurd 'Ali, *Khitat al-Sham* (Damascus, 1927), 4:90.

18. Luwis Shaykhu, *al-Adab al-'Arabiya fi 'l-Qarn al-Tasi' 'Ashar* (Beirut, 1926), 2:50.

19. Ibid., p. 43.

20. Elie Kedourie, *The Chatham House Version* (London, 1970), pp. 320–21.

21. Henry Jessup, *Fifty-Three Years in Syria* (New York, 1910), pp. 483–84.

22. Salim 'Anhuri, *Sihr Marut* (Damascus, 1885); see also Niqula Yusuf, *A'lam min al-Iskandariya* (Alexandria, 1879), pp. 464 seq.

23. See dispatch from French Consul Patrimonio with attached newspaper clippings in Archives du Ministère des Affaires Etrangères, *Correspondence politique des consuls, Beyrouth*, 27, no. 210: Beirut, 6 September 1884.

24. Shaykhu, op. cit., p. 133.

25. See text of a letter from the *maktubji* of the *vilayet* in *Hadiqat al-Akhbar*, 1884, and Elie Kedourie, "The Death of Adib Ishaq," *Middle Eastern Studies*, 9 (January 1973): 99.

26. Shibli Shumayyil, "Hurriyat al-Tiba'a wa Qanun al-Matbu'at" in his *Majmu'a* (Cairo, 1908), 2:328.

27. See the weekly *al-Ittihad—l'Union*, no. 3, 7 October 1880.

28. Ibid., no. 2, 24 September 1880.

29. Ibid., no. 3, 7 October 1880.

30. Al-Jundi, op. cit., p. 43.

31. Ibid., p. 41.

32. Ibid.

33. Zaydan, op. cit., p. 57.

34. First appeared on 24 June 1882; available at the Bibliothèque Nationale in Paris.

35. Al-Jundi, op. cit., p. 45.

36. On its founder see 'Abd al-Latif Hamza, *Adab al-Maqala al-Suhufiya fi Misr*, vol. 4 (Cairo, n.d.), which is specifically concerned with 'Ali Yusuf and his publication.

37. Zaydan, op. cit., pp. 60–61.

38. Alias Baron Jacques François de Menou, successor of Kléber as general commander of the French expeditionary force to Egypt, repatriated by terms of the Treaty of Amiens of 1802 following his defeat by the British at Alexandria in March 1801. For more on the press during this period, see Salahiddine Boustany, *The Press during the French Expedition in Egypt, 1798–1801*, (Cairo, 1954).

39. See Abu al-Futuh Radwan, *Ta'rikh Matba'at Bulaq* (Cairo, 1953), for the extent of its publications.

40. G. B. Brocchi, *Giornale Esteso in Egitto nella Siria . . .* (Bassano, 1841), 1:370.

41. Ibrahim 'Abduh, *Tatawwur al-Sahafa al-Misriya, 1798-1951*, 3d printing (Cairo, 1951), p. 260.

42. For full text see 'Abdin Archives, *Mahfaza, Daftar Majmu' Idara wa Ijra'at*, p. 207.

43. 'Abdin Archives, *Mahfuzat*, no. 31, *Sijill* 525 (Ma'iya Turki), p. 64, section 11.

44. On Ottoman legislation concerning the press, see Hariciye Arshivi, vol. 3, nos. 1–25 (Archives of the Sublime Porte) and 'Abd al-Majid Sadiq Ramadan, *Evolution de la législation sur la presse en Egypte* (Cairo, 1935).

45. 'Abduh, op. cit., pp. 264–65.

46. Ibid., p. 266.

47. Ibid., p. 267.

48. 'Abduh (op. cit., p. 268) cites the case of one Muhammed Hashim, subject of the Algerian 'Abd al-Qadir al-Jaza'iri, who had established without license a movable-type press. When the police sought to take action, the governor prevented it on grounds that "not all are equal before the law."

49. Ibid., pp. 268–69.

50. Ibid., p. 269.

51. 'Abdin Archives, no. 9 of 26 M 1293.

52. 'Abdin Archives, no. 374, *Mahfaza* 29 (*Ma'iya Turki*) of 15 J 1283; for details concerning this bureau see no. 11, *Daftar* 560 (*Ma'iya Turki*), note of 1 Sh 1283 from the vali to the foreign ministry.

53. 'Abdin Archives, *Mahfuzat*, no. 9 of 26 M 1293.

54. See the reaction of the supervisor of *al-Waqa'i' al-Misriya* to a practice "which is against what Ottoman and other civilized nations observe" in *al-Tijara* of 15 May 1879.

55. 'Abdin Archives, *Mahfuzat*, no. 31, *Sijill* 525 (*Ma'iya Turki*), section 2.

56. 'Abdin Archives, *Mahfuzat Ta'rikhiya*, nos. 65 and 110; the original is in *Mahfaza* 30 (Ma'iya Turki) of 3 Zl 1279.

57. 'Abdin Archives, *Mahfuzat*, no. 381 and *Mahfaza* 47 (Ma'iya Turki) of 6 Z 1292.

58. 'Abdin Archives, *Mahfuzat*, no. 1280 of 13 S 1280, *Daftar* 1, p. 61 and no. 8 of 14 S 1286 for khedival rejection of offer by Perenier to publicize news of the stage and cafés and of Alexander Panotsi to publish discourses on belletristic literature (*adab*).

59. For a sample see *al-Watan* of 17 November 1877.

60. For text see *al-Waqa'i' al-Misriya* of 29 November 1881; details also in Radwan, op. cit., p. 391.

61. In many ways it echoed the French law of 1853, which was the opposite of the French law on publications of 1881; see Mahmud 'Azmi, *Mabadi' al-Sahafa al-'Amma* (Cairo, 1941), p. 39.

62. *Al-Waqa'i' al-Misriya*, 19 January 1883.

63. See 'Abd al-Rahman al-Rafi'i, *Muhammad Farid, Ramz al-Ikhlas wa 'l-Tadhiya* (Cairo, 1942), p. 188.

64. 'Abduh, op. cit., p. 276.

65. See note 26 above.

66. Lawyer and editorialist of the *Bosphore Egyptien*, and occasionally a dabbler in agriculture and finances; see Jacques Berque, "The Establishment of the Colonial Economy" in W. R. Polk and R. L. Chambers, eds., *Beginnings of Modernization in the Middle East* (Chicago, 1968), pp. 225-26.

67. Shumayyil, op. cit., p. 328.

68. Ibid., p. 334.

69. See P. J. Vatikiotis, *The Modern History of Egypt* (London, 1969), p. 146.

70. Cited by W. S. Blunt in his *My Diaries* (London, 1919-20).

71. Al-Jundi, op. cit., p. 48.

72. Ibid., p. 53.

73. Ibid.

74. Ibid., pp. 53-54.

75. First published in *al Muqattam* in 1901.

76. Shumayyil, op. cit., p. 335.

77. Ibid., p. 337.

78. Khalil Sabat, *Ta'rikh al-Tiba'a fi al-Sharq al-'Arabi*, 2d printing (Cairo, 1966), p. 71.

79. Ibid., p. 72.

80. Among those who frequented the club were men like Ahmad Shawqi, Hafiz Ibrahim, Mustafa al-Manfaluti, Khalil Mutran, and other littérateurs, poets, and such.

81. For a biographical synopsis see Yusuf As'ad Daghir, *Masadir al-Dirasa al-Adabiya* (Beirut, 1955), 2:454-55.

82. Namely in the decade of the 1870s, when according to Shaykhu, op. cit., p. 67, owners were not subjected to pressures of censorship or prevented from criticizing current developments.

83. Ibid., p. 68.

84. George Antonius, *The Arab Awakening* (Philadelphia, 1938), p. 87.

85. Sabat, op. cit., p. 70.

86. *Adab*, 2:69.

87. Organizer in 1899 and head of the Islamic Educational Committee (*Lajnat al-Ta'lim al-Islamiya*) (Shaykhu, op. cit., p. 67).

88. Op. cit., pp. 22–23.

89. See note 12 above.

90. Abdülhamid would have had his life had it not been for the intervention of the British and French. He was exiled to the Hijaz, where he died under mysterious circumstances. For more on him see Ali Haydar Midhat, *The Life of Midhat Pasha* (London, 1903).

91. The germinal place of the Young Turk movement and a sensitive area of contention with foreign powers and native agitators.

92. Another sensitive subject that had culminated in the Armenian massacres during the reign of Abdülhamid.

93. The sultan was suspicious of this month, when Murad V was deposed after a very brief reign having succeeded Abdülaziz following the latter's alleged suicide.

94. Comte Am. de Persignac, "Les Gaîtés de la censure en Turquie," in *La Revue* 67 (April 1907): 390.

95. Ibid.; cited by E. E. Ramsaur, *The Young Turks: Prelude to the Revolution of 1908* (Princeton, N.J., 1957).

96. Ramsaur, op. cit., p. 105 n. 24.

Russell Yates Smith

The British and Sa'd Zaghlul, 1906–1912

Although Sa'd Zaghlul is revered as the leader of
Egyptian nationalism after World War I, his countrymen do
not identify him with that movement in the prewar years,
especially during his career in the Egyptian cabinet between
1906 and 1912. He was philosophically outside the main
stream of the prewar nationalist movement led by Mustafa
Kamil and Muhammad Farid, and was often the object of
their criticism. At best, Zaghlul is identified in this period as
a moderate nationalist who believed in the British connection
in Egypt and cooperated with his country's occupiers because he approved of their attempts to reform Egypt. However, the record shows that after Cromer's departure from
Egypt in 1907, the British did not view Zaghlul as a moderate
or as pro-British. Sir Eldon Gorst identified him as the potential leader of the extremist element in Egyptian nationalism
—an opinion that was voiced increasingly as his prewar career
unfolded, and was realized before the outbreak of war in
1914.

Egypt was nominally part of the Ottoman Empire, although the Mehmed Ali dynasty had been *de facto* autonomous rulers in the nineteenth century. The English occupation of Egypt in 1882 established a further complication in the tangled web of the question of Egyptian sovereignty.

Throughout 1906 the British in Egypt faced a rising tide of Egyptian animosity toward the occupation. Tensions began to mount in January when Mustafa Kamil, proprietor of the popular nationalist journal *al-Liwa'*, seized upon a dispute between Britain and the Ottoman Empire over the Egyptian frontier in the Gulf of Aqaba area in order to arouse support among his compatriots for the Ottoman sultan on pan-Islamic grounds. The danger of a religious outburst posed by this support moved the British consul general and head of the occupation, Lord Cromer, to call for reinforcement of the British garrison. In February a strike of the law students, incited by Kamil, further unsettled the situation. These incidents created an uneasy atmosphere that persisted into late spring and climaxed in June with the events at Dinshwai.

The death of a British officer during a dispute with fellahin at that village produced sentences of startling severity imposed on twenty-one of the villagers including four hangings and a number of floggings—all carried out in full view of the accused's families and neighbors. The reaction to these harsh judgments was an intensification of feeling in Egypt against the occupation and, in England, criticism of Cromer in the press and in Parliament. The Liberal Government in London decided that the time had come for some changes in occupation policy to reduce the unrest in Egypt and to assuage English opinion. The first such change was Lord Cromer's appointment of Sa'd Zaghlul as minister of education in October 1906.

Prior to this action there had been no minister of education since 1894. Egyptians had complained that Cromer deliberately neglected this area as part of a plan to retard their advancement toward self-government. During 1906 the field of education had provided the setting for lively activity against the occupation. In the schools the influence of Kamil over the students, manifested in the law students' strike, continued to increase; the students were becoming completely unmanageable. Outside the schools a group of leading Egyptians formed a committee, headed by Zaghlul, to found a national university—an objective that the British had resisted for years. Egyptians also resented Cromer's policy of passing over Egyptians for ministerial posts and filling them instead with men drawn from the Turco-Circassian ruling class and other minority groups. A further aggravation was that the ministers ceased to have any influence in government as operations passed increasingly into English hands.

Cromer was aware of these grievances, and his inclusion of Zaghlul, an Egyptian of fallah origins, in the government marked a step toward alleviating them. The appointment succeeded in reducing the tensions produced during the year. Cromer reported to the foreign secretary in London, Sir Edward Grey, that the move had to some extent gratified Egyptian national prejudices and aspirations and had obliterated Dinshwai from their minds.[1] The consul general, however, expressed some reservations about Zaghlul. In a private letter to Grey, Cromer, noting that the other ministers had become "cyphers," said that Zaghlul, "by all accounts," was "not likely to be a cypher." It remained to be seen, he continued, whether Zaghlul would cooperate with the British or whether he would follow the advice given him in the local press "to resist English opinions merely in order to show that he is not a dummy."[2]

Cromer's concern was soon set at ease. He was very pleased with Zaghlul, who showed himself to be open-minded and who even changed some of the opinions he had held about education before coming into office. Cromer's major case in point was Zaghlul's speech before the Egyptian General Assembly on 3 March 1907 in which he objected to an assembly resolution to conduct all education in Arabic. Cromer pointed out to Grey that Zaghlul, "who came into office as a strong patriotic reformer and somewhat of an Anglophobe," had formerly been of a different mind about this question, but had changed his views. Cromer added "that all the best men in the country are with us, but very few of them have, like Saad, the courage to say so."[3] Zaghlul's changes of opinion earned him bitter criticism from nationalists such as Kamil, who, warning him that he would lose the support of the country, said that it was known that the prospect of becoming prime minister was being held out to him. Kamil asked Zaghlul if this post was "really worth all the moral loss he cannot fail to suffer if he continues on the path on which he has entered?"[4] Zaghlul, however, continued in Cromer's good graces, and, during the consul-general's farewell speech, was one of only five Egyptians singled out for a final word of praise: "Unless I am much mistaken, a career of great public usefulness lies before the present Minister of Education, Saad Zaghlul Pasha. He possesses all the qualities necessary to serve his country. He is honest; he is capable; he has the courage of his convictions; he has been abused by many of the less worthy of his own countrymen. These are high qualifications. He should go far."[5] Zaghlul, of course, would go far, but not in the directions that Cromer had envisioned for him.

The first official signs of trouble between Zaghlul and the British appeared when a new Egyptian government was formed in November 1908. In July the Ottoman sultan had restored the constitution of 1876 as a result of the Young Turk revolution, and the Egyptian nationalists were clamoring for constitutional rule in Egypt. Sir Eldon Gorst, Cromer's successor, sought to counter their agitation by effecting a rapprochement with Khedive 'Abbas Hilmi, whom Cromer had antagonized years before and driven into league with the nationalists. An autocrat by training and nature, 'Abbas was ready to cooperate with the British, but he wanted a new government on whom he could rely. For the first time since coming to the throne in 1892, he was allowed some influence in selecting his cabinet. He replaced Mustafa Fahmi, the prime minister forced upon him by Cromer, with Butrus Ghali, and included a personal favorite, Muhammad Sa'id, as minister of justice. Both the khedive and Butrus wished to exclude Zaghlul from the cabinet. Although Butrus's reason for this is unknown, the khedive had not been enthusiastic about Zaghlul's entrance into the government back in 1906, and they had since quarreled openly during a cabinet meeting in March 1907. Nevertheless, Zaghlul was retained on the recommendation of Gorst, who admitted that the minister of education "has many defects, and causes me more trouble than all his colleagues put together, but at the same time he is honest, and always ends by yielding when matters come to a crisis." Gorst's clinching argument for retaining Zaghlul, however, was "that he would be a great danger if left outside the Government, and might be able to place himself at the head of all the hostile elements in the country."[6]

The Ghali cabinet, made up of men who were new to office except for the prime minister and Zaghlul, symbolized the new relationship between the British agency and the khedive, as well as the implementation of Gorst's new policies for governing Egypt known as the Liberal Experiment. Gorst hoped to make British rule more amenable to Egyptians by cutting back on the number of Englishmen flooding into the country to work in government offices and by encouraging Egyptian officials to take a more active role in their respective departments. In the spring of 1908, he had explained his policy to a group of senior English administrators. These men, who had enjoyed positions of authority, "now found themselves demoted and forced to defer to the Egyptians who were their nominal superiors."[7] Between 1908 and Gorst's death in 1911, he not only upgraded the authority of Egyptian ministers, but he also was to revitalize the theretofore powerless legislative bodies—the Legislative Council and the General Assembly. The door to increased participation by Egyptians in their own affairs having been opened, a number of them resolved to keep it open and, moreover, to broaden the scope of Egyptian control of the nation's destiny beyond what the British envisioned. In the course of the Liberal

Experiment, it became increasingly apparent that Zaghlul was among the foremost of them.

His activities in the Ministry of Education under the new government were marked by a pronounced aggressiveness that was missing before. Almost from the beginning of his tenure in office, Zaghlul had struggled to assert his authority over that of the British adviser, Douglas Dunlop, who had been entrenched in his position since 1889. Dunlop had been "on his mettle" and treated Zaghlul tactfully while Cromer was still in Egypt,[8] but with his departure it had soon become apparent that the adviser was blocking Zaghlul's attempts at reform—especially in increasing the number of Egyptian teachers in the system. Allegations to this effect were published in the *Egyptian Standard*, the English-language edition of *al-Liwa'*, during the late summer of 1907.[9] They were reinforced when Edouard Lambert, who had resigned as director of the Khedival Law School in June, wrote that he had played a role in Dunlop's machinations against Zaghlul. Lambert told how Dunlop had compelled him and others to form a group intended to paralyze the actions of the minister and to reduce him to impotence. The former director of the Law School admitted that his reports to the minister were first outlined and then corrected by the adviser, who also compelled him to give "an unfavorable report concerning all the candidates" applying for admission as teachers in response to Zaghlul's appeal for Egyptians to present themselves for jobs in the schools.[10]

With the Liberal Experiment in force, however, Zaghlul dismayed the British by disciplining the English headmistress at the Sanieh School for Girls, who had disobeyed his orders to reinstate a student dismissed from the school. The *Egyptian Gazette*, the leading British newspaper in Egypt and organ of the English community there, criticized Zaghlul for this action,[11] and also for the rapidity with which he brought Egyptian teachers into the system. The newspaper pointed out that only 251 out of 750 candidates for the Secondary School Certificate had passed the recent examinations, and blamed such poor results on enforcing changes before the country was prepared for them.[12]

Zaghlul's forcefulness in the Ministry of Education carried over into his work in the cabinet, where he and two of his colleagues—Muhammad Sa'id and Husayn Rushdi—refused to let either the British or the prime minister push through projects without first discussing them seriously with the cabinet. The British adviser to the Ministry of Finance encountered this attitude when he asked the cabinet to approve the government's purchase of the Oasis Railway. Zaghlul, Sa'id, and Rushdi believed that the matter had been presented hurriedly and asked that discussion on this project be delayed until another session. The adviser became angry and demanded that it be discussed immediately. The ministers gave in at the request of the khedive, but when the adviser pushed them to give their approval of other matters without discussion, they heatedly insisted upon delaying their consideration until another meeting. Afterward the khedive mentioned to Ahmad Shafiq, one of the members of his court, that he had never before witnessed such sharp talk in the cabinet. Shafiq replied that the adviser now knew that the ministers, unlike their predecessors, would not accept projects without discussion and without being convinced of their utility.[13]

The prime minister, Butrus Ghali, received similar treatment when it appeared that he was determined to reactivate without discussion the unpopular Press Law of 1881 in order to stifle agitation in the nationalist newspapers for a constitution in Egypt. This agitation had led to serious student strikes and demonstrations ever since the government had been formed in November. In March 1909 the demonstrations had culminated in a student mob that literally tore to pieces a British-sponsored agricultural exhibition. The *Gazette* blamed the press for this outburst, saying that it must be brought to reason and "must not be allowed to pander to the vilest passions of an illiterate and inflammable populace."[14] Zaghlul, Rushdi, and Sa'id threatened to resign unless the matter was discussed. The khedive called his cabinet together, and the ministers finally agreed to the resurrection of the law, but in a modified form.[15] The original version provided that a paper could be suppressed by the government after receiving two warnings; the modified version required the consent of the cabinet. This provision worked in favor of the press, and after a short lull the *Gazette* complained that the tone of the nationalist papers had not improved because the government was not willing to implement the law.[16]

Although the activities of these ministers put more authority into the hands of the cabinet, the project for extending the concession of the Suez Canal Company was to place new power into the hands of the General Assembly. It was also to signal the failure of Gorst's Liberal Experiment and to bring on a second warning about Zaghlul that would be echoed in succeeding months.

In the autumn of 1909, the Suez Canal Company put before the government for its approval a project to extend the company's concession from 31 December 1968 to 31 December 2008. In return for the extension, the government, whose coffers were low, was to receive four million pounds over the next four years and a share of the revenue. The British favored the project, but in the Egyptian cabinet the usual triumvirate of Zaghlul, Sa'id, and Rushdi were against it. The cabinet was agreed, however, on the necessity of submitting the project to the General Assembly, the most representative body in the country, in response to an inundation of telegrams and petitions from various Egyptian groups and individuals demanding that this be done. Gorst agreed to this and, further, that the assembly's decision would be final and binding with the proviso that Zaghlul, the most able debater and speaker in the cabinet, defend the project.[17]

Egypt became the scene of high emotion. The national press mounted a strong campaign against the project. It became apparent to the British that its rejection was a foregone conclusion.[18] In the midst of the emotional clamor aroused over this matter, Butrus Ghali was assassinated by a fanatical nationalist, Ibrahim al-Wardani, who justified his action on several grounds, among which was Ghali's role in the revival of the Press Law and his advocacy of the concession extension.[19] The new Egyptian government, headed by Muhammad Sa'id, continued to pursue the project. On 7 April 1910 the assembly overwhelmingly rejected the Suez Canal Company's proposal. The manner in which it was rejected, however, raised suspicions that the new cabinet had acted in collusion with the assembly.

Zaghlul had defended the government's arguments for accepting the extension during the assembly's meeting on 4 April. Three days later the assembly sat again to give the answer. As this meeting opened, Fath Allah Barakat, a member of the assembly and Zaghlul's nephew, took the floor saying that the assembly's committee for the canal project had framed its reply to the government's arguments. He moved that this reply be read and the vote taken immediately. After the reading of this report, which advised a rejection of the scheme, Zaghlul rose to answer, but was reminded there could be no more discussion. The vote to refuse the extension of the concession was overwhelming.[20]

According to the *Gazette* correspondent who covered the meeting, Barakat's maneuver was prearranged[21]—an opinion that persisted and was reinforced when the nationalist newspaper *al-Sha'b* published a story to that effect. The *Gazette* called the story "extraordinary," but said that this view was commonly believed. High officials and former ministers were declaring that the present government had not desired the extension of the canal concession and that its agreement with the assembly was a "matter of course."[22]

In a private letter to Grey at the foreign office, Gorst admitted that the assembly's refusal was expected, but he had not foreseen "such an open and indecent refusal even to discuss the question." To him, the assembly's action was proof "of the present incapacity of the Egyptians for any sort of autonomy, and of the futility of expecting from them reasonable discussion or argument on important matters of public interest." He lamented the death of Ghali and said that he felt "every day more and more how difficult it is to get along without the assistance of an experienced and capable Egyptian in whom one can have confidence. All the other Ministers are poor creatures (except Zaghlul who may become dangerous), and they are no real help."[23] Although Gorst was expressing his warning about Zaghlul in private, the same opinion was aired publicly only a few months later in stronger terms.

In September a report appeared in the *Egyptian Gazette* that nationalist criticisms of the Muhammad Sa'id cabinet were a hoax designed to guarantee the British agency's support of this government. Soon afterward,[24] there appeared in the same paper an anonymous letter signed simply "An Ex-Official." The writer agreed with the report, but said that the correspondent "deliberately avoided touching on certain facts which ought to be made officially public one day and of the truth of which I have no doubt." He remarked that his facts were "really startling," and might draw denials from certain quarters, but that "the world will be convinced of their truth in the course of the following season."

He began his exposé by commenting that there was a mistaken belief among the British in Egypt that Muhammad Sa'id was contemplating taking over the leadership of the nationalists as soon as he was compelled to resign from his post as prime minister. "This is incorrect," said the writer, "for although Mohamed Said is a nationalist at heart . . . he prefers to remain the faithful servant of his august master, the Khedive. . . . " The letter continued: "But the present Ministry is not without such a dangerous member who threatens to lead the Extremists the moment he quits his ministerial place." This member was revealed to be Zaghlul. The writer continued that no one who had followed Zaghlul's career for three decades could doubt "for a moment" that he was a "Nationalist of the Nationalists" or that one day he would prefer the leadership of that party to official life.

The letter further disclosed that Butrus Ghali had repeatedly complained of Zaghlul's conduct and that the late prime minister had once openly accused his minister of disclosing a state secret to the nationalists. The "Ex-Official" explained that Zaghlul's removal was contemplated on various occasions, but that he was retained in the cabinet although the khedive and Ghali "were never on his side." Referring to the impression that Sa'id and Zaghlul were an inner circle in the cabinet working together, the writer declared that the two men were not even on friendly terms, and had not been since Muhammad Sa'id had attained the rank of prime minister, which Zaghlul had coveted for himself.

Subsequent events proved that the "Ex-Official" knew what he was talking about. In April 1912, after months of rumors that relations between Sa'id and Zaghlul were strained, he resigned from the cabinet.

In the course of the next two years, he was to gain the backing of moderate and extremist Egyptian nationalists and to be the most popular figure at the elections in 1913 for the legislative assembly established by Gorst's successor, Lord Kitchener. During its short life, interrupted by the outbreak of World War I, Zaghlul would dominate that body as its elected vice-president the highest elective office in the country at that time—and as leader of the opposition to the government. At the end of the war, he was in position to take up where he had left off.

1. Great Britain, Public Record Office, Foreign Office (hereafter F.O.) 371/68/287-289, Cromer to Grey, 2 November 1906.

2. F.O. 800/46/182, Cromer to Grey, 2 November 1906.

3. F.O. 800/46/296, Cromer to Grey, 3 March 1907.

4. *Egyptian Standard*, 8 March 1907, p. 1.

5. *Egyptian Gazette*, 7 May 1907, p. 3.

6. F.O. 800/47/117, Gorst to Grey, 15 November 1908.

7. Peter Mansfield, *The British in Egypt*, (London, 1971), p. 184.

8. F.O. 800/46/204, Cromer to Gorst, 22 November 1906.

9. These allegations appeared in a number of letters signed "Abu Hafs" that

were published almost daily on page 3 of the *Egyptian Standard* beginning 18 September 1907, and ending 29 September 1907.

10.   *Egyptian Standard*, 10 October 1907, p. 1; *Egyptian Gazette*, 11 October 1907, p. 5.

11.   *Egyptian Gazette*, 2 March 1909, p. 3.

12.   Ibid., 22 May 1909, p. 2.

13.   Ahmad Shafiq, *Mudhakirati fi nisf qarn*, (Cairo, 1934), vol. 2, pt. 2, pp. 172–73.

14.   *Egyptian Gazette*, 8 March 1909, p. 3.

15.   Shafiq, op. cit., pp. 173–77.

16.   *Egyptian Gazette*, 6 July 1909, p. 2.

17.   Shafiq, *op. cit.*, pp. 186–87.

18.   *Egyptian Gazette*, 12 February 1910, p. 3.

19.   Mansfield, op. cit., p. 187.

20.   *Egyptian Gazette*, 8 April 1910, p. 3.

21.   Ibid.

22.   Ibid., 13 April 1910, p. 3.

23.   F.O. 800/47/299, Gorst to Grey, 10 April 1908.

24.   *Egyptian Gazette*, 13 September 1910, p. 3.

Rashid Khalidi

Arab Nationalism in Syria
The Formative Years, 1908–1914

It is generally agreed that modern Arab nationalism
first developed as a significant political movement in Syria in
the opening years of this century. Although the influence of
Syrian émigrés in Cairo on the rise of Arab nationalism cannot be ignored, there can be little question that Syria was the
first scene of the expression of Arab nationalism as a mass
movement, with a considerable political impact, rather than
just a developing intellectual current.[1] For Syria (defined in
the context of this article as including modern Syria, Palestine, Jordan, and Lebanon) during the years from 1908 until
World War I witnessed the growth of a political movement
without parallel until that time in the politics of the region.
This movement can, of course, be dismissed as a collection
of disgruntled members of the upper classes without any clear
political ideology, and with little popular support, particularly
in view of its ineffectiveness in opposing the Turks during the
opening stages of the war.[2] Nevertheless, as will be seen,
this movement for local reforms, for decentralization, for resistance to the "Turkifying" Committee of Union and Progress

(C.U.P.), and for some form of Syrian autonomy, was in fact the forerunner of the Arab nationalist movement that in the 1920s and 1930s resisted British and French rule. The prewar conflict with the Turks, the belated wartime Arab revolt (launched ostensibly in the name of Arab nationalism), and the postwar episode of the Arab government in Damascus, together provided modern Arab nationalism with its ideology, its initial leadership, its immediate grievances, and its first martyrs.

The 1908–14 period was, of course, preceded by numerous stirrings of autonomist and even nationalist feeling in Syria. While recording them, and noting their importance as well as that of the cultural and linguistic movement aptly titled "the Arab awakening," it is essential to keep in mind both that these earlier developments involved little or no serious political organization, and that they did not represent or involve the majority, or even a large proportion, of the people of Syria. Whatever may be said about the movement that developed from 1908 to 1914, these charges cannot be leveled against it. The inauguration of the era of party politics following the 1908 revolution and the growth of the press in the same period (thirty-five new papers were founded in Syria in the twelve months after the revolution, and about sixty in Beirut from 1908 to 1914)[3] meant a qualitative change in the nature of the politics of the area. The same class, divided into opposing coalitions similar to those formed in the past, continued to dominate local politics in the cities and towns of Syria. But their domination had to be expressed through entirely new organs of power and in a new idiom, thus giving individuals and groups from outside this class some access to the political arena, notably through the press.

Furthermore, the reimposition of the Constitution in 1908 resulted in the involvement of the urban masses in politics in a changed fashion. They had, of course, always been a part of the political process, mainly in the form of a wave of public opinion favoring now one and now another faction of "notables" in the local struggle for power.[4] Now, however, with elections, with a free press, and with more than one political party in the empire to compete for public favor, the political field was drastically widened, thereby broadening the potential role of public opinion and of the urban masses.

Before proceeding any further with the discussion of these developments, it would be appropriate to mention briefly some of the earlier manifestations of Arab nationalist sentiment in Syria. The beginnings of such feeling were directly linked to the decline in Syrian and Arab loyalty to the Ottoman Empire, and to an increasing Arab unwillingness to be ruled by the Turks. Such developments, of course, presupposed the loosening of the primarily religious bonds that held the non-Turkish Muslim population to the empire.

As a result of the weakening of the empire in the eighteenth and early nineteenth centuries, and with the secular reforms of the period thereafter, this had in fact occurred by the last third of the nineteenth century. Once the Ottoman Empire had ceased to be a strong Muslim state, once the Sultan had ceased to govern as a Muslim ruler in traditional fashion, and once the Ottoman polity included Christians and Jews as equal members, those factors that had disposed the Arabs to acquiesce in Ottoman rule in spite of their subordination to the Turkish element in the empire disappeared or lost their weight. Thus the years following the introduction of modernizing reforms in the empire saw increasing disaffection among the Arab population of the empire, a disaffection intensified by the economic dislocation caused by the pervasive impact on the local economy of the European economies.[5]

The first nationalist manifestations of this dissatisfaction were detected by foreign observers during the 1850s, although it seems clear that at this early stage such feelings were not widespread. Nevertheless, according to reports from foreign observers in Aleppo, Beirut, and Jerusalem, there were certain common themes running through all expressions of Arab discontent at this stage: a dislike of Turkish rule and, increasingly, of the Turks; a desire for some form of Arab self-rule; and a growing Arab racial or national consciousness that expressed itself in pride in the Arabic language.[6] All of these factors, incidentally, could be shared by many if not most Christians, and we shall see that all of them were to play an important role in sparking off the first large-scale open expressions of Arab dissatisfaction in the years after the reinstitution of the constitution in 1908.

However, during the decades between the first overt signs of an "Arab awakening" in the 1850s and 1860s, and the growth of a significant Arab political reaction to Turkish domination after 1908, there was in fact very little to indicate burning unrest among the Arab population of the empire. Aside from the opposition to the sultan of a few of the Arab deputies elected to the short-lived Parliament of 1877–78, and the writings against Abdülhamid's autocratic rule by men such as 'Abd al-Rahman al-Kawakibi, Neguib Azoury, and other exiled intellectuals, this period was one of relative quiescence among the Arabs of the empire. Paradoxically, one of the reasons for this was probably the very autocracy and religious conservatism that many of the sultan's most bitter opponents criticized. For by giving the appearance of resisting the West and opposing modernization, by his displays of ostensible piety and respect for the *shari'a* and men of religion, and finally by his consciously pan-Islamic policy, Abdülhamid seems to have succeeded in laying to rest the fears of conservative Muslims who had been shocked and outraged by the reforms and policies of his father, Sultan Abdülmecid. Abdülhamid thus neutralized any possible appeal dissidents may have made to the populace. In addition, the sultan appears to have devoted special attention to Syria, perhaps out of fear of the potential discontent he realized existed there. His reign saw the opening of numerous new schools and mosques in Syrian cities and towns; and in addition to choosing several Syrians as his closest confidants, Abdülhamid included a large force of Syrian troops in the palace garrison. Moreover, one of the most important of the initiatives of Abdülhamid's reign, the construction of the Hijaz Railway, was a project of great economic benefit to

Syria, and enhanced the sultan's position as protector of the holy cities of Mecca and Madina.[7]

Thus by winning the support of the conservative Muslim sections of the population and by driving abroad the discontented liberals who opposed him, Abdülhamid for a time strengthened his personal rule and increased his popularity in Syria. All of this did not, of course, prevent his overthrow, nor did it do any more than retard the growth of Arab nationalism. For the army and the government service, which Abdülhamid had strengthened and modernized, could not forever remain free of the radical political ideas that were inseparable from Western technology and forms of organization. When in July 1908 the sultan's personal rule was ended by a revolt of the armed forces, the rebels, organized in the C.U.P., were mainly discontented young army officers and junior government officials.[8]

The seizure of power by these radical young modernizers (whose hold on power was strengthened when they defeated an attempted counterrevolution in April 1909 and deposed the aged sultan) did not solve the national problems that had been suppressed or ignored during Abdülhamid's reign. They were, in fact, exacerbated, for the 1908 revolution had meant all things to all men. To the Young Turks who had made the revolution, it meant a last chance for the Ottoman Empire to modernize, regain its strength, and ward off the dismemberment with which it was threatened. To do all these things, the state would have to be strengthened, the armed forces expanded, and the outlying areas of the empire brought under the direct control of the capital; and this in turn meant greater centralization of the empire's administration, implicitly around a Turkish core. Another group of those who initially supported the revolution (most of whom later gravitated into opposition to the C.U.P.) advocated greater provincial and national autonomy as the means to save the empire. Such a policy was warmly welcomed by many members of the empire's national minorities (among them the Arabs) as more congenial to their national aspirations.

Resistance to this decentralizing tendency, coming mainly but not solely from the empire's Turkish element, was based on the fear that decentralization would accelerate the disintegration of the empire and thus further the designs of the waiting European powers. When, however, the C.U.P.-dominated government followed up its victory over the forces of reaction in April 1909 by attempting to implement its program of provincial reorganization and administrative centralization, it provoked a strong reaction in the Arab provinces. As has already been suggested, this reaction was an expression of dissatisfaction not only by a faction of the wealthy and educated upper classes, but also by significant numbers of the urban lower and middle classes.

It would be wrong to assume that the popular and quasi-nationalist opposition to the C.U.P. that developed in Syria after 1908 represented a coherent and organized nationalist movement. Despite general unrest over the issues of language and nationality and the question of local autonomy, which took the form of demonstrations, petitions, newspaper campaigns, and parliamentary disputes, the structure of Syrian society remained essentially unchanged. It was true that before and during this brief constitutional period there had been a marked expansion of the various Syrian school systems—state, private, foreign, and traditional[9]—and after the lifting of Abdülhamid's censorship, there was a tremendous increase in the number of newspapers, periodicals, and books published. Yet the traditional domination of local politics by the landowners, merchants, and religious scholar-dignitaries not only continued but found new expression in a new era of unhampered political activity, symbolized by the reinstituted Ottoman Parliament. In the elections of 1908, 1912, and 1914, members of the upper classes were, with few exceptions, elected to represent Syria, many of them joining the opposition, others the C.U.P. It is therefore possible for us to say, with C. Ernest Dawn, that "the conflict between Arab nationalist and Ottomanist in pre-1914 Syria was a conflict between rival members of the Arab elite."[10]

Notwithstanding the aptness of this description, there was
another factor that, in combination with the increase in political freedom and the development of communications, contributed to the involvement of much of the urban population
in this conflict. This was the immediate effect of the centralizing reforms of the C.U.P., particularly on the populace
of the cities and towns. For the first time Turkish instead
of Arabic was mandatory in courts and government offices,
and its use became obligatory in state schools. Small and
large businessmen had to follow court proceedings in Turkish,
school children had to learn the language (even Arabic was
taught from books in Turkish),[11] and numerous officials had
suddenly to deal with government functionaries in an alien
tongue, or worse, through an interpreter. For to implement
these reforms (as well as to ensure the political reliability
of the provincial administration), the government replaced the
predominantly Syrian local officials chosen during Abdülhamid's reign with new men generally ignorant of Arabic
and of the local conditions and customs of the Syrian provinces.[12]

As a result of these annoying and insensitive measures,
most particularly the replacement of the Arabic language by
Turkish, which especially outraged religious Muslims, the
population was alienated from the new regime, and from the
C.U.P., which dominated it. They were therefore receptive
to the reactionary and religious agitation of disgruntled members of the upper classes who had formerly benefited from
the Hamidian regime, as well as to a new kind of agitation.
This new appeal was made largely by men who had held positions of importance under both old and new regimes (many
of them were deputies in the 1908 Parliament), and who
spoke in terms of Turkish discrimination against the Arabs,
of the insensitivity of the central government to the needs
and demands of the Syrian provinces, and of the need for
these and other problems to be solved if the empire were not
to be dismembered by the rival European powers. In view
of the great influence already acquired in Syria by France

and Britain, and of their history of meddling in Syrian affairs, the warnings of the Syrian reformers were meant seriously, and were accepted as such by their C.U.P. opponents, although the latter did not accept the suggested solution of greater regional autonomy.

In a sense what was at stake was a conflicting view of what the Ottoman Empire was and what it ought to become after its traditional organization and ideology had clearly grown outmoded. The leaders of the C.U.P., most of them sincere, if somewhat narrow-minded, patriots, conceived of the empire in the post-Hamidian era as a state more or less like any other, and one in which European precedents and political theories could be applied more or less freely. As a result, they borrowed extensively from French political thought and German governmental models. They seem to have been pragmatists with little explicit idea of what they wanted, aside from strengthening the empire to enable it to stave off the collapse and dismemberment with which it was threatened. But the measures applied by the Young Turks in their years in power indicate their lack of sympathy for nationalism, particularly minority nationalism, and their partly unconscious identification of the interests of the empire with those of the Turks. The predominance within the committee and the government of the more uncompromising military wing, which held these beliefs and others more extreme, increased as time went on at the expense of other more flexible civilian leaders.

Military predominance in the party was almost complete from 1913 onward. A fundamental point upon which all factions of the C.U.P. were agreed—the refusal to share state decision-making power with any other party or national group—formed the main point of contention between them and the "Arabists" (to use Dawn's term for the early supporters of Arab nationalism).[13] The latter were naturally interested in a share of political power at the center of the empire, and were also committed to winning a greater measure of local autonomy and self-government for the Syrian provinces, which meant in effect that the Ottoman state would for the first time voluntarily share its revenues and its decision-making power. This the C.U.P. could not accept for reasons rooted in their ideology and in their fear of the designs of the Great Powers, specifically Britain and France. Underlying this conflict was a struggle for control of the political and material resources of Syria between the forces dominating the central administration and a local elite.

The first signs that the potential disagreement over such issues would be reflected on a mass level appeared only after the full effect of the reorganization of the Ottoman administrative system was felt in Syria in late 1909 and early 1910. Following the widespread dismissals that were part of this reorganization, the conviction spread that, since those being fired were primarily of non-Turkish nationality, they were being removed from their posts to make room for Turks. When disgruntled former officials, many of whom were Syrians, returned to their homelands, they helped to spread the idea that the C.U.P.'s reforms were intended primarily to foster Turkish national supremacy in the empire.[14] Public opinion in the Syrian provinces was quick to come to the same conclusions after the new measures had been fully implemented.

By February 1910 the language issue had become a matter of extensive controversy. In Beirut, for example, there were numerous public protests against the regulations specifying Turkish as the sole official language in government offices and demands that Arabic continue to be allowed, particularly in the courts.[15] The controversy grew as the extent of the new measures became apparent, and by the summer of 1910 there was great discontent in many sectors of Syrian society over the new government's handling of the language issue and the question of nationality that lay behind it.

In one of the most notable expressions of this discontent, a furor developed in Beirut when a student protest (allegedly instigated not by the students themselves but by inhabitants of Beirut) over the appointment of "a man from Anatolia" as professor of Arabic at the state preparatory school led to public demands that a Syrian be appointed to the post.[16] Bitter press polemics followed, first in Beirut and later in the capital, over this issue that, in touching on the question of the Arabic language and its place in the Ottoman state, went to the heart of the matter.

The emotions engendered by this bitter dispute were summed up in a report by a British observer in Beirut:

> Amongst the Ulema and Notables, and indeed among the population in general, a good deal of bitterness and discontent is caused by the policy of the present Government in sending to Syria officers and officials who for the most part know only Turkish and affect to scorn the language and customs of the country. . . . In any case, popular feeling (which has been much irritated of late by the attitude of the government in any question touching the Arabs) is just now rising sharply against the local Authority.[17]

These feelings, and the insensitivity of the government, were not confined to Beirut. From Damascus, where the same measures met with the same response, the British consul wrote that "the antagonistic sentiment as between Arab and Turk is beginning to permeate downwards to the lower classes, and will soon no longer be confined to the Ulema, notables and grandees, and official circles."[18] In Damascus one of the incidents that most annoyed local public opinion, and that perhaps best highlights the type of problems caused by the C.U.P.'s new administrative policies, was the appointment of a Turkish official who was allegedly virtually ignorant of the Arabic language as *Mustantiq*, or examining magistrate. Since knowledge of the local language was obviously an indispensable requirement for proper execution of official duties and since ignorance of it could easily lead to grave injustice, this appointment met with widespread public indignation.[19]

The over-all effect of this Arab reaction on the policies of the C.U.P. seems to have been relatively slight. However, there was appearing among the Arabs, particularly those of Syria, a phenomenon new to their modern history: the

growth of numerous societies, some public, like *al-Ikha'*
al-'Arabi, or *al-Muntada al-'Arabi*, and some secret, such as
al-Fatat, *al-Qahtaniya*, and *al-'Ahd*. These societies, founded
mainly in Istanbul by Arab intellectuals, officers, students,
deputies, and government officials (the same class, incidentally,
that was represented in the initial Turkish membership of the
C.U.P.) but with branches and influence throughout the
Arab provinces of the empire and in Egypt, played a major
role in the development of Arab nationalist thinking. The
secret organizations among them were the nursery of the
nationalist revolutionary movement that developed later.[20]

At this early stage the major effect of the public clubs
and societies was to enhance and spread a notion of Arab
national identity, first among their members, and then through
them among the Arabs of the empire. This essentially cultural impact on educated members of the upper classes was
matched at a popular level by the increasing discontent with
the policies of the central government insofar as they applied
to the questions of language and nationality. Moreover, until
the outbreak of the Tripolitanian and still more of the Balkan
wars shook the confidence of the people in the C.U.P. and
in the power of resistance of the Ottoman Empire, the small
organized groups of dissatisfied Arab officers and intellectuals
were well in advance of Syrian public opinion. The leading
role in the development and representation of the rising
popular movement for reforms, and later decentralization,
fell instead to such figures as Shafiq Bey Mu'ayad, leader
of the Arab deputies in the Ottoman Parliament; 'Abd al-
Hamid al-Zahrawi, deputy-speaker of the chamber; and
Shukri al-'Asali, deputy for Damascus.[21] These men were all
members of several of the most important public and secret
Arab societies, and were among the most prominent Arabs
in the Chamber. They soon became loosely affiliated with the
opposition party, from 1911 the "I'tilaf wa Hurriya" (usually
translated "Entente Libérale"), which stood for greater decentralization.

To understand the role such men played, and how they

brought together the growing popular, upper-class, and parliamentary discontent with the C.U.P., we shall focus on Shukri al-'Asali, who symbolized much of what was best in the nascent Arab nationalist movement, as well as some of its weaknesses. After a career in the Ottoman civil service in which his last post had been as *qaimmaqam* of the district of Nazareth in the southern part of the Beirut *vilayet*, at the age of 43 al-'Asali defeated the C.U.P. candidates in a January 1911 by-election. He came to Parliament fresh from a prolonged but ultimately unsuccessful struggle to prevent the transfer of some 10,000 dunums of land in a north Palestine village in his district from its Arab tenants to Zionist colonists who had purchased it from an absentee landlord. Al-'Asali entered Parliament on an electoral platform that pledged him to fight Zionism "to his last drop of blood."[22] That such a stand met with a positive response in Damascus is a measure of the importance of the Zionist question in the politics of the period, not only in Palestine, but throughout the Syrian provinces.[23]

This was demonstrated once al-'Asali transferred his energies to Istanbul, where he reinvigorated the Arab parliamentary bloc, leading them in attacks on the government's policies, particularly in regard to Zionism. The majority of the Arab deputies, sensitive to the newly aroused anti-C.U.P. sentiments of many of their constituents, were won over by al-'Asali and other concerned deputies to the idea that the government was negligent regarding Zionist colonization in Palestine, and that this was a matter of importance for all Arabs.[24] The Zionist issue was concurrently the focus of the attacks on the government by a *de facto* alliance of opponents of the C.U.P. These opportunistic attacks were launched by the opposition as a means of bringing under fire the so-called extreme elements of the C.U.P., alleging that they were "selling the country to the Jews." This maneuver was made practicable by the fact that a few leading members of the committee were Jewish.[25]

The parliamentary attack in which the Arab deputies participated, with Shukri al-'Asali in the lead, was important not because it seriously weakened the government, although the C.U.P. was momentarily shaken, nor because the Arabs' critique of Zionism was accepted: they were in fact listened to "amidst great indifference" by the chamber when they themselves took the floor in May 1911. It is a landmark, rather, because this was one of the first occasions on which the Arab deputies acted together as a bloc on a question of national importance to them as Arabs.[26] It had importance also because the failure of the C.U.P.-dominated government and Parliament to heed the urgent requests of the population of an Arab part of the empire, forwarded through their deputies, contributed to the feeling among many Arabs that the new regime represented little if any improvement over the old.

The parliamentary and press debates at this time that opposed "Arabists," "Ottomanists," and anti- and pro-C.U.P. factions, and that centered in some measure on the government's "soft" line on the question of Zionism, had an impact in Syria that can be gauged from a report of a secret meeting of the Beirut branch of the C.U.P. convoked early in April 1911. An attempt by a special envoy from the C.U.P. Central Committee to have the Beirut branch of the committee censure publicly the attacks of al-'Asali was "resisted by the Arab members present who, on the contrary, in a very decided manner expressed their approval of their Parliamentary representatives, whom they felt it was their duty to support." During a second meeting held after categorical instructions were received from the C.U.P. Central Committee regarding adoption of a resolution censuring al-'Asali, there were further recriminations, and the meeting "ended in the tearing up of the drafted telegram by one of the Arab members."[27] This was not simply an internal C.U.P. squabble, nor was it even a dispute related specifically to the actions and statements of Shukri al-'Asali, as was recognized by the British consul-general, who reported on the meeting. The opposition of the Arab C.U.P. members was, he wrote, a reflection of

> the growing spirit of discontent in Syria at the neglect by the Government of what they consider their Constitutional rights as regards appointments in the Government Service, especially in Arabic-speaking districts, and as regards the use of Arabic in Courts of Justice and in Public Offices, not to mention the alleged neglect of their local interests. . . . [28]

The evidence seems compelling that by the end of the third year of constitutional rule in the Ottoman Empire there had developed a strong feeling of dissatisfaction in large sectors of Syrian society with the ruling C.U.P. and the purely Turkish interests it was seen to represent. The situation was so clear that a not particularly acute foreign observer could write from Damascus in July 1911 of "the rather evident anti-Turkish sentiment and prejudice, which began to appear throughout Syria some eighteen months ago," adding that al-'Asali was playing a major role in the attacks on the Arab policy of the government.[29] The same observer noted shortly afterward that al-'Asali's intervention had foiled a scheme to silence, through bribery, various leading anti-Zionist newspaper editors' opposition to further Zionist land purchases in Palestine.[30] It was clear that al-'Asali had become one of the leaders of a growing wave of Syrian popular feeling. Anti-C.U.P., anti-Zionist, and anti-centralization, it had yet to develop into a nationalist or even autonomist movement. The decline in prestige of the constitutional regime with the defeat of the Ottoman armed forces in the Libyan war, and even more with the debacle in the Balkans, would speed that development.

The effect of the war in Libya on the Arab provinces of the empire was great, particularly after it became clear that, faced with Italian naval superiority and the acquiescence of the Great Powers, the government intended to reconcile itself to the loss of the North African provinces. The negative effect on Arab public feeling of the willingness of the government to cede an Arab land to a European power and its inability to defend it was reinforced when war broke out a year later in the Balkans. With another Ottoman military failure, the politico-military-religious ties that held Arab Muslims to the empire were further weakened. And when citizens were exhorted to make a supreme effort to recover the territories lost in the Balkans, the contrast with the indifference to the loss of Libya was soon noted by Arab malcontents. The central place of Macedonia and Rumelia, and particularly of Adrianople (Edirne), in Ottoman history, as well as the proximity of these regions to the capital, of course, made such comparisons invidious. But the fact that Rumelia and Macedonia were not only Turkish provinces but the homeland of most of the leaders of the C.U.P., and of a large proportion of the Turks of the empire, were the factors that were foremost in the minds of Arab critics.[31]

These latter had increased in number in the period between the beginning of the Libyan war and the outbreak of the Balkan wars. For in the interim, the C.U.P. had won resoundingly in what has gone down in Turkish history as the "big stick election," that of April 1912.[32] In the process of bribing and bullying its way to a resounding "electoral" victory, which most foreign observers agreed had been rigged ("The C.U.P. have court-martialled themselves into a thundering majority", wrote one of them afterward),[33] the committee had confronted a serious electoral challenge in the Arab provinces from the Ententist opposition party. Inasmuch as this party included the most formidable Syrian opponents of the C.U.P., many of whom were excellent speakers, and all of whom were given a fresh opportunity to expound their opposition to the committee, its challenge in Syria could not go unanswered. In response to the highly successful speaking tours in Beirut, Damascus, Hama, and Aleppo by the Ententist candidates, who were accompanied by a Turkish member of the party and by Shukri al-'Asali, the C.U.P. held rallies in the major cities of Syria.[34] In marked contrast to the earlier Ententist electoral meetings, these met with a mixed reception. It was the opinion, in fact, of virtually all British and French consular officials at this time that the C.U.P. would definitely lose in a free election.[35] The committee, of course had no intention of holding one, having already filled the cabinet and the local administrations with committee members who could be relied upon to prevent any possibility of an electoral defeat.[36]

Not satisfied with these precautions, and perhaps embarrassed by the bad showing it was making in the election campaign, the C.U.P. initiated a policy of repression, designed to cow the populace. About a week after a successful speech in Beirut, al-'Asali was the victim of a botched assassination attempt near his home in Damascus.[37] One of the most outspoken opposition newspapers in Damascus, *al-Muqtabas*, was suppressed soon afterward and its owner-editor, Muhammad Kurd 'Ali, forced to flee abroad under a charge of treason for attempting to subvert the caliphate.[38] In Haifa court proceedings were begun against a group of eight shaykhs of doubtful nationality who had just arrived from Beirut, and who were charged with preaching an Arab caliphate.[39] The trials in Damascus and Haifa shed light on the preoccupations of the C.U.P. at this stage. The committee clearly feared not only ordinary political opposition: it seems to have been worried by the possibility of wholesale Arab opposition to the Turks and to the empire itself. This fear had definitely not existed two years earlier, for when Kurd 'Ali was then tried on almost identical charges based on similar newspaper articles, he was easily acquitted.[40]

It would be an oversimplification to say that the political conflict in Syria in this period had resolved itself into one of Arab against Turk. There was a large party among the Syrian upper classes closely linked to the C.U.P., and among the populace the political and religious legitimacy of the empire had still not lost its hold, although propaganda for an Arab caliphate clearly was seen by the Turks as a threat to the ideological pillar of Ottoman rule. Nevertheless, a large proportion of the politically conscious population was already strongly opposed to the C.U.P. and saw its opposition in national terms. Although they probably did not include "the dominant faction of the Arab elite," as has been shown by Dawn, the Arabists had the backing of an articulate and numerically significant section of the Syrian population.[41] This is evidenced by the large number of Syrian, Palestinian, Cairo, and Istanbul newspapers that consistently opposed the C.U.P. and expressed Arab nationalist sentiments. By a rough count there were at least twenty such major newspapers in the period after 1910 that took a generally Arabist, anti-C.U.P., and anti-Zionist line.[42] Whatever the over-all leanings of the Arab upper classes as a whole, there was manifestly therefore a widespread tendency toward sympathy with Arabism among the literate part of the Syrian population, a tendency that was reflected in public opinion.

In the face of this potential threat, not only to its own rule but to continued Ottoman domination of the Arab provinces, the C.U.P., as we have seen, resorted to repression. It pursued this course even after the elections, with the result that most of the prominent members of the opposition, including al-'Asali, Shafiq al-Mu'ayad, and 'Abd al-Hamid al-Zahrawi, were forced to flee to Egypt.[43] The triumph of the committee was short-lived though, for in July 1912 they fell from power, to be succeeded by an Ententist government, and became in their turn the victims of the repression of the regime while their former victims returned from exile. Inter-party friction in Syria and the rest of the empire was, however, overshadowed in October 1912 when the Turkish army in Europe crumbled before the sudden advance of the Bulgars, Serbs, and Greeks. In the wake of these humiliating defeats and the "abandonment" of Libya (peace was signed with Italy the day before the war broke out in the Balkans), many in Syria began to contemplate the end of the domination of Syria by the Ottoman Empire, which at the end of 1912 looked to many to be on the verge of final collapse. This was staved off for a few more years because of the intervention of the military hard core of the C.U.P., which in early 1913 overthrew the weak Ententist government, which it sensed was about to surrender Edirne, and was incapable of preventing the disintegration of the empire. But the casting about of the Syrians for alternatives to Ottoman rule continued unabated, discreetly encouraged by those who stood to gain from a partition of the empire, particularly the French.

The growth of Arab nationalism was only natural in these circumstances, and it was encouraged by the spread of Turkish nationalist ideology in the Ottoman army and in other spheres of official life, including the educational system. An example of the sort of thinking that had begun to win adherents among the Turkish members of the officer corps, and that provoked a strong reaction from Arab officers, is the following remark by a Turkish lecturer at the Military Academy in Istanbul to a group of cadets:

> We shall soon rise again in the name of Turkey and under the Turkish banner. . . . You and your kinsmen should realize that you are Turks and that there is absolutely no such thing as an Arab people or an Arab homeland.[44]

In response both to this ideology and to what they saw as their exclusion from the top ranks of the armed forces for political and racial reasons, many Arab military officers were beginning to organize themselves in nationalist secret societies under the leadership of prominent officers such as 'Aziz 'Ali al-Masri and Salim al-Jaza'iri. Al-'Ahd, the most important of the groups they formed, had a vitally important role to play in the growth of Arab nationalism, which we will touch on below.[45] At this stage, however, the growing dissatisfaction with Turkish rule and the critical state of the empire's political fortunes combined with the ambitions of the European powers to produce an unusual and significant reaction among the population of the Syrian provinces. The reform committees that sprang up in the towns and cities of

Syria as part of this reaction, and the Syrian Arab Congress in Paris in which it culminated, marked the high point reached by the new political current of Arabism. Before discussing these events, a few words on the beginnings of this reaction are in order.

The reports of both the British and French consuls in all the major cities of Syria are unanimous in describing the universal wave of despair, worry, and agitation that swept first the Syrian littoral and later the interior of the region in the two months following the initial Ottoman defeats in the Balkans. Prompted by the belief that Syria was about to fall in its turn under the domination of the European powers, this agitation centered around the question of which of the two powers most directly concerned—Britain or France—would dominate Syria in the event of the possible collapse of the Ottoman front lines, only miles from the capital.[46] There lay behind the choice that seemed to present itself to the people of Syria in November and December 1912 a long history of Anglo-French rivalry that went back to the days of Napoleon and of Mehmet Ali. Although this rivalry may in some measure explain the exaggerated nature of a few of the reports about alleged Syrian enthusiasm for either Britain or France, this exaggeration can easily be disregarded after comparison between conflicting reports. In a sense, moreover, neither the British nor the French consuls were actually falsifying their descriptions of a Syrian desire for either British or French rule. For just as fear of France for her partiality to the Christians made some Muslims of the Syrian littoral willing to accept Anglo-Egyptian tutelage, so many Christians favored a French occupation in preference to British indirect rule.[47]

This phase in any case passed quickly, once it was clear that neither the Ottoman army nor the empire would imminently collapse. It was succeeded by a strong movement of administrative reform and decentralization, with branches in most of the important cities of the Syrian provinces, and working in coordination with the Ottoman Administrative

Decentralization Party (Hizb al-Lamarkaziya al-Idariya al-'Uthmani) in Cairo, which included many of the most important Arab nationalist figures. Under the influence of al-Lamarkaziya, the reform groups, the most important of which was in Beirut, beginning in January 1913 concentrated on drawing up a plan for provincial reform and decentralization. Their plans, which were to be implemented in Beirut in the first instance, and then to be extended to all the Arab provinces of the empire, met with the guarded approval of the Ententist government.[48] They were, however, naturally anathema to the C.U.P., which seized power on 23 January 1913. The stage was therefore set for a contest between the Arabists—strengthened now by public support organized by reform committees in the various cities of Syria—and the C.U.P., resistant as ever to decentralization in any form. This struggle, whose nature was in part muted by the continued emergency caused by the Balkan situation, led to what initially appeared as a victory for the Arab nationalists. As we are about to see, it was in fact nothing of the kind, and spelled the end of the short-lived reform movement

By the end of January 1913, the newly formed Beirut Reform Committee, whose administrative committee was composed of forty-two Muslims, forty-two Christians, and two Jews, had formulated its initial program. This called for provincial decentralization and the employment of foreign advisers in the local administrations, which would be entitled to use most locally raised revenues.[49] The final proposals of the committee were presented on 12 March 1913. They were published in all Beirut newspapers, Unionist and non-Unionist, together with leading articles on the necessity for provincial reform under identical titles, and each written by the editor of a rival paper. In addition to the points mentioned in the initial program, the reform scheme as finally adopted called for a widening of the powers of the provincial general councils, which were to control most spending in each *vilayet*. Most controversially, it called for Arabic to become the official language of the *vilayet*, with all officials including the *vali* required to speak it within a period of five years.[50]

The appeal of this program, not only to the Arab upper classes but to growing numbers of Syrians just educated in the many new schools set up during the preceding decades, is obvious. The provision regarding Arabic, which was also included in a reform program proposed by al-Lamarkaziya in Cairo at about the same time, was of particular importance.[51] This can be seen from the fact that a government-sponsored reform project presented at this time noticeably failed to include it, calling for Arabic to be admissible and for Turkish to remain the official language in government offices.[52] It was to the growing number of literate Syrians, the class of teachers, clerks, small merchants, and shopkeepers, as well as to urban workers and artisans, that the Reform Committee's proposals were directed, and to them that the substitution of Arabic for Turkish meant the most. In the months following, these groups were to play an important role in supporting the reformists' proposals.

It should be noted that the Beirut Reform Committee was no more homogeneous politically than it was religiously. This can be seen from a secret petition by five of the twelve Christian members of the reformers' twenty-five-man executive forwarded to Paris by the French consul-general. In it they declared their desire for a French protectorate over Syria, and said that their only motive for joining the committee was to ensure that the program called for the appointment of foreign advisers in Syria.[53] The presence of such tendencies among many Syrian Christians, particularly Maronites, was known to many of the reformers, and was suspected by Arab nationalists in Cairo, such as Rashid Rida. Writing in *al-Manar* soon after publication of the reform program in Beirut, Rida warned that in demanding foreign advisers it was vital to specify precisely what their powers and functions were to be. Between the lines of his commentary is the unspoken fear that once having invited foreign advisers, the Syrians might not be able to get rid of them.[54]

Notwithstanding these tensions, which evidently also existed in al-Lamarkaziya in Cairo, the entire reform movement in Syria, in Egypt, and in Iraq managed in public to display a high degree of unanimity. They needed all the solidarity they could muster, for in March 1913 the C.U.P. introduced two provisional laws on the organization of the *vilayets* that were far from meeting the demands of the Syrians.[55] In protest to the government's attempts to avoid implementing the demanded reforms, numerous public figures refused to accept posts newly offered to them, or resigned from posts that they held.[56] The C.U.P. utilized some of the better-known tactics of the Hamidian regime in trying to split or discourage the reformers by attempting to stir up sectarian dissension in Damascus and other places,[57] and by trying to appeal to the opportunism of some of the reformers by offering them posts. It is a measure of the popular support and unanimity of the movement, rather than of any other factor, that these maneuvers failed (for many of the same men were to succumb to the same blandishments a few months later).

This was remarked upon by the British foreign secretary, Sir Edward Grey, who minuted on a report of the events: "Union of Moslems and Christians for reforms rather interesting."[58] One of the reasons for Grey's interest was the fact that this unity, and the desire for reforms, had spread throughout Syria by the end of spring 1913, and similar reports were being received from Aleppo, Damascus, Jaffa, and Jerusalem. It was clear that if the movement were to succeed in its objectives, Britain would probably be called upon to provide advisers.

There can be little doubt that both the nearly unanimous rejection of the C.U.P.'s proposals by the reformers and the public support they managed to retain irked the unionists. This can be discerned, for example, from the passages in Cemal Pasha's autobiography that refer to leaders of the movement.[59] The government's next move—the closing down of the newly opened Beirut Reform Club on 9 April 1913—

can only be explained as an overreaction by the sorely pressed C.U.P.

In closing the club the Turkish *vali* acted with the support of what the French consul-general called "l'élément turbulent de Beyrouth." Finding themselves momentarily deprived of mass support ("la classe inférieure," the same observer called them), the leaders of the reform movement seem to have been momentarily at a loss.[60] They rallied the next day, however, leading a highly effective shopkeepers' strike and prompting all Beirut newspapers (except the two C.U.P. organs) to appear on 10 April with black borders and the official announcement of the dissolution of the Beirut Reform Club on their front pages. This in turn led to the suppression of a leading reformist paper, *al-Mufid*, and the arrest of its editor and four other leaders of the movement.

The reformers had captured the imagination and (evidently) the support of the Beirut crowd, for these incidents sparked off several days of large popular demonstrations that ended only after consular intervention secured the release of the arrested men on 14 April. Yet even after their release, popular feeling remained high, and many newly opened shops were forcibly shut by demonstrators.

An interesting fact noted by the most acute observers was that the leaders of the reform movement were carried away, rather than led, by popular feeling. The French consul wrote:

L'unanimité avec laquelle les Beyrouthins ont protesté contre le coup de force du Vali est d'autant plus significatif, qu'ils ont obéi plutôt à une idée qu'aux ordres de chefs d'une autorité contestable . . . ; elle indique que la petite classe elle-même s'intéresse aux réformes, et revendique l'autonomie de son pays, que le mouvement a gagné le peuple et s'y propage; elle indique aussi , . . qu'une certaine solidarité s'est créée entre chrétiens et musulmans en vue d'atteindre un but commun.[61]

These words bear out the assertions made earlier that the reformists' program appealed to broad sections of the population and cut across sectarian lines.

Surprised by the strength of the local opposition to its tough measures, the C.U.P. (probably under the influence of its pragmatic wing)[62] gave in somewhat in Syria, allowing the use of Arabic in courts and government offices and its teaching in the schools, although Turkish remained the sole official language.[63] These measures did not retard the growth of the reform movement, which after circulating massive petitions in protest against the April arrests and receiving cables of support from Basra, Damascus, and Cairo, planned a new step. This was the dispatch of six delegates to Cairo, Paris, and London to secure more support for the cause of reform in Syria.[64] Simultaneously, a loosely affiliated group of Syrian students and intellectuals in Paris decided to hold a congress there.

More trials, new repression, and further Turkish attempts to split the reformers on sectarian lines, as well as to dilute the concessions made in April, followed a new victory within the C.U.P. of its hard-line faction.[65] It was at this stage that there appeared an entirely new development. A plan for an Arab rising was formulated by a group led by 'Aziz 'Ali al-Masri and Salim al-Jaza'iri and composed of about forty Arab officers serving in the Ottoman front line armies in the Balkans. Their preparations reached the stage of sending a small group of young officers to Beirut to study the situation.[66] The plan interested many Beirut Muslims, but in the end it came to nothing, although they did avoid discovery by the Turks.

More fruitful, at least in the short term, were the visit of the reform group to Europe and their participation in the Arab Congress, which sat in Paris from 18 to 23 June. The Beirut group called at the Quai d'Orsay, but did not go on to London so as to be able to participate in the Paris Congress. The latter body studiously avoided offending the Turks, calling for reforms on the lines of those recommended in Beirut.[67] Perhaps influenced by this relative moderation, and undoubtedly wary of the possibility of European intervention in

Syria if they did not come to terms with the reformers, the C.U.P. decided to negotiate with them.

In negotiations with a C.U.P. representative in Paris in July 1913, most of the reformers' demands were met and with them virtually all the demands voiced in Syria since the inception of Arab discontent in 1909. According to the agreement, education was to be in Arabic in all regions with an Arab majority, local control of the administration was to be strengthened, Arabic was to become obligatory for officials in the Arab provinces, and foreign inspectors were to be appointed in every *vilayet*. Other provisions indicate that popular grievances were not the sole concern of the Arab negotiators, for three ministers, five *valis*, and ten *mutasarrifs* were to be Arabs, and two Arabs from each *vilayet* were to enter the Senate.[68] Although the Arabs were certainly entitled to a share of the empire's highest offices, the upper-class leaders of the reform movement would have been (and in fact were) the first to benefit from the wholesale elevation of Arab dignitaries to high office.

Perhaps because they never intended to make any real concessions to the Arabs in the first place, or perhaps because less-compromising counsels prevailed within the C.U.P., the government immediately began to chip away at the Paris agreement. In later agreements in Paris with three reform leaders (all of whom afterward received government appointments or electoral support), many of the points agreed upon at Paris were omitted, and in the law as adopted all the important concessions were hedged with conditions.[69] The anger of the Syrians at the failure of the C.U.P. to change its administrative ways, or even to implement the emasculated provisions of the July agreement that had become law, was exacerbated by the desertion of many of the reform leaders who had promised not to accept government office until the implementation of their demands.[70]

Among those who were won over at least momentarily by Turkish promises and government posts were the Christian and Muslim co-presidents of the Beirut Reform Committee, Yusuf Sursuq and Ahmad Bayhum; the president of the Arab Congress, 'Abd al-Hamid al-Zahrawi; Shukri al-'Asali and his friend 'Abd al-Wahhab al-Inglizi; and 'Abd al-Karim al-Khalil, a member of the executive of al-Lamarkaziya and president of al-Muntada al-'Arabi, as well as other public leaders of the movement.[71] For most of them their apostasy was only temporary, and many, including al-Zahrawi, al-'Asali, and al-Inglizi were to give their lives for the Arab cause in 1916. Nevertheless, their momentary opportunism enabled the C.U.P. to divide and discredit the entire reform movement, without making any substantial concessions.

In an equally blatant, and equally successful, maneuver, the Unionists managed to weaken the opposition in the spring 1914 elections by promising to support several Syrian opposition figures, and then securing the election of their own party stalwarts. To their ranks were added several nonentities whose main distinction was that they were of the same families as prominent Arab nationalists. Among them were an obscure cousin of Shafiq al-Mu'ayad; an aged relative of Salim al-Jaza'iri, one of the founders of al-'Ahd, and of his cousin, also a nationalist officer; and relatives of 'Ali al-Nashashibi and Salim 'Abd al-Hadi, both members of the executive of al-Lamarkaziya, and the latter a leading nationalist officer.[72] All of these men resisted the temptation to compromise with the C.U.P., and all died on the gallows in 1916. The appointment of their relatives to Parliament (a more accurate term than election) is evidence not only that the C.U.P. was intent on pursuing the same uncompromising course as ever: it shows also how many nationalists it was still necessary to neutralize in this time-honored fashion.

After the elections of April 1914, the ranks of those who had not wavered in their opposition to the C.U.P. were swelled by those disgusted with the ruling party's latest manipulation of the election process. There was, however, little they could do. The news that so many of their leaders had abandoned them had had a demoralizing effect on the people of Syria,

who had been led to expect so much of the reform movement, and who naturally felt cheated.[73] As a result, they could
not have been expected to respond to the appeals of these
same men who had earlier shown such weakness and such
lack of political maturity. Because the nationalist movement
was fragile and politically unsophisticated and there was a
wide gulf between leaders and led, the nationalists had only
one other alternative—to appeal to a foreign power. But here a
dilemma faced them, for their benefactor against the Turks
would be sure to demand something in return.

For a few this risk was acceptable, and some went ahead
and collaborated with a European power. But for the majority
the decision to collaborate with Britain or France was not
made easily, and their desire to see Syria and the rest of the
Arab lands free of the Turks was matched by their reluctance
to submit to partition by Europe. Unfortunately, it was impossible to obtain European aid without being burdened with
European interference, although many of the nationalists
were to go to the gallows without realizing how true this was.

The Arab nationalists of al-'Ahd, al-Fatat, and al-Lamarkaziya eventually did approach the British in 1915, albeit with
many reservations. But their approach was made too late in
the war for a military rising in Syria to achieve the effect it
might have earlier. It was relayed, moreover, through the
sharif of Mecca, who had private dreams that bore little
resemblance to those of the more idealistic nationalists or
of their Syrian followers. For strategic reasons Britain welcomed the approaches of the Arabs. But Britain was not at
ease with the Syrian popular movement, which had shown
its strength in 1912 and 1913. Although she needed them
against the Turks, Britain was reluctant to work with determined and dedicated Arab nationalists, for it was obvious
that they would never accept the tutelage that she sought to
exercise over her new "ally."

Through her alliance with the Hashemites, however, Britain
was spared having to do so. Cooperation with them promised
most of the advantages and none of the drawbacks of a direct

involvement with the Arab nationalist movement centered on Syria. Because of this alliance, because of the political immaturity and inconsistency of the nationalist movement and of many of its leaders, and finally because of its misfortune in losing so many of them at the hands of Cemal Pasha in 1916, the "victory" won by Arab nationalism during World War I was a hollow one, the effects of which in Syria were long-lasting and pernicious. Instead of gaining independence or even autonomy, Syria was divided into four states, separated from its neighbors to the east and west, and subjected to decades of British and French colonial rule. In the years after World War I, however, the central force struggling against these developments, and in some measure overcoming them, was the popular nationalist movement, which first came to life during the period we have just analysed. For all its weaknesses and failures, it should be seen as the beginning of a seminal trend in modern Arab history.

1. For the best treatment of the growth of Arab nationalism, see George Antonius, *The Arab Awakening* (London, 1939), and Albert Hourani, *Arabic Thought in the Liberal Age* (Oxford, 1962), especially pp. 260–85. To these should be added several of the articles by C. Ernest Dawn collected under the title *From Ottomanism to Arabism* (Urbana, Ill., 1973).

2. See, e.g., the now rather dated account in E. Kedourie, *England and the Middle East* (London, 1956), pp. 59–65.

3. See Filib Tarrazi, *Ta'rikh al-Sahafa al-'Arabiya* (Beirut, 1913–44), vol. 1.

4. See Hourani's "Ottoman Reform and the Politics of the Notables" in W. R. Polk and R. L. Chambers, eds., *Beginnings of Modernization in the Middle East* (Chicago, 1968), pp. 41–68.

5. D. Chevalier, "Western Development and Eastern Crisis in the Mid-Nineteenth Century: Syria Confronted with the European Economy" in Polk and Chambers, op. cit., pp. 205–22.

6. A. Hourani, *Arabic Thought*, pp. 266–67; Antonius, op. cit., pp. 53–60; Tibawi, *A Modern History of Syria* (London, 1969), pp. 158–61; and M. Maoz, *Ottoman Reform in Syria and Palestine* (Oxford, 1968), pp. 245–48; all give different approximate dates for the beginnings of this Arab separatist feeling in Syria. They are in agreement, however, that it first became noticeable in the 1850s.

7. Tibawi, op. cit., pp. 179–98, gives an appraisal of Abdülhamid's reign and its effects in Syria.

8. The best study of the C.U.P. to date is that of Feroz Ahmed, *The Young Turks* (Oxford, 1969).

9. Tibawi, op. cit., pp. 182, 194–96.

10. C. E. Dawn, "The Rise of Arabism in Syria," *Middle East Journal* (1962), pp. 145–68. The article is reprinted in Dawn's book cited above.

11. Suleiman Mousa, *al-Haraka al-'Arabiya* (Beirut, 1970), p. 59.

12. Regarding these personnel changes, see Ahmed, op. cit., pp. 22–24, and Amin Sa'id, *Al-Thawra al-'Arabiya al-Kubra* (Cairo, 1934), 1:4.

13. See Dawn's definition at the beginning of his article cited in note 10 above, p. 145.

14. Sa'id, op. cit., 1:4.

15. F.O. 195/2342/16, Cumberbatch to Lowther, 12 February 1910. (All documents cited in this form are to be found in the Public Record Office in London. French diplomatic documents cited are in the Quai d'Orsay, Paris.)

16. F.O. 195/2342/85, Cumberbatch to Lowther, 16 June 1910; *Lisan al-Hal* (Beirut), 3–6 June 1910.

17. F.O. 195/2342/87, W. Young to Lowther, 10 June 1910.

18. F.O. 195/2342/116, Devey to Lowther, 12 July 1910.

19. Ibid.

20. There is an account in Antonius, op. cit., pp. 108–12 and 119–20, of the formation of these societies, whose alleged activities are also described in *La Verité sur la question syrienne* (Istanbul, 1916), which was printed at the order of Cemal Pasha. See also Hourani, *Arabic Thought*, pp. 280–85, and A. Sa'id, op. cit., pp. 9–11, 14–23 and ff.

21. Elected over C.U.P. opposition, al-'Asali, who became one of the most dynamic and forceful of the Arab leaders, was described as follows: "Of superior intelligence, he knows both Turkish and Arabic, and law remarkably well; in the offices he has held ever acted with justice and energy. His views are liberal and wide-minded, and there can be no doubt that by far the best of the candidates has been elected on this occasion, a man of high character, and of opinion strongly progressive and possibly even rather ultraradical, but who has always gained for himself universal esteem and sympathy" (F.O. 195/2370/27, Devey to Lowther, 25 January 1911).

22. Ibid.

23. For this incident, and an appraisal of the opposition of the people of Palestine to Zionism before 1914, see N. Mandel, "Turks, Arabs, and Jewish Immigration into Palestine, 1880–1914," Ph.D. thesis, Oxford University, 1965, and the article of the same name in *St. Antony's Papers* 17 (1965): 77–108.

24. Mandel, op. cit., p. 245. Among the other deputies were Ruhi al-Khalidi and Sa'id Bey al-Husayni of Jerusalem and Rida Bey Sulh of Beirut.

25. For this debate see Mandel, op. cit., pp. 240–45, and Ahmed, op. cit., pp. 86–90.

26. The Arab deputies had earlier, in 1909 and 1910, opposed a project to give a river concession in Iraq to a British firm. This was perhaps the first time they acted as a national bloc. See Ahmed, op. cit., pp. 55–57, 66–67; F.O. 800/192/43, Lowther to Hardinge, 5 January 1910, and F.O. 800/193A/233, Hardinge to Lowther, 21 February 1910.

27. F.O. 195/2370/60, Cumberbatch to Lowther, 13 April 1911.

28. Ibid.

29. F.O. 195/2371/123, Devey to Lowther, 13 July 1911.

30. F.O. 195/2371/131, Devey to Lowther, 12 August 1911. This is confirmed

by the report in Ministère des Affaires Etrangères (hereafter M.A.E.), *Turquie*, Politique Intérieure, Palestine, Sionisme, N.S. 38; Guy to de Selves, 14 September 1911.

31. See Ahmed, who quotes a statement by the grand vizir that is quite revealing (op. cit., p. 93). See also Mousa, op. cit., pp. 28–29, and K. T. Khairallah, *Les Régions arabes liberées* (Paris, 1919), p. 32.

32. Ahmed, op. cit., pp. 103–4.

33. F.O. 800/193B/82, Fitzmaurice to Tyrrell, 5 June 1912. According to one source, the opposition was able to win no more than four seats (Mousa, op. cit., p. 29).

34. For the 1912 election campaign, see M.A.E. *Turquie*, N.S. 116, Couget to Poincaré, 15 February 1912; F.O. 195/2389/24/885, Fontana to Lowther, 19 February 1912; M.A.E., *Turquie*, N.S. 116, Couget to Poincaré, 23 February 1912; F.O. 195/2389/24/1341, Devey to Lowther, 11 March 1912; and F.O. 195/2389/24/1338, Cumberbatch to Lowther, 13 March 1912, as well as the newspapers of the period.

35. E.g., ibid., and F.O. 195/2423/1475, Devey to Lowther, 19 March 1912.

36. Ahmed, op. cit., pp. 98–104; see also F.O. 195/2425/1688, Satow to Lowther, 25 April 1912; M.A.E., *Turquie*, N.S. 116 Grapin to Poincaré, 31 January 1912, for examples of the provincial changes carried out by the C.U.P. before the elections.

37. F.O. 195/2423/1475, Devey to Lowther, 19 March 1912, and F.O. 195/2411/308/2091, Devey to Lowther, 1 April 1912.

38. F.O. 195/2427/1958, Devey to Lowther, 18 April 1912; M.A.E., *Turquie*, N.S. 116, Ottavi to Bompard, 1 August 1912.

39. F.O. 195/2414/418/1544, Cumberbatch to Lowther, and M.A.E., *Turquie*, N.S. 116, Guy to Poincaré, 1 March 1912. There are some differences between the two accounts.

40. F.O. 195/2312/175, Devey to Lowther, 18 September 1909, and F.O. 195/2342/7, Devey to Marling, 2 January 1910.

41. Dawn, op. cit., pp. 163–64.

42. See Sa'id, op. cit., 1:11–12, and Tarrazi, op. cit., p. 1, as well as M.A.E., *Turquie* N.S. 121 Guy to Pichon, 30 April 1913. The latter is a report on the press in Syria. See also Mandel, op. cit., pp. 222–25.

43. F.O. 195/2389/24/2690, Devey to Lowther, 19 May 1912.

44. Anonymous [Asad Daghir], *Thawrat al-'Arab* (Cairo, 1916), pp. 144–46.

45. For an extensive discussion of *al-'Ahd*, see Hassan Saab, *Arab Federalists of the Ottoman Empire* (Amsterdam, 1958), pp. 225–41; see also Majid Khadduri, "Aziz 'Ali al-Misri and the Arab National Movement," *St. Antony's Papers*, 17 (1965): 140–63.

46. These reports are too numerous to cite individually; dozens of them can be found in F.O. 371/1506–8; in F.O. 195/2445–6 and in M.A.E., *Turquie* N.S. 117–18.

47. Sa'id, op. cit., 1:18, explains some of these fears.

48. M.A.E., *Turquie*, N.S. 119, Couget to Poincaré, 2 January 1913; Sa'id, op. cit., 1:18–19.

49. F.O. 371/1775/253/6020, Cumberbatch to Lowther, 24 January 1913.

50. F.O. 371/1775/253/14474, Cumberbatch to Lowther, 12 March 1913.

51. Ibid.

52. Ibid.

53. M.A.E., *Turquie*, N.S. 120, Couget to Jonnart, 18 March 1913.

54. *Al-Manar*, 16:4, 280, 7 April 1913; see also Sa'id, op. cit., 1:24.

55. Ahmed, op. cit., p. 134; F.O. 371/1775/253/17975, Cumberbatch to Lowther, 27 March 1913.

56. Ibid.; M.A.E., *Turquie*, N.S. 120, Ottavi to Pichon, 27 March 1913; Khairal-lah, op. cit., p. 40.

57. M.A.E., *Turquie*, N.S. 120, Ottavi to Pichon, 29 March 1913; ibid., 4 April 1913.

58. The minute is on Cumberbatch's dispatch of 27 March 1913, cited above.

59. Djemal Pasha, *Memories of a Turkish Statesman* (London, 1922), p. 57. He calls al-'Asali "impertinent," and is highly critical of him and other Arab leaders.

60. This account is based on M.A.E., *Turquie*, N.S. 120, Couget to Pichon, 11, 13, 15 April 1913; and on F.O. 371/1775/253/18583, 16900, 16966, and 20328, Cumberbatch to Lowther of 10, 13, 14, 17 April 1913.

61. M.A.E., *Turquie*, N.S. 120, Couget to Pichon, 15 April 1913.

62. M.A.E., *Turquie*, N.S. 120, Bompard to Pichon, 21 April 1913.

63. Ibid., Ottavi to Pichon, 23 April 1913; F.O. 371/1775/253/22581, Cumberbatch to Lowther, 28 April 1913.

64. Ibid.

65. F.O. 371/1775/253/24349, Cumberbatch to Lowther, 13 May 1913.

66. M.A.E., *Turquie*, N.S. 120, Defrance to Jonnart, 13 March 1913; Bompard to Pichon, 19 April 1913; Couget to Pichon, 2 May 1913.

67. *Al-Mu'tamar al-'Arabi al-Awwal*, (Cairo, 1913), pp. 113–21.

68. Ibid., pp. dal to ha.

69. Ibid., pp. ha to za.

70. M.A.E., *Turquie*, N.S. 123, Coulondre to Pichon, 25 August 1913.

71. See Antonius, op. cit., p. 117; F.O. 195/2457/316, Cumberbatch to Mallet, 16 January 1914; and M.A.E., *Turquie*, N.S. 124, Couget to Doumergue, 13 January 1914, as well as Ottavi to Doumergue, 19 February 1914, and Couget to Doumergue, 6 February 1914.

72. The 1914 election results can be found in F.O. 195/2457 and in M.A.E., *Turquie*, N.S. 124.

73. See e.g., M.A.E., *Turquie*, N.S. 124, Ottavi to Doumergue, 19 February 1914.

Suleiman Mousa

The Rise of Arab Nationalism and the Emergence of Transjordan

THE OTTOMAN STATE AND THE ARABS

Early in the sixteenth century, the Ottoman Turks seized control of the Arabic-speaking lands that had been ruled by the Egyptian Mamlukes. For four centuries the Ottomans remained in control of the Asian Arab lands. This control might well have lasted longer had it not been for the fact that the Ottomans took the side of Germany in World War I.

The ties of Islam had, all along, considerably influenced the Arabs in their acceptance of Ottoman rule and, vice versa, in the attitude of the Muslim Ottomans toward their Arab subjects. Religious fervor was then much stronger than national consciousness. No doubt the Arabs were regarded with special consideration because they were the first Muslim nation, the one into which the Prophet Muhammad was born and which included his descendants and the great caliphs of Islam. However, that consideration never amounted to entrusting them with real responsibilities in the central government; only a relatively small number of Arabic-speakers held key posts in Istanbul.

The social structure remained at its old traditional level of princedoms, fief landlords, and shaykhdoms. In consonance with the traditional concept of government, the Ottomans were concerned with governing their subjects much more than with bettering their conditions. In the nineteenth century the gendarmerie was an instrument to achieve security by terror wherever it could be applied. The ruling oligarchy paid little attention to the masses. Ottoman subjects in the Arab provinces were equally objects of neglect until late in the nineteenth century. After the Committee of Union and Progress (C.U.P.) took power in 1909, many new laws were exclusively in the interests of the Turks; they were aimed at giving them control over the other races of the empire. In economic development programs preference was accorded to Turkish provinces—so much so that perhaps as much as eighty per cent of the public funds was spent exclusively in Turkish areas.[1]

Coupled with this Ottoman neglect of the non-Turkish provinces was the gradual seizure by the European powers of some Ottoman provinces and an attempt to extend their influence to the rest. The latter was done through the capitulations, pressure, diplomacy, and Western education. Thus the European powers began to establish schools in geographic Syria (Syria, Lebanon, Palestine, and Transjordan). Those schools helped to raise the literacy rate so "that the level of Arab literacy in towns and villages was probably ten per cent higher than in Turkish areas."[2] The prevailing mass ignorance prior to this had perhaps made any social unity impossible. The state schools, however, fostered a grievance of a special kind. The Ottoman government began to recognize Turkish as the official language in Arab lands. Not only in government matters but also in the state schools, Arabic was given a secondary place. Meanwhile, missionary schools were according Arabic a privileged position. The government's language policy caused the Arabs to feel that there was a plan to eradicate their national structure and to Turkicize them by the passage of time. It must be admitted, however, that Ottoman education left its impact among the Arabs and produced a number of brilliant leaders and administrators. Eight prime ministers of Iraq were graduates of the military college in Istanbul; in Jordan seven prime ministers were graduates of Ottoman military and civil schools.

THE RISE OF ARAB NATIONALISM

The movement of Arab nationalism sprang essentially from national and racial feelings. Two main factors were behind its emergence at the beginning of the twentieth century: the Arabs' contact with European culture and ideas, and a natural reaction against the Turkish national movement.

Turkish-speakers held most administrative posts in the Ottoman Empire, in spite of the fact that all subjects of the state were considered "Ottomans" in their formal nationality. At the same time, the Arabs had a sort of autonomy in many provinces, particularly in the Arabian Peninsula, where the sharifs ruled in the Hijaz, the Saudis and Rashidis in Najd, and the Zaydis and Idrissis in Yemen and Assir. The first rising of the Saudis late in the eighteenth century had been essentially a national movement with a façade of religious reform.

The Arab national movement started in Syria and Iraq with the demand for reform and a certain degree of autonomy so that those provinces might be able to effect reforms. In the beginning of the movement, reformers did not entertain the idea of separation since that would carry with it the danger of European domination. This fear of European domination increased after the African Arab countries began to fall—starting with the French occupation of Algiers in 1830 and culminating with the Italian occupation of Libya in 1911. The Ottomans, in contrast with the Europeans, at least, kept the unity of the Arab countries and gave the Arabs the satisfaction of feeling that they were living under a Muslim sovereign state. Hence the Arabs' welcome of the constitution of 1908 and the C.U.P.'s motto of freedom, justice, and equality.

The C.U.P. deposed Sultan Abdülhamid II in 1909. Their tough policies brought about a succession of risings in Yemen, Assir, Jabal al-Druze, and Karak. The government forces crushed the revolts in Jabal al-Druze and Karak, but were unable to do so in Yemen and Assir. It is noteworthy that Sharif Husayn, amir of the Hijaz, fought on the side of the Ottomans in Assir and Nejd. He believed then that "the state is not confined to the Turks but we have the larger share in counsel and right of opinion in matters relating to its interests. . . ."[3]

Before the deposition of Abdülhamid, the Arabs saw the sultan as the Muslim caliph and the head of the Ottoman state. After he was ousted, it became clear that power was in the hands of the C.U.P. and not in the hands of the sultan-caliph. The C.U.P. initiated a racial policy. The Arabs generally felt disappointed to discover that, despite the restoration of the constitution, the C.U.P. had assumed absolute power and were following a Turkification policy instead of the policy of decentralization that the Arabs had expected. What the Arabs had wanted was greater autonomy within the Ottoman state, but now many of them announced that the bond of the caliphate no longer existed and that the question was one of Turk against Arab and no more.[4]

Arab nationalists at first pursued an open policy in their endeavors to obtain reforms, but C.U.P. measures obliged them to seek outside platforms to express their views. Thus they formed in 1912 the Decentralization party in Egypt and held in June 1913 the first Arab Congress in Paris. At the same time two secret societies were formed: al-Fatat ("the Young Arab") and al-'Ahd ("the Covenant"), both of which aimed at Arab independence.

We must bear in mind that the Arab movement was essentially of a national character. Christians as well as Muslims participated in both its open and secret activities. The terms of the movement were plain: a common tongue, a common history, a common homeland, and common interests. The Decentralization party took a further step in including a number of Palestinian Jews in its membership, on the plea that "if the Jews accept the country's nationality, they would become ordinary citizens of this homeland."[5] Pioneers of the Arab movement made their motto "Religion is for God, homeland is for all."

The resolutions of the Arab Congress in Paris gave an indication about Arab demands at the time. They were mainly a call for (1) the implementation of reforms, (2) active Arab participation in the central administration and the exercise of their political rights, (3) establishment of decentralized rule in the Arab provinces, (4) the Arabic language to be recognized as an official language in the Arab provinces and in Parliament, (5) military service to be performed by Arabs in their respective provinces, except in cases of extreme necessity by the state. However, at almost the same time, al-Fatat adopted the decision that its ultimate aim would be "to free the Arab nation, according to conditions and circumstances, step by step, through legitimate means or otherwise."[6] It followed this by selecting the colors of the Arab flag— white, black, and green—in March 1914.[7]

The coming of World War I brought about new situations and caused both Turks and Arabs to face hard decisions. Sharif Husayn advised against involvement, but the C.U.P. joined hands with Germany and sent Cemal Pasha to Damascus as commander of all troops in Syria and Arabia. He had wide powers to carry on the war against the British in Egypt. The Arabs, faced with this situation, decided to postpone their demands and declared that they would cooperate fully with the Ottoman government in the war effort. But Cemal Pasha, in the wake of his failure in Egypt, began to pursue a policy of oppression and persecution. He arrested a number of suspected anti-Ottoman leaders and had them hanged on 21 August 1915; there followed a campaign of repression, banishment, arrests, and military courts. This policy estranged the Arabs and caused them to believe that the Turks were bent on crushing their national identity once and for all.

In this atmosphere of doubt and uncertainty, the British government approached Sharif Husayn, proposing support if the Arabs would rise against the Ottomans. At first the sharif declined, but some months later two events occurred that made him change his mind. National leaders in Damascus informed him of their movement and invited him to assume its leadership; at almost the same time a plot of the Turkish governor of the Hijaz to overthrow the sharif and put an end to its autonomy was revealed. The grand sharif delegated his third son, Faysal, to proceed to Damascus, where he consulted with the Iraqi and Syrian leaders of the movement. They assured him of their ability to stage a successful rising in co-operation with strong Arab elements in the Ottoman army. Faysal then informed them of Britain's proposal to his father. After this, they drew up a protocol authorizing the grand sharif to negotiate with Britain on behalf of the Arab nation on the condition that Britain recognize Arab independence in all Asian Arab countries (excluding Aden) in return for granting Britain a preference in economic projects.

On the strength of this protocol, the sharif began his negotiations with Britain, but he did not wish to commit himself irrevocably before exhausting all possible means for an understanding with the Ottoman government. Thus in March 1916 he asked them to agree to the following: (1) a declaration of a general amnesty for political prisoners, (2) to grant Syria and Iraq an autonomous administration, and (3) to recognize the sharif's position in the Hijaz as a hereditary right. The answer he received was a rebuff. He was told very bluntly that such demands were not his concern and that he had better improve his behavior. Cemal Pasha had a second group of leaders and intellectuals hanged on 6 May 1916. The die was cast, and a month later the Arabs began their revolt.

TRANSJORDAN UNDER THE OTTOMANS

Under the Ottomans, Transjordan was an integral part of geographic Syria, but it had a comparatively small population and was far from the main centers of commerce and routes of communication.

The Ottoman government established in 1851 a governorship in the district of Irbid; ten years later it established the governorship of Salt. The district of Karak remained independent until 1893. The whole area would have been forgotten land had it not been for the fact that the Syrian *Hajj* ("pilgrimage") passed through there on the way from Damascus to the holy cities of Mecca and Madina and the return trip to Damascus.

The pilgrimage road at that time ran through areas most of which were under the control of Bedouin tribes. Therefore the Ottomans found it expedient to pay the shaykhs of those tribes money in return for the tribes' keeping order and refraining from maltreatment of the pilgrims. The government built a scrics of forts and stations along thc road and stationcd troops in some of them so that pilgrims could rest there and replenish their stocks of water for the next stage. The agreements with the Bedouin provided for guarding the wells and cisterns at those stations and having them filled with water during winter. Every year the government would appoint a senior official to accompany the pilgrimage and supervise the welfare and safety of the pilgrims. This senior official was entrusted with the task of distributing the gifts and sums of money among the Bedouin chiefs in accordance with traditional agreements. Sometimes the pilgrimage chief ignored that tradition, which in turn caused the tribes to attack the pilgrims. Ahmad al-Budayri relates how in 1756 the Banu Sakhr tribe attacked the Syrian pilgrimage and "committed deeds that even worshippers of fire would not commit."[8] In 1909 the chief of the pilgrimage did not dare to return by land from thc Hijaz to Damascus; the grand sharif had to dclcgatc his brother, Nasir, and second son, 'Abd Allah, to accompany the pilgrims and see that they returned safely.[9]

Descriptions by travelers who visited Transjordan late in the nineteenth century indicate the general conditions prevailing in the various Ottoman provinces. Selah Merril relates the difficulty he encountered in finding someone to carry a letter from Ajlun to Salt, a journey of thirty to forty miles, because of the lack of security. He tells how a young man in Salt wished to study in the American college in Beirut and how his parents dissauded him from his ambition because they were concerned about the long distance and serious dangers! When one of Merril's comrades fell ill, since there was no medical treatment available, he had to send a messenger from Salt to Jerusalem to get a stretcher to carry the sick man. After two days men arrived with the stretcher. The ill man was carried on their shoulders to Jerusalem—a twenty-two hour journey.[10] It should be remembered that the inhabitants of Transjordan used very primitive methods of medical treatment, such as pouring boiling olive oil or animal butter on wounds caused by swords or bullets or applying hot rods of iron to various parts of the body. When Robinson Lees and his companions decided to travel from 'Amman to Hawran, they could not find a Bedouin who would venture to accompany them. The Circassians hesitated because the country was full of danger; only after much hesitation and deliberation did two of them agree to make the journey for a payment of ten pounds (which was then a small fortune).[11] Gray Hill met with great difficulties when visiting Karak. When he informed Salih al-Majali, paramount shaykh in the district, that he would complain to the queen of England and to the sultan of Turkey, the shaykh did not show any concern and said that Gray could complain to anyone he liked but that in Karak he himself was the king.[12]

Generally the inhabitants were divided into two main categories: Bedouin and villagers. The Bedouin were in control of the semi-desert area east of the pilgrimage routes (later the Hijaz Railway). They lived in goat-hair tents and were mainly concerned with raising camels, sheep, and fine breeds of horses. They moved their encampments from one place to another, seeking sufficient sources of water and grazing. The area west of the railway, too, was once inhabited by nomadic tribes. The Jordan Valley was inhabited by tribes who would spend the summer in the hilly plateau to the east. Each tribe had a certain wide area of its own to live in with other allied tribes. The Hawitat were masters of the south around Ma'an, Aqaba, and Petra; the Banu Sakhr lived in the middle and the north; and the Adwan lived in the Jordan Valley and the eastern plateau around Salt and 'Amman.

Villagers lived in areas suitable for the cultivation of wheat, barley, and other grains. They were not as numerous as the Bedouin. In the areas of Karak, besides the town itself, there were only three villages. About 1880 Circassians from the Caucasus arrived and established settlements where spring waters were abundant: at 'Amman, Jarash, al-Zarqa, and elsewhere. In the north the number of villages was small. There would be a population ranging from 40 to 700 persons in each village.[13]

Life was indeed very primitive, and the code of nature prevailed, with the strong overpowering the weak and small tribes allying themselves with the large ones in peace and war. Even villagers found it expedient to ally themselves with the strong tribes around them, as, for example, the inhabitants of Salt allied themselves with the Adwan tribe. Sometimes villagers and tribes fought each other, as the villagers of the north fought against the Banu Sakhr. Other villagers found no alternative but to pay a tribute (*khawa*) to avoid tribal onslaughts. Villagers were no match for the Bedouin, who made fighting their pride in life and who excelled in horsemanship and in the use of swords and spears. The tribesmen also had more freedom of movement. They would make a sudden attack on their sedentary neighbors, seize their cattle, and vanish into the wilderness. A German explorer tells how the villagers of Ajlun intended to abandon their villages under the pressure of the Bedouin. The government sensed the danger and sent a military force that in cooperation with the villagers, attacked the aggressive tribe and "exterminated the whole bedouin tribe down to its last member."[14] Villagers also made alliances among themselves in a tribal fashion under the leadership of strong families. In hilly areas where trees were abundant, the Bedouin were at a disadvantage and were unable to penetrate. Increased use of rifles and firearms gave the villagers an effective weapon of defense against Bedouin lancers.

It should be added that fighting was not limited to villagers against tribesmen. In fact, matters were much worse because the tribes raided each other. The raiders sometimes went a long way. Jordanian tribes raided as far as Iraq, and Arabian tribes penetrated as far as Jabal al-Druze and the Hawran. For the Bedouin fighting was a way of life.

Thus we see Transjordan toward the end of the nineteenth century sparsely populated and cultivated, with few roads, no medical facilities, no postal service, no newspapers, and only very few schools. Beasts of burden were the only means of transporting goods, and traveling was done on horse or mule. Literacy probably did not exceed one per cent.

THE LATE OTTOMAN PERIOD

During the first six years of this century, the construction of the Hijaz Railway line began in Damascus, passed through Transjordan, and reached Madina in the Hijaz in 1908. It did little to affect the way of life in the country, but it did affect the rising in Karak when the military forces of the Ottoman government were conveyed at an unprecedented speed to crush the revolt.

That rising was a clear proof of the wide gulf separating the ruler from the ruled. The semi-sedentary inhabitants of this district had lived many years without a regular government. Suddenly they found themselves a target for Ottoman regulations and rules. The government, for its part, did not attempt to understand their particular state of mind; it did not even bother to study their grievances regarding the new order imposed so suddenly upon them. The central government had decided in 1910 to carry out a census of the male population in preparation for conscription, to increase taxation, to enforce a partial disarming of the population, and to register land-ownership. These measures, especially the prospect of conscription into the Ottoman army, caused apprehension. The Majali, the leading family in the district, also believed that the government meant to deprive them of their dominant position. The people, led by the head shaykh, Qadr al-Majali, rose in revolt on 21 November 1910. They occupied the main government building in Karak and disposed of most of the troops within the town, including patrols and troops guarding the census committee. Railway stations were attacked, and Bedouin tribesmen joined the rising, which spread to Ma'an and Tafilah.

The Ottoman authorities hastened to deal with the situation. A large body of troops was sent by the railway. This force was able to enter the town of Karak on the tenth day of the rising. They managed to crush the resistance and ruthlessly inflict heavy casualties on the inhabitants. Although the rising failed and the people suffered considerably, the Ottoman government was soon preoccupied with the war against Italy and declared a general amnesty in Karak.

When World War I came, the government introduced military conscription, except in Karak. Since imported goods were cut off, the Ottomans began a policy of confiscating agricultural produce and livestock. Gangs of men were organized to cut down trees to replace coal as the fuel for the Hijaz Railway. In general there was much distress and a scarcity of commodities; the prevalent feeling was one of restlessness, fear, and hate.

THE ARAB REVOLT

Sharif Husayn declared the Arab Revolt on 10 June 1916 in the name of the Asian Arabs. He had made an agreement with Great Britain as the Arabs' representative and leader. Although the revolt did not materialize in Syria, as originally planned, the forces of the revolt included regular troops and irregular volunteers from all Asian Arab countries. Most of the regulars were from Iraq and Syria.

The news of the revolt spread in Arabia. The first active response in Transjordan came from 'Awda Abu Tayih, the famous shaykh of the Hawitat tribe. To the Hawitat, as to many other Arabs, the sharif was the direct descendant of the Prophet Muhammad and much closer to them than the Ottoman sultan, who did not speak their language and was in the habit of sending his troops to attack them. 'Awda and other shaykhs went inland to the Hijaz and urged Faysal, third son of Sharif Husayn and the nearest Arab commander to them, to begin operations in their country. Faysal eagerly delegated one of his outstanding commanders, Sharif Nasir, to proceed north, and T. E. Lawrence accompanied the expedition. Upon arrival 'Awda collected a force of volunteers, attacked Ottoman garrisons around Ma'an, and captured Aqaba on 6 July 1917.

Soon after Faysal transferred himself to Aqaba, he was followed by his younger brother, Zayd. Faysal's army began to expand its sphere of operations northward to Tafilah, Shobek, and Hasa. Tribesmen supported the Arab army, whose units raided as far north as the Yarmuk River and established an advance post at Azrak. The loyalty of the Jordanians to the Arab army was such that not a single incident of betrayal occurred; not only were the men of the revolt safe but so also were the British and French military missions who were giving support to the Arab forces. It happened that the Ottoman commander instigated raids by the people of Karak on certain tribes loyal to the revolt, but when the true facts underlying the revolt came to light, the Karakis refrained from taking further action. Most Jordanians actively supported the revolt, and thousands enlisted in its ranks. The loyalty and dedication of the Jordanians was a major factor in the successful outcome of the revolt.

Arab forces cooperated fully with the British army in the final campaign against the Ottomans in Syria in September 1918. The Arabs made a bold thrust behind the lines of the enemy and cut his lines of communication around the junction town of Dir'a. During that expedition the people supported the Arab forces until finally the Ottoman withdrawal turned into a rout. Most of the Arabs in Arabia and the Fertile Crescent countries supported the revolt, which promised to bring about their freedom.

It should be noted, also, that the revolt, according to the sharif's proclamations, was not declared against the sultan but only against the Committee of Union and Progress, whose leaders were charged with being renegades, narrow-minded men, and racial bigots.[15] The sultan was mentioned in the Friday prayers for more than one year after the beginning of the revolt. The Arabs continued to recognize the caliphate, then vested in the sultan, until the Turks abolished it in 1924. The sharif visualized the possibility of a federal state comprising Arabs and Turks, under the crown of the sultan, that would naturally exclude the C.U.P. In 1918 Cemal Pasha the Lesser made peace overtures. In response Faysal suggested the formation of an Arab-Turkish state, under the sultan, similar to that of Austria-Hungary.

TRANSJORDAN AFTER THE WAR

During October 1918 Ottoman forces were driven out of Syria, and soon after the war came to an end. The Allies established three military administrations: (1) the British in Palestine, (2) the French in Lebanon and along the northern Syrian coast, (3) the Arabs in the interior from Aleppo in the north to Aqaba in the south. Amir Faysal became the head of the Arab administration in his capacity as the commander of an Allied army.

For the Arabs the emergence of the Arab administration meant the establishment in Syria of an independent Arab state for the first time in hundreds of years. Arab nationalists then had high hopes for an eventual British and French withdrawal that would enable Palestine, Lebanon, and the coast to join the young Arab state. It seemed to those nationalists that the establishment of a united Arab state comprising Syria, Iraq, and Arabia was not very far off. The Arabs had heard of the Sykes-Picot Agreement, concluded in May 1916, which divided Iraq and Syria into complicated spheres of influence between France and Britain. The Arab nationalists were shocked at these arrangements, which aroused doubt and fear in their hearts. The Allies had, however, issued a number of pledges and assurances to the effect that the inhabitants would not have to submit to any rule that did not meet with their approval. The Arabs could not believe that their friends, the British, would betray them after all the cooperation manifested during the war.

Transjordan formed a part of the Syrian state, and Jordanian deputies participated in the activities of the Syrian Congress. The Congress, which represented all of geographic Syria, declared the country independent on 8 March 1920 and proclaimed Faysal constitutional monarch.[16] However, only four and one-half months later, on 24 July 1920, French forces occupied Damascus and forced Faysal to leave his kingdom.

The period of independence was brief and confused. The Arabs were directing most of their attention to warding off the danger of foreign designs. Nevertheless it was a period of Arab rule, full of national pride. In April 1920 Jordanians made a raid into Palestine to show their objection to the British Zionist policy. Airplanes bombed and strafed their groups after they had crossed the Jordan and Yarmuk rivers toward the west. Ten men were killed, among them a notable leader, and the raiders were forced to retreat and disperse.

The Arab government was not able to pay sufficient attention to its internal problems. Therefore its prestige depended on Faysal and his brother Zayd. Security was not as good as the government wished, and raiding continued. Deficits in the budget caused delays in paying wages to officials and policemen. Early in 1920 the government attempted military conscription, but the response was poor. Even in the town of Salt, people opposed this new measure, and a clash took place in which some men lost their lives. The government was, however, very anxious to improve conditions. An example of this was the repair of the demolished sectors of the Hijaz Railway; and as a result railway communication was resumed between Damascus and Madina.

When the French occupied Damascus, they did not continue their advance to the territory of Transjordan because it was assigned as a British mandate in the Sykes-Picot Agreement and by the decision taken on 25 April 1920 at the San Remo Conference. Accordingly, Sir Herbert Samuel, the high commissioner for Palestine, visited the town of Salt and held a meeting on 21 August 1920 with the leading notables of Transjordan. The British government had decided by then that it was committed to recognize an Arab administration in Transjordan in accordance with its pledge to Sharif Husayn. Therefore Samuel informed the notables that Transjordan was under British mandate, and the British government did not intend to attach the country to the Palestine administration. They intended to help the notables establish a separate administration through which they could rule themselves, with the help of British political officers.

As a result, three local and separate administrations were formed during the month of September 1920 in Irbid, Salt, and Karak. The district of Ma'an-Aqaba was considered part of the Hijaz. These three administrations were so weak that influential shaykhs here and there refused to give their allegiance and declared their own administrations. The collection of taxes was very slack; as a result, wages to policemen were not paid. Local clashes flared up, and there were no troops to put them down. Bedouin tribes kept up their traditional raiding. In the north they attempted to impose their authority over the villagers and plundered their cattle. The villagers retaliated and engaged the Bedouin in a fierce battle near the village of Ramtha; at least eighty men from both sides were killed. The tribes were defeated and soon after retreated into the semi-desert areas. Enmity between the two sides persisted until after the establishment of the amirate, when

Amir 'Abd Allah delegated one of the sharifs to conclude peace and settle blood claims on both sides.

The high commissioner finally appointed a number of political officers to work with the local administrations. He also entrusted Captain Frederick Peake with the task of forming a small military force. Peake remained as the commander of the small force, which subsequently was augmented and in 1923 became the Arab Legion.

ESTABLISHMENT OF THE AMIRATE

The Transjordan amirate was a living example of the unjust policy of the World War I Allies toward the Arabs. The Arabs had risen in revolt to achieve independence and establish a united state, but Britain and France divided the country between them, crushed Arab resistance by force of arms, and inflicted upon them injuries from which they still suffer. The worst aspect of the arrangement was the partition of geographic Syria into four entities: Syria, Lebanon, Palestine, and Transjordan. This was done despite the objections of most of the inhabitants and against their interests. Still worse, Britain adopted the policy of supporting a Jewish national home in Palestine.

The Syrians, including the people of Transjordan, resisted the French invasion. Resistance continued until after the fall of Damascus when the villagers of Hawran murdered the prime minister and one of his ministers, who were collaborating with the French. The Hawran leaders held a meeting soon after in which they decided to continue to resist the French. They sent messages to King Husayn appealing for aid and asking him to send one of his sons to lead their movement. At the same time Jordanian leaders in 'Amman and Ma'an, together with Syrian nationalists, sent similar appeals to the king.

King Husayn, who had been exceedingly worried by the turn of events, was heartened by this evidence of popular resistance. He chose his second son, 'Abd Allah, to proceed north in order to study the situation and participate with the Syrians in their struggle. Amir 'Abd Allah had worked with his father in planning the Arab revolt and had played an active role in its military operations. He had commanded the Eastern Army, captured Ta'if, and beseiged Madina until it surrendered. At the same time, he held the post of minister for foreign affairs in the Hijaz state, and in March 1920 an Iraqi congress proclaimed him king of Iraq. Such was the situation when the amir left Mecca for Madina and proceeded from there by train to Ma'an, which he reached on 11 November 1920, accompanied by several leading sharifs and a force of about five hundred men.

Upon his arrival, which caused considerable excitement, he proclaimed that he had come in response to the Syrians' call so that he might participate in the honor of fighting the aggressors. The amir said that he considered himself a deputy to his brother Faysal and urged the Syrians to rise in rebellion. The French in Syria were disturbed because rumors exaggerated the strength of the force at the amir's disposal.[17] They feared that his presence at Ma'an might stimulate the Syrians to rise in general rebellion. Accordingly they assembled their forces in Hawran and asked their allies the British to find a way for the amir's return to the Hijaz. They went so far as to threaten sending a military force to expel the amir if the British were not prepared to do so.

The British, however, took no measures against the amir beyond informing him that they would not consent to any steps he might take to use their mandated territory as a base for operations against the French. The British distributed statements urging Jordanians to refrain from communicating with the amir. Under this pressure the governors in Salt and Karak informed the amir that they would oppose him if he proceeded northward "for political aims." At the same time, the British Foreign Office informed Faysal, who had arrived in London early in December, that the movements of his brother were causing concern, and asked him to dissuade his brother from taking any action against the French.

The British government had invited Faysal to visit London, where discussions were initiated concerning the possibility of reaching an understanding with the Arabs. There was widespread antipathy toward British policy that erupted in the summer of 1920 in a violent uprising in Iraq. Faysal cabled his father urging restraint and at the same time asked a friend in Palestine to proceed to Ma'an and press upon 'Abd Allah the advisability of restricting his activities while discussions with the British were in progress. But the Jordanians were not convinced, and their activities caused the French to cut the railway line near Dir'a as a precautionary measure against a possible attack. The amir also found it expedient to boost the morale of his supporters. He sent Sharif 'Ali al-Harith to proceed to 'Amman and Salt. Sharif 'Ali met a wide popular welcome in both towns and among Bedouin tribes of the area. He sent messages to the notables of the north asking them to be prepared "to save the country from the French."

On 12 December Sir Herbert Samuel, the British high commissioner for Palestine, telegraphed to London that shaykhs of southern and central Transjordan had received and accepted a summons from the amir and Sharif 'Ali and that it was possible that 'Abd Allah "may proclaim a Shereefian government over Trans-Jordania. . . ." Samuel warned that such a step might lead to inter-tribal disorder and "recurrence of raids into Palestine," and called attention "to the seriousness of situation which may be now developing."[18] The French intimated that the situation "might necessitate French force pursuing Sherifians across the frontier of British zone. . . ." This was considered a serious threat by the British—so much so that Lord Curzon requested the French government to instruct their high commissioner in Syria "to refrain from military action in our zone unless and until he considers such action unavoidable. . . ."[19] Samuel, in order to eliminate the possibility of French interference, suggested to his government on 27 December that they approve the dispatch of a British military force to Transjordan. We may deduce from this that Samuel wanted the force to tilt the balance against the amir and to intimidate the people.

On 7 January 1921 Samuel again recommended to his government that British control over Transjordan should be "direct and complete." At the same time, 'Abd Allah assured the envoy of his brother that he had no intention of alienating the British government and that he would suspend his operations temporarily and wait for the outcome of the political negotiations. The French renewed their threat of using military force against 'Abd Allah. On 30 January Samuel assured Lord Curzon that 'Abd Allah was preparing to attack the French and that it had become imperative to occupy Transjordan militarily. Ten days later he suggested withdrawing British political officers from Transjordan to create difficulties for the amir in case he proceeded to 'Amman. However, the Foreign Office urged him not to do so but to delegate Ronald Storrs, the governor of Jerusalem, to welcome the amir if he arrived in 'Amman. Samuel, nevertheless, persisted in pointing out his views. He assured his government that the activities of the amir had weakened the authority of the local administrations and that some tribes had stopped the payment of taxes.

The British government continued its deliberations with Faysal. Meanwhile, at the beginning of the new year, the British changed their policy toward the Arab countries. Administration of mandated territories (Iraq, Palestine, and Transjordan) was transferred to the Colonial Office. Winston Churchill, secretary of colonies, decided to hold a conference in Cairo with the purpose of discussing all matters relating to those countries and finding suitable solutions. When preparations for the holding of the conference were in progress, Samuel telegraphed Churchill, on 24 February 1921, that Amir 'Abd Allah was the "active leader" of the movement against the French, and that the presence of his deputy, Sharif 'Ali, in 'Amman "has weakened authority of local governments in Transjordan." He added, "Have you considered inviting 'Abd Allah to Cairo Conference? His movement is not making headway and that would enable him to withdraw from Transjordan without loss of prestige. . . ." On 28 February Churchill replied that Samuel could inform the amir "that I will be glad to see him later if meeting can be arranged and provided tranquility is preserved meanwhile. . . ."[20]

Amir 'Abd Allah had meanwhile found it more expedient to accept the advice of his father and brother, especially because he did not possess the resources to start a widespread movement against the French. The people were not sufficiently prepared to wage effective military operations. The enthusiasm of the Jordanians had encouraged him to continue to stay more than three months at Ma'an. That enthusiasm culminated in a delegation's urging the amir to come to 'Amman and save the country from its chaotic situation. So it came about that the amir proceeded by train from Ma'an to 'Amman and, on 21 March 1921 was received there with ovations. He was looked on as a deliverer and liberator. Soon delegates and deputations began to visit 'Amman from all parts of Transjordan, Hawran, and Jabal al-Druze, to pay homage and offer loyalty and allegiance.

In a letter to Samuel a few days later, the amir wrote of his new position in 'Amman. When he learned that Churchill had arrived in Cairo, the amir sent a letter to him explaining how the Arabs were disappointed at the partition of their country into small states and how they aspired to obtain freedom and independence in Syria, Palestine, and Iraq.

Churchill opened the Cairo Conference on 12 March. On the seventeenth the conference began its discussions of questions relating to Palestine and Transjordan. The conference considered the military occupation of Transjordan. On 18 March Churchill telegraphed to the prime minister that he considered it "necessary immediately to occupy militarily Trans-Jordania. . . ." He further said that military arrangements for occupation of Transjordan were proceeding on the assumption that a satisfactory arrangement with Amir 'Abd Allah was reached. He went on to say that there was "no alternative to this policy as we cannot contemplate hostilities with Abdullah in any circumstances." He believed that the amir would be "fortified and restrained" by the presence of British troops.[21] On 21 March Churchill arranged for the modification of the Mandate so that Transjordan was excluded from the application of the clauses relating to the creation of a Jewish national home.

Churchill decided to visit Palestine, and Amir 'Abd Allah received an invitation to meet him in Jerusalem. The amir, accompanied by a number of Syrian and Palestinian nationalists, held four meetings with Churchill. In the first meeting Churchill explained that his government was not able to carry out its policy of supporting the Arabs in Syria and Palestine "owing to the decisions of the Allies and to promises made to third parties." He said that the British government recognized the Arab character of Transjordan, and he proposed that it be constituted as an Arab province under an Arab governor responsible to the high commissioner for Palestine. The amir counterproposed that Palestine and Transjordan should constitute one state under an Arab amir, and that relations between the British government and this state be similar to that with Iraq. Churchill insisted that his government would not adopt the amir's proposal. At this juncture the amir said that he would very much like to know what British policy really aimed at. "Did His Majesty's Government mean to establish a Jewish Kingdom west of the Jordan and to turn out the non-Jewish population? . . . The Allies appear to think that men could be cut down and transplanted in the same way as trees." Here Samuel interposed to assure the amir "that there was no intention either to cut down or to transplant, but only to plant new ones." Churchill also said that there was a great deal of "groundless apprehension" among the Arabs in Palestine. Samuel again explained British policy in Palestine, stating there "was no question of setting up a Jewish Government there." The amir repeated four times his original proposal of combining Palestine and Transjordan, but Mr. Churchill was adamant in declining to consider it. The amir suggested later that Transjordan be combined with Iraq, but "he was told that this was also impossible." At another meeting Churchill suggested that the amir himself remain in Transjordan and take charge of its administration. After consulting with his companions, the amir agreed to accept the proposal on condition that his father be consulted also. It was agreed that there should be a trial period of six months and that the British should assist financially. Churchill insisted that Transjordan should not be a base from which attacks might be directed against the French in Syria or the British in Palestine. Churchill further said that, if 'Abd Allah would accept Transjordan, there might be in the near future a reconciliation with the French, which might lead to the amir's being installed as amir of Syria in Damascus. Churchill promised that the British government "would do everything they could to assist towards the attainment of this object."[22]

The amir returned to 'Amman and began his rule by unifying the various districts of Transjordan. On 11 April the first council of ministers was formed. This council was Arab in character, since only one of its members was a local Jordanian. This procedure was continued for many years. The British helped fund the government with a modest grant, most of which was expended on the formation of a military force to keep order.

Six months passed, and the amir decided to remain, despite internal and external difficulties that were facing him. Herbert Samuel and his staff in Jerusalem kept urging the British government to work for the expulsion of the amir and the Syrian nationalists from Transjordan so that the mandatory administration in Palestine might assume direct rule in Transjordan. Churchill was not convinced, and he delegated Colonel Lawrence to go to Transjordan and study the situation. Lawrence spent almost two months in Transjordan. He recommended adherence to the first arrangement and accused the staff in Jerusalem of writing misleading and deceiving reports. Churchill accepted his views.

Internally the new state had to overcome a difficult situation. In only the second month of its establishment, some villagers in the north rebelled and defeated the small force sent to subdue them. It took the government more than one year to muster sufficient troops to quell the insurgents. Toward the end of June 1921, a group of armed men attacked General Gouraud, the French high commissioner for Syria, injuring him and killing his aide-de-camp. The French authorities alleged the assailants came from Transjordan and demanded the arrest of a number of Syrian nationalists who were residing there. The Transjordan government refused to accede to the French demand on the plea that the crime was political. Disturbances and local strife broke out at Karak, but the military force was able to suppress them and impose order.

International recognition was obtained when the League of Nations, on 23 September 1922, approved a British memorandum excepting Transjordan from the application of the Jewish national home clauses in the mandate for Palestine. This was followed on 25 May 1923 by British official recognition of Transjordan's independence. Samuel declared in 'Amman on that day that Great Britain recognized Transjordan as an independent state under British mandate. This day has since become Jordan's Independence Day.

The government of Palestine, however, persisted in its endeavors to curb the measure of independence enjoyed by Transjordan. That government found, early in August 1924, the necessary justification when a number of Syrian nationalists attacked some French positions in Syria. The French authorities claimed the assailants had come from Transjordan and demanded that the British, as the mandatory power, take the necessary action. The Palestine government dispatched two columns of British troops to 'Amman and Irbid, declared martial law in the Irbid area, and sent the amir an ultimatum demanding that he agree to British financial control, expulsion of Syrian nationalists, approval of an extradition agreement with Syria, and that Jordan's troops be under British command. The amir found no alternative but to accept the ultimatum. In this way the new state lost that measure of independence it had enjoyed.

The final stage in the establishment of the amirate was the inclusion in June 1925 of the southern region of Ma'an-'Aqaba. This had been a part of the Hijaz until King 'Ali (elder brother of 'Abd Allah) renounced it in favor of his brother, as a result of the Sa'udi attack on his country.

Thus Transjordan came into being as a separate entity. The subsequent struggle of this small country to better the conditions of its inhabitants, to instill a measure of security not witnessed before, to make great strides in the areas of human progress, and to achieve full sovereignty—all this falls outside the scope of this essay.

In conclusion, the state of Transjordan was founded as a result of two main factors: the political interests of Great Britain and France on the one side and the Arab national movement on the other. The boundaries of the new state were generally fixed by foreign bargaining and power politics, but its national character was preserved by Arab effort. The leadership of the Amir 'Abd Allah contributed effectively to the permanent exclusion of Zionist penetration. We have seen how Great Britain undertook to protect the "civil and religious rights" of the Arabs of Palestine and to preserve their freedom, "both economic and political," and how—during a relatively short period—they were deprived of everything. Transjordan, too, could have easily fallen prey to the Zionists had it not been for the efforts of Amir 'Abd Allah during the period of transition from Ottoman rule to statehood. The progress of Transjordan into nationhood and full sovereignty may also be considered an example of the outcome of constructive cooperation between a European power and an Arab country. Had such cooperation taken place at the end of World War I between Great Britain and France on the one hand and the Arab countries on the other, the situation in the Middle East today would indeed have been very different.

1. *Memoirs of King Abdullah* (London, 1950), pp. 97–98.

2. Ibid., p. 142.

3. Letter sent by the sharif in 1913 to his brother, quoted in Suleiman Mousa, *al-Harakah al-'Arabiyah* [The Arab Movement] (Beirut, 1970), p. 56.

4. Memorandum, British ambassador in Istanbul to British foreign secretary, 28 June 1910, F.O. 371/1007, Public Record Office, London.

5. Letter, 20 June 1914, Rafiq al-'Azm, chairman of the Decentralization party (Cairo) to Mahmud al-Mahmasani (Beirut), quoted in Mousa, op. cit., p. 64.

6. Letter, 2 January 1913, 'Abd al-Ghani al-Arisi (Paris) to Muhib al-Din al-Khatib (Cairo) (both members of *al-Fatat*), ibid., p. 33.

7. When the Arab revolt began, the sharif used a red flag because red was the traditional color of the sharifs. After a year, in June 1917, he adopted the three colors of al-Fatat in addition to the red.

8. A manuscript written by Ahmad al-Budayri (Damascus). See the comments by Dreid al-Mufit in *Huna London* (a magazine published in Arabic by the BBC Arabic Service), August 1973.

9. *Memoirs of King Abdullah*, pp. 67–68.

10. Selah Merril, *East of the Jordan* (London, 1881).

11. Robinson Lees, *Life and Adventure beyond Jordan* (London, 1890[?]), pp. 236–39.

12. Gray Hill, *With the Beduins* (London, 1890).

13. Gottlieb Schumacher, *Northern Ajlun* (London, 1890), pp. 97, 98, 120, 123, 141, 147, 149, 179, and 184.

14. Ibid., pp. 28–29.

15. Message, Sharif Husayn to Sultan Mehmed Reshid, 12 July 1916, F.O. 882/19.

16. This same congress had adopted some months before a resolution rejecting Zionist claims in Palestine. It is worthy of note that its membership included two native Jewish leaders who were representing all Jews in geographic Syria.

17. For example, Allenby sent a telegram on 4 December saying that 'Abd Allah had 7,000 men with him and that 'Awda Abu Tayih had joined him.

18. Samuel to Curzon, in *Documents on British Foreign Policy, 1919–1939*, First Series, Vol. 13, ed. R. Butler and J. Bury (London, 1963), p. 413.

19. Telegram, 19 December 1920, Curson to Hardinge, ibid., p. 417.

20. F.O. 371/6371, Samuel to Churchill, 24 February 1921; Churchill to Samuel, 28 February 1921.

21. Ibid.

22. Report on the Middle East Conference held in Cairo and Jerusalem, 12–30 March 1921, Public Record Office, London, File AIR 8/37.

Ann Lesch

The Origins of Palestine
Arab Nationalism

Nationalism emerged as a major political force in the Palestine Arab community in the 1920s and 1930s in reaction to the growing strength of the Jewish community and the British denial of the Arabs' aspiration for independence. The Palestine Arabs made invidious comparisons between their deteriorating political position and the gradual acquisition of self-government by the neighboring Arab communities. Although relatively late in its development and ultimately unsuccessful, the Palestine Arab national movement was vigorous at its height, not only organizing political parties and delegations to London, but also fanning mass demonstrations and a three-year uprising.[1] The roots of this movement may be traced to the period before World War I, when the area comprising Palestine was ruled from Istanbul. Although the movement was then only at an incipient stage, the outline of its aspirations and methods is discernible.[2] Moreover, the Arab community was already subject to some of the external pressures from European powers and the Zionist movement that were to influence its development in later years.

In the late nineteenth and early twentieth centuries, three major external forces impinged on Palestine. First, the European powers competed vigorously for influence in the main towns. They asserted special religious prerogatives at the holy places on behalf of the Christian sects, and their consuls provided diplomatic protection to the indigenous non-Muslim groups. These local interests were used to support their political claims, which were to be advanced if the Ottoman Empire disintegrated. Second, Zionism, which emerged in Eastern Europe in the 1880s, sought to transform Palestine by means of immigration and political concessions from Istanbul or European powers. Finally, Ottoman administrative reforms in the 1880s resulted in substantial material improvements in Palestine. Serious tension between Istanbul and the local Arab leadership arose only after the 1908 Young Turk revolution, as the new regime turned from Ottomanism to pan-Turanism and sought to curb all expression of local nationalism.

Arab reactions to these pressures took diverse forms. Although the Europeans provided educational and economic benefits to the urban Arabs, the local leaders sought to limit the consuls' political influence and tried to play off the rivalries among the European powers in order to offset their political claims. These leaders also petitioned Istanbul to stop Jewish immigration and prevent land-buying by Zionist organizations. After 1908 they initiated political societies and newspapers to enhance this pressure and to widen public awareness of the situation. The Arab leaders worked in concert with Ottoman authorities to limit European and Zionist influence. However, the inability of the authorities to withstand all foreign pressure exacerbated the strains between Arabs and Turks.

The Arabs were relatively successful in pressuring the Ottoman regime to curtail Jewish immigration and land-buying. They were less successful in limiting European involvement and winning national political rights. Nevertheless, the Arab leaders retained considerable local authority in town and district councils and through the rural clan networks. Moreover, after 1908 they gained important public forums through newspapers and political societies. Control from Istanbul was thereby limited, and the Arab elite established the rudiments of political organization and action.

European interest in Palestine grew rapidly in the nineteenth century. The territory was both the Christian Holy Land and a potentially valuable part of the Ottoman Empire, whose demise was being predicted—and hastened—by the Great Powers. Although European religious and political interests were based on disparate impulses, in practice competition for influence in the holy places and among the local Arab groups tended to mask political aims.

European consular offices were opened at the ports of Jaffa and Haifa in the early nineteenth century, but no consulates were permitted by the Ottoman regime in Jerusalem at that time. A British consulate only opened in 1838, when Palestine was under Egyptian rule. This opened the door for other European states to expand their diplomatic and religious representation. Britain and Prussia established a Protestant bishopric in 1841, the Catholic powers revived the Latin patriarchate of Jerusalem in 1847, and Russia stepped up its support for the Greek Orthodox institutions. Britain also extended diplomatic protection over such small non-Muslim groups as the Druze, Copts, Abyssinians, Samaritans, and Jews.

Competition for influence within each Christian sect somewhat mitigated the political impact of European activities. The British-Prussian bishopric, for example, split in the 1860s into separate Anglican and Lutheran establishments, which built their own churches, hospices, and schools in Jerusalem. Similarly, in the mid-1850s France supported the Latin patriarch, headquartered in Bayt Jala, whereas Austria aided the convent monks in Bethlehem, and Spain sponsored another Latin convent at 'Ain Karim.[3] Serious strains also arose between Russia and the Greek Orthodox monks. Russian Orthodox funds and pilgrims were the church's primary support, but the monks and patriarchs were exclusively Greek. The

Russian archimandrites in Jerusalem backed the demands of the local Orthodox Arabs for a greater role in the religious hierarchy and for substantial social services. Although designed to weaken the Greek patriarchate, this Russian involvement indirectly promoted separatism among the Arabs.[4]

Competition between the sects was also intense, particularly at Christmas and Easter, when the struggles for priority at the holy places reached their height. Franco-Russian rivalry on behalf of the Latin and Orthodox communities, respectively, was most bitter in the 1840s and 1850s and was a precipitating cause of the Crimean War. On a small scale, tension simmered in Haifa between the French Carmelite convent and German pietist settlers, the Templars, who settled there in the 1870s. In at least one instance, the Templars allied with the local Muslim Arabs against the convent in a land dispute.[5]

The direct influence of European consuls in Palestine reached its height from the 1840s to the 1860s, while Ottoman provincial rule was weak. The consuls interceded actively on behalf of their client communities and even helped to mediate (or took sides in) clan warfare in the rural areas.[6] British influence was the most substantial, partly as a reflection of the power wielded by the British ambassador in Istanbul, Stratford Canning, over Sultan Abdülmecid, while Britain was the empire's principal ally. Moreover, London supported the small Protestant community, rather than the powerful Latin and Orthodox establishments, and was therefore attractive to the authorities as a balance against French and Russian influence.

Although the direct intervention of the consuls waned in the 1880s and 1890s as provincial rule tightened and resentment at foreign interference grew, European competition did not abate in Palestine. Russia, Britain, France, and Germany constructed hostel and hospital complexes for the growing numbers of pilgrims and opened schools for Arab children. In the 1880s the czarist government even joined Britain in supporting the immigration rights of Jewish settlers, although many Jews were fleeing Russian pogroms.[7] The Sublime Porte continued to be hostile toward Russia, with which it had fought in the 1850s and 1870s, and its friendship with London waned after the British occupation of Egypt in 1882. In contrast, French and German influence within the empire grew substantially. French economic and cultural influence was particularly evident in Lebanon and northern Palestine, and Germany received important economic concessions and established significant military influence in Istanbul. France constructed the Jaffa-Jerusalem Railway in 1893, and French experts drew up plans for major harbor works at Haifa and Jaffa. France sought concessions to develop these ports and to extend the Dir'a-Haifa branch of the Hijaz Railway south to Jaffa. Such concessions would have established France as a major power in the Eastern Mediterranean. Meanwhile, British defense analysts concluded in 1906 that Haifa would provide the best port for the British fleet, although it already had access to Alexandria and Cyprus, and London began to consider Palestine as a potential buffer zone east of Egypt.

Parallel to the growing European involvement in Palestine, Zionism emerged as an organized political movement that directed its attention to Palestine. Zionism received its particular focus from the ancient Jewish longing for the return to Zion, and it received a strong impetus from the increasingly intolerable conditions of the Jewish communities in Rumania and czarist Russia.

In 1880 the Jewish community in Palestine (the *Yishuv*) numbered perhaps 35,000 out of a total population of 584,000. Over eighty percent of the inhabitants were Muslim Arabs, ten percent Christian Arabs, and six percent Jews. Half of the Jews lived in Jerusalem, and virtually all the rest lived in Safad, Tiberias, and Hebron. Although the old community of Arabic-speaking Sephardic Jews had a certain social and economic status in these towns, the newer European element relied largely on contributions (*halukah*) from European Jewry for sustenance and had a very low status. Philanthropists such as Sir Moses Montefiore tried to encourage these residents to undertake remunerative employment; but the rabbis opposed such work, and the Ashkenazi community remained an isolated, pious, and impoverished enclave.[8]

A new wave of immigration began in the 1880s that differed fundamentally from the "old" *Yishuv*. The First *'Aliyah* (ascent) of the 1880s and 1890s added 15,000 Jews to the population, so that the Yishuv totaled 50,000 in 1900, out of 640,000 residents. The immigrants came in two waves, the first after the 1881 Russian and Rumanian pogroms, and the second after the expulsion of the Jewish community from Moscow in 1891. The first wave consisted largely of members of Hovevei Zion ("Lovers of Zion"), young idealists who sought to work on the land and held grandiose political aspirations.[9] Some worked initially on two old Yishuv settlements, Petah Tiqva (founded by Jerusalem Jews in 1876) and Mikve Israel, an agricultural training school opened by the Alliance Israélite Universelle in 1870. The immigrants lacked agricultural training or financial support, and their new colonies were saved from complete collapse only by emergency financial aid from Baron Edmond de Rothschild of Paris.

Perhaps the greatest obstacle was the Ottoman regime, which tried to prevent Jewish immigration and land purchases.[10] In 1882 the sultan banned all Russian Jewish immigration into Palestine, rescinding the decree only under pressure from European ambassadors in Istanbul.[11] Official prohibitions of Jewish immigration and land purchase were again decreed in 1891, after Jerusalem Arab notables protested against the second wave of immigration.[12] Further regulations in 1892 and 1900 radically curtailed Jewish land purchases in the Jerusalem-Jaffa area. Once a colony was established, the Ottoman authorities tried to prevent the settlers from constructing permanent buildings, because that would strengthen their legal claim to the land.[13] In most cases the settlers erected the buildings without receiving or even applying for—the required permits.

The settlers also had to contend with hostility from neigh-

boring Arab villagers. In cases where the land had been purchased from Arab moneylenders who had acquired it from
debt-defaulting villagers, the villagers' resentment was transferred from the moneylenders to the Jewish colonists.[14]
Boundary disputes were also common, as a result of the in-
accuracy of Ottoman land registers and the lack of any land
survey. Moreover, the Jewish colonists inadvertently violated
customary rights, forbidding Arab neighbors to graze their
sheep on the uncultivated pasturelands. They also dispensed
their own direct justice on trespassers, rather than using the
Ottoman courts.[15] Petah Tiqva was attacked by neighboring
villagers in 1886, and Rehoboth was attacked in 1892. Over
time, however, the Arabs became accustomed to the Jewish
colonists, and some were hired as workers or guards.[16] So
long as the colonies were scattered and small, and the settlers
were willing to employ Arabs, rural hostility remained minimal and basically apolitical.

In 1900–1902 a Jewish colonizing agency negotiated the purchase of nearly half of the Tiberias district from the Sursuqs,
wealthy Christian bankers in Beirut. The family had acquired
land titles from the Arab villagers in the 1870s and 1880s
over most of the plain of Esdraelon, the granary of Palestine.[17] This huge purchase was resisted successfully by the
Tiberias *qa'immaqam* ("district officer"), Amir Amin Arslan,
who was a leader of the Druze Arabs in Syria. Although
the Beirut *vali* ("governor") approved the sale, unrest in the
Tiberias district caused the Istanbul government to overrule
the vali and invalidate the sale. The Sursuqs, however, sold
another large tract in the Esdraelon, south of Nazareth, to
the colonizing agency in 1910, which the qa'immaqam of
Nazareth was unable to prevent.[18] These sales had a major
impact on the Palestine Arabs, as they raised the specter of
large-scale alienation of Arab land.

Rural labor issues were also politicized as a result of the
policy of *'Ivrit 'Avodah* ("Hebrew labor"), introduced by the
Second 'Aliyah settlers of 1903–14. This 'Aliyah added 25,000
Jews to the Yishuv, so that it reached a total of 75,000 out

of nearly 690,000 by 1914. Among the immigrants were zealous youths who criticized the First 'Aliyah settlers for becoming landed gentry and eschewing manual labor. A 1906 immigrant, David Ben-Gurion, later wrote: "We waged the struggle for Jewish labor. We regarded Arab labor in the Jewish villages as a grave danger, for we knew that the land would not be ours if we did not work it and develop it with our own hands."[19] The immigrants also stressed the use of Hebrew, rather than Yiddish or Arabic, a move that furthered the cohesiveness of the Yishuv but set it apart from the Arabs. The Templars, in contrast, had rapidly learned Arabic so that they could converse with the Arab inhabitants, and they even farmed some land in joint shares with Arab villagers.[20]

Zionism acquired a formal structure after the first congress, held in Basel in August 1897. The brainchild of Theodor Herzl, a Viennese journalist, the congress initially served as his vehicle for seeking diplomatic support in European chanceries and Istanbul. Herzl sought German assistance, proposing to Kaiser Wilhelm II that the Zionists colonize Palestine under German protection. He also offered Ottoman officials a substantial loan, if the Jews could obtain Palestine as a semi-autonomous state. In 1901 he proposed directly to the sultan that a Zionist land company acquire crown land (*chiftlik*) in Palestine in return for helping the empire liquidate its £85 million debt. The sultan would only consider Jewish immigration to Anatolia, not Palestine, and undoubtedly realized that Herzl had no funds to support his scheme.[21]

Herzl turned to London in 1902, suggesting to the colonial secretary that the British territories of al-'Arish in Sinai or Cyprus be set aside for Jewish immigration. Although these ideas were vetoed, the British government formally offered the Zionists land in East Africa in August 1903. Herzl, shaken by the recent Kishinev pogrom in Russia, felt that East Africa could serve as an emergency haven until land in or near Palestine was available. Despite the pogroms the Russian Zionists adamantly opposed the East Africa project and, after Herzl's death in 1904, they insured the rejection of this idea.

The 1905 Zionist congress resolved that all settlement efforts should be directed toward Palestine.

The organization of a formal Zionist movement alarmed Istanbul, which feared the alleged wealth of the Jews and their potential mass migration from Europe to Palestine. The government therefore suspended all land transfers to Jews throughout Palestine. Turkish and Arab officials noted with concern the opening of a Palestine Office in Jaffa in 1908 that assisted new immigrants and encouraged agricultural settlement; the ground-breaking for an all-Jewish town, Tel Aviv, in 1909; and the report by the head of the Palestine Office to the 1913 congress on the results of the colonizing activities.

The European Zionists appeared to have little awareness of the opposition that was brewing in Palestine. Rural violence and a March 1908 Arab-Jewish clash in Jaffa were viewed as nomadic plundering or anti-Semitic outbursts.[22] In the early 1890s, however, a leading member of the Odessa Hovevei Zion society, Ahad Ha'Am (Asher Ginsburg), had warned:

> We abroad are accustomed to believe that the Arabs are all savages who are living on the level of animals, and who do not understand what is happening here around them. This, however, is a great mistake. . . . The Arabs, and particularly the urban population, see through our activity in the country and its purpose but they keep silent, since for the time being they do not fear any danger for their future. When, however, the life of our people in Palestine will have developed to such an extent that the indigenous population will feel threatened, then they will not easily give way any longer.[23]

The Zionist press in Europe did note the manifestoes issued in Paris by such Arab intellectuals as Najib 'Azuri, a former Ottoman official in Jerusalem, that aired the concept of an Arab national "awakening." The Zionist press noted that an Arab national movement would hinder the realization of their own aims.[24] But most of the articles in the Zionist press were designed to arouse the support of European Jews, and they therefore minimized the obstacles to Zionism and paid scant attention to Arab politics.

The Zionist leaders made little effort to counter Arab fears or to come to grips with the fact that Palestine was already inhabited. The leaders in Europe felt that their relations with the Palestine Arabs were less urgent than their need to win the support of European powers or the Ottoman government. Moreover, they felt caught in a vicious circle: overt Zionist support for Arab national movements would arouse Ottoman opposition and, conversely, an Ottoman-Zionist entente would alienate the Arabs.[25]

The Zionists who ran the Palestine Office in Jaffa and the liaison office in Istanbul were more fully aware of the extent of Arab opposition. Dr. Arthur Ruppin, head of the Palestine Office, argued that the Zionists must establish friendly relations with the Arab elite, take greater care in their land purchases, adopt Ottoman citizenship, and hire some Arab laborers.[26] He wrote in 1912: "Insofar as Jewish labourers seek employment in our farms we shall give them preference, but it would be very dangerous . . . for us to give employment only to Jews."[27] Nevertheless, Ruppin felt that rapid immigration and land settlement were essential in order to ensure the permanence of the Yishuv, and he believed that the Arabs would ultimately acquiesce to the presence of a large Jewish community in Palestine.

By 1914 it was becoming clear to the Zionist officials in Palestine that they could not fulfill Arab demands to curtail land purchases and end their exclusivist economic and social policies. The officials began to realize that the Arabs viewed them as dangerous economic and political competitors, with whom there were virtually no grounds for negotiation.[28]

The third factor affecting Palestine, in addition to the European powers and the Zionist movement, involved changes in Ottoman rule and in the relations between Arabs and Turks. The Ottoman Empire was subject to severe strains during the nineteenth century, from internal pressures as well as European territorial and financial encroachment. In order to counter the centrifugal forces in the Balkans and to arrest European penetration, the sultan sought to modernize the Ottoman armed forces and to establish more efficient rule in the provinces. These efforts were facilitated by the communications revolution, which introduced the telegraph, the railway, and the steamship to the empire.

Centralization accelerated under the reformist Young Turks, who engineered a *coup d'état* in July 1908 and deposed Sultan Abdülhamid II in 1909. A primary aim of the Young Turks was to prevent European powers from seizing additional Ottoman territories. But they became involved in debilitating wars in the Balkans and Tripolitania, which severely drained the empire's debt-ridden economy. Moreover, the Young Turks' initial promise of political equality to all Ottoman subjects without distinction of religion or race was vitiated by administrative measures that decreased provincial autonomy and decrees that outlawed political groups based on ethnic or national identity. The dominant Committee of Union and Progress (C.U.P.) also shifted its political ideology from Ottomanism, which implied equality among the different parts of the empire, to pan-Turanism and Turkification, which glorified the pre-Islamic Turkish tribes.[29] Turkish was imposed as the sole language of administration, courts, and schools in the Arab provinces, as well as in Anatolia. The Arabs' religious bond to the Ottoman Empire was also weakened by the C.U.P.'s stress on the pre-Islamic Turks.[30] Islam had been the strongest tie between Arabs and Turks; the Arabs had remained loyal to the sultan as head of Islam even though differences in race and language separated the two peoples.

There had already been hints of Arabism and a growing consciousness of the differences between Arabs and Turks in the 1890s and 1900s. Arab and Turkish leaders and intellectuals sought to erase the humiliations imposed by expanding European power and to reassert the superiority of Islamic culture over European Christian life.[31] Many thinkers argued that a return to the roots of Islam was essential in order to restore its purity and strength, roots that lay in Arabia.[32]

Thus a new tendency arose among Arab intellectuals to turn from Istanbul to Mecca as the vital center of Islam. When this Islamic search joined with European territorial notions of "patriotism," a separate political Arabism began to take shape.[33]

Turkification greatly accelerated this Arabist reaction, especially within the provincial elites and commercial and professional middle classes. In addition, the Young Turks' reestablishment of an imperial parliament in Istanbul provided the seventy-two Arab delegates with an opportunity to mingle with fellow Arabs from distant provinces. They could discuss common grievances and present common demands to the government. The ideas of imperial decentralization and national autonomy spread quickly, and decentralization provided the main plank of the Entente Libérale party.

The Young Turks also enabled the provinces to form their first overt political societies and newspapers. The Reform Societies in Beirut, Basra, and Jaffa opposed Turkification, but affirmed their loyalty to the empire. The Reform Society in Jaffa was organized by a former Entente Libérale delegate, Hafiz al-Sa'id, who sought greater provincial autonomy but refrained from calling for independence.[34] Societies that were formed outside the empire could be more outspoken, such as the Ottoman Decentralization Society in Cairo and the Young Arab Society (al-Fatat), which was initiated by Arab students in Paris in 1909, including 'Awni 'Abd al-Hadi and Rafiq al-Tamimi of Nablus.[35]

Arab political activities were spurred by the loss of additional Balkan provinces in 1912–13. An Arab congress, convened in Paris in June 1913, called for imperial decentralization, the appointment of Arabs to the central cabinet, and the use of Arabic in schools within the Arab provinces. Although the Ottoman government initially agreed to the demands, it failed to implement them, partly because it was preoccupied by the Balkan wars and partly because it felt that the congress represented only a small, marginal element in Arab society.

The failure of this reformist effort served to radicalize some members. A group of Arab officers in the Ottoman army, disenchanted with the Young Turks for their inability to strengthen the empire and their dismissal of Arab grievances, formed a clandestine society called al-'Ahd ("the Covenant") on the eve of World War I and established ties with al-Fatat. The two groups were unable to take any action before the war broke out, and the officers were then dispersed to non-Arab provinces for their military tours. It took the wartime repression by the Turkish governor, Cemal Pasha, and the European Allies' encouragement of an Arab rebellion to bring Arabs to the point of a complete break with the Ottoman Empire. Nevertheless, the bulk of the Arabs remained loyal until British and Arab troops actually occupied the provinces in 1917–18.[36] Some Muslims feared that ending Ottoman rule would only expose the Arabs to the full force of European imperialism and therefore clung to the empire as the last defense against the Christian Europeans or, in the case of Palestine, the Zionists.

Palestine itself had undergone major internal changes in the late nineteenth century. Previously, it had been ruled loosely from Istanbul and had suffered from clan warfare, Bedouin raids, and economic dislocations. In the 1870s and 1880s, however, the sultans sent skilled governors to the districts, who prevented the Bedouin from raiding the fertile plains, enhanced public security, and encouraged economic growth.

In the past, Turkish governors were appointed to the districts for one-year terms and therefore had little opportunity to become acquainted with local political alignments and problems, much less rule the districts effectively. Moreover, they had paid high fees for the appointment and were primarily interested in recouping the cost. The towns were run, in practice, by councils of local Arab notables. The rural areas were controlled by large clans and their Bedouin allies. Ottoman rule was so weak that the government did not dare enforce conscription or increase taxes for fear of a rural revolt, probably in collusion with the urban notables.[37] Only Ibrahim Pasha of Egypt, who ruled Palestine from 1831 to 1840, attempted to impose military conscription on the Muslim Arabs, a move that resulted in revolt from Hebron to Nablus, which he suppressed only with great difficulty.[38]

The centuries-old division between Qaysi and Yemeni was pervasive in Palestine, involving Christian villages as well as Muslim, Bedouin as well as fellahin.[39] In the Hebron-Bethlehem area half a dozen large families engaged in frequent skirmishes. Hebron and Bayt Jala were predominantly Qaysi, and Bethlehem was largely Yemeni;[40] but the conflicts sometimes cut across this line. Thus the territorial battles of the 1850s between the Abu Ghosh, who controlled the mountain passage between Jerusalem and Jaffa, and 'Uthman al-Lahham of Bethlehem involved two Yemeni families.[41]

In the north the families of Tuqan (Qaysi) and 'Abd al-Hadi (Yemeni) vied for influence on Jabal Nablus. The Tuqans, a conservative Muslim clan, remained staunchly pro-Ottoman during Ibrahim Pasha's rule and wielded substantial influence in the rural areas. The 'Abd al-Hadis, in contrast, supported the Egyptians in the 1830s, were relatively tolerant of non-Muslims, and exercised their greatest influence within the towns of Nablus and Janin.[42] Each family established alliances with lesser families and with Transjordan Bedouin, who raided the Jordan Valley and the plains of Esdraelon and Sharon.

As a result of the constant clan warfare and Bedouin depredations, the plains were largely depopulated in mid-century.[43] Interior towns such as Nablus and Jerusalem and coastal ports such as Acre and Jaffa maintained walled fortifications and closed their gates at night in order to ensure their residents' safety. Lacking permanent roads, there was little communication among the districts.[44] Grain and other goods had to be transported by camel to the coast, and villages that controlled the mountain routes could exact a high price for passage across their land.

The situation began to change in the 1860s, and economic growth accelerated under Sultan Abdülhamid II. Substantially expanded Ottoman forces prevented the Bedouin from raiding the plains and quelled the clans' private forces. Improved administration resulted in increased trade and the growth of towns beyond their medieval walls. The Palestine population, which had actually decreased in the first half of the century, began to climb rapidly. Jaffa and Nablus each had 20,000 inhabitants by the early 1880s. Acre had 9,000, and Haifa 6,000.[45] Acre, Haifa, and Jaffa had expanding ports; Jerusalem was the religious center; and Nablus boasted a flourishing soap industry, based on oil from the surrounding olive groves. Peaches, almonds, and cotton also brought revenue to the town. Moreover, Abdülhamid patronized Nablus, subsidizing the soap industry and paying for the advanced education of Nablus children in Istanbul in preparation for their employment in the Ottoman civil service.[46]

Orange groves were introduced along the maritime plain, and a large village such as Umm al-Fahum supported a population of 2,000 on its olive groves. Nazareth, a Christian Arab center, served as the market town for the villages on the plain of Esdraelon. The plain was described in the 1880s as "a huge green lake of waving wheat, with its village-covered mounds rising from it like islands; . . . one of the most striking pictures of luxuriant fertility which it is possible to conceive."[47] Even Jericho, a mud-hut village in the depths of the Jordan Valley, experienced a boom in the 1890s, initially as an attraction for Christian pilgrims[48] and subsequently as a winter resort for wealthy Jerusalem Arab families.

The construction of roads and railways provided a crucial underpinning for this economic growth. The Jaffa-Jerusalem road, extensions to Bethlehem and Jericho, and the Haifa-Nazareth road, all opened up the interior areas to commerce. Moreover, a railway was completed between Jaffa and Jerusalem in 1893 and another between Dir'a (Syria) and Haifa in 1908, which crossed the Esdraelon.[49] Coastal beaches were also used as carriage-ways, but the interior roads were the main means to end the districts' isolation and facilitate the export of grain, fruit, and olive oil.

As part of his provincial reorganization, Abdülhamid redrew the district lines in Palestine. The districts of Acre and Gaza had previously extended along the coast, and all the central areas were included in the vilayet of Damascus.[50] In the 1880s a new *sancak* (*mutassariflik*) of Jerusalem was formed, extending west from Jericho to Jaffa and including both Gaza and Hebron to the south. This sancak was independent of the vilayet of Damascus and was tied directly to Istanbul. To the north the districts of Acre and Balqa were established as part of the new vilayet of Beirut. Acre district included Haifa, the inland towns of Safad, Nazareth, and Tiberias, and the plain of Esdraelon. Balqa district encompassed Samaria, where Nablus was the principal town, and a coastal zone including Tulkarm.[51] Three-quarters of the Palestine population, and the largest land area, were in the sancak of Jerusalem, but the best agricultural lands were in the northern districts.

The separation of the Jerusalem district from the Syrian province was accompanied by the enhancement of the relative stature of Jerusalem's leading Arab families. They eclipsed in influence such rural families as the Abu Ghosh and rivalled the Nablus clans. In the eighteenth century the most influential Jerusalem families were the 'Alamis, Jarallahs, and Khalidis. In the next century they continued to provide judges, government officials, and educators, but the principal rivalry centered on the Khalidis (Qaysi) and Husaynis (Yemeni).[52] By the end of the century, the Husaynis controlled the positions of mufti and mayor, which were the most important local offices. The Husaynis passed the positions from father to son, holding the muftiship until 1937 and the mayoralty until 1920, except for 1906–9 when Faydi al-'Alami held the post.[53] In the early twentieth century, a fifth family, the Nashashibis, began to acquire local influence. They had rapidly expanded their land holdings, but their wealth was not yet reflected in commensurate political influence.[54] The elections to the Ottoman parliament in 1908, 1912, and 1914 saw members of the Husayni, Khalidi, 'Alami, and Nashashibi families elected as deputies from Jerusalem.[55] Leading individuals, such as Musa Kazim Pasha al-Husayni, both served in the imperial foreign service and acquired local influence. Similarly, Ruhi 'Abd al-Hadi of Nablus-Janin served as Ottoman consul in the Balkans, Greece, and Switzerland from 1905 to 1920, and Haydar Tuqan was both an Ottoman official and a deputy from Nablus to the imperial parliament.[56]

The Muslim Arab elite as a whole felt secure in its position, although the families engaged in intense competition. As provincial autonomy increased and the region began to prosper in the 1890s and 1900s, the families could anticipate influential political roles and substantial wealth. Lesser families and the civil servants could also expect a more stable and prosperous life. Similarly, Christian Arab merchants and professionals expanded their activities and looked forward to growing roles in export trades and education. In some towns with mixed populations, Christian Arabs even served as deputies to the Muslim mayors.

The only unsettling aspects were the penetration of European states into the region and the political ambitions of the nascent Zionist movement. The European penetration had its positive side: pilgrims and tourists provided substantial revenue for the Arab merchants; some missionary schools attracted Muslim as well as Christian Arab students.[57] Nevertheless, the openly stated political aims of the European powers disturbed, in particular, the Muslim Arabs, who began to fear that the Ottoman regime could not prevent an eventual European conquest. The Zionist movement foreshadowed the potential displacement of the local population and was therefore viewed as an even greater danger than European occupation. Most Arab complaints to Istanbul in the 1890s were therefore directed against Jewish settlement.

The aftermath of the Young Turk coup d'état in 1908 upset some of the assumptions of the Arab elite about the

mutuality of Arab and Turkish interests and thereby accelerated tendencies toward a separate Arabism in Palestine, as in other Arab provinces. The Turkification policies
of the C.U.P., its opposition to the expression of minority
nationalism, its ineffectiveness in dealing with the Balkan
secessions, and its vacillation toward the Zionists, all contributed to Arab disenchantment and a growing awareness
of divergent interests. The financial burdens imposed by the
unsuccessful military campaigns also contributed to public
unrest.

Orthodox Arab opposition to the Greek hierarchy, fueled
earlier by Russia, began to assume an anti-Turk coloring
after 1908. The tensions over the Greek monopoly of offices
and funds erupted immediately after the Young Turk coup.[58]
The Arabs' demand for a communal council to administer
the patriarchate finances was rejected by the Greek clergy,
whereupon the Arabs closed down churches, occupied monasteries, and held demonstrations in Jerusalem, Bethlehem, and
Jaffa. Ottoman officials initially sought a compromise between the two sides, but in late 1909 the government forced
a settlement that largely supported the Greek officials, out of
its growing fear that the Orthodox Arab unrest was only
another manifestation of the wider Arab national ferment.
In 1911 activists in al-Nahdah al-Urthuthuksiyah found a
forum in *Filastin*, the newspaper founded by Orthodox Arab
brothers Yusuf and 'Isa Da'ud al-'Isa. They also had a spokesman in the teacher Khalil al-Sakakini.[59]

Nevertheless, anti-Turk politics did not provide the rallying
point for the Palestine Arabs. The political elite remained
uncertain in its attitude toward Istanbul, with supporters of
both the C.U.P. and the decentralizing Entente Libérale
found in the ranks of the leading families. Rather, opposition to Zionism provided the common ground for local politics, the basis upon which political societies were formed and
newspapers were supported.

Before the Young Turk coup, the Arabs' means for expressing and organizing their opposition to the Zionist movement

were extremely limited. Nevertheless, Arab notables in Jerusalem did protest to Istanbul and did use their local positions in order to contain Jewish immigration and settlement. In May 1890, for example, a Jerusalem protest against the governor's approval of a land purchase by the Rishon le Zion settlers resulted in the recall of the governor. Similarly, the June 1891 telegram that Muslim and Christian notables sent to Istanbul urging a complete ban of Jewish immigration and land purchases resulted in imperial edicts prohibiting them.[60]

Although modified under European pressure, these edicts radically curtailed Zionist land-buying in the sancak of Jerusalem in the 1890s and 1900s. Enforcement of the edicts, however, depended on local officials, who were sometimes susceptible to bribes. A notable exception was the mufti of Jerusalem, Tahir al-Husayni, who not only protested to Istanbul against land transactions but presided over a commission on land transfer applications and thereby effectively stopped Jewish purchases for several years. In the northern districts a similar exception was Amir Amin Arslan, the qa'immaqam of Tiberias, who resisted the Sursuqs' effort to sell a large tract to the Zionists. Finally, after the 1905 Zionist congress resolved to direct all colonizing efforts to Palestine and to acquire national sovereignty there, the sultan suspended all land transfers to Jews. In late 1906 he sent a new governor to Jerusalem and a new district officer to Jaffa, who sought to curb Zionist activities.

Although a few private efforts to warn Jewish settlers of the seriousness of Arab opposition to their political aims took place, the Arabs had only rare contacts with the European Jews who were promoting Zionism. In 1899 the elderly Yusuf Diya al-Din Pasha al-Khalidi, a former mayor of Jerusalem, wrote the chief rabbi of France, Zadoc Kahn. He warned that the Ottoman government would not be able to quell the popular movement against the Jews that would result from the Zionist incursion.[61]

Not until the initiation of electoral politics and newspapers after 1908 were the Arabs able to organize and articulate their grievances. Anti-Zionism became an increasingly important aspect of the election campaigns for the imperial parliament that were held in October 1908, April 1912, and April 1914. Although the campaigns were fought more along family and religious lines than on broad political issues, candidates for both the C.U.P. and (in the 1908 election) the Entente Libérale opposed the Zionist movement.[62] In 1914, for example, Raghib al-Nashashibi argued that he would "dedicate my strength day and night to remove the damage and danger awaiting us through the Zionists and Zionism."[63] In contrast to the Jerusalem representatives, the three-term deputy from Acre, Shaykh As'ad al-Shuqayri, did not oppose Zionism. A conservative Muslim, he was primarily concerned about Latin influence in Palestine and felt that the Zionists could help the Arabs to resist European encroachment.[64]

Arab deputies aired the issue of Zionism in parliament in 1909 and 1911. In the summer of 1909 a deputy from Jerusalem demanded that Jewish immigration be checked and succeeded in winning a renewal of the old regime's restrictions.[65] In March 1911 the finance minister was forced to resign after he was accused of accepting loans from Jewish bankers in return for which the Zionists received special favors in Palestine. The Turkish deputies lost their interest in the issue once this minister was deposed, and therefore they became impatient with the Arabs' discourses against Zionism in May.[66] In these debates the lead was taken by the Jerusalem deputies, in particular Ruhi al-Khalidi, and two Syrian Arab deputies, Amir Amin Arslan and Shukri al-'Asali, representing Latakia and Damascus, respectively. Both deputies had been qa'immaqams in northern Palestine and had sought to prevent Sursuq land sales to the Zionists.

Within Palestine anti-Zionist societies sprouted in the 1910s, often in reaction to particular land sales or to vacillation on the part of the Ottoman authorities. Faydi al-'Alami and Ruhi al-Khalidi were active in 1911 trying to prevent the sale of a village near Jerusalem, and the Ottoman National party (al-Hizb al-Watani al-'Uthmani), founded at the same time in

Jaffa, concerned itself with the prevention of land sales. Its founders included the barrister and landowner Shaykh Sulayman al-Taji al-Faruqi.[67] The former parliamentary deputy Hafiz al-Sa'id formed a branch of the Beirut Reform Society in 1912–13, after his failure to win reelection on the Entente Libérale slate and at the time of Ottoman discussions of possible financial aid from the Zionists. Finally, in May and June of 1914, when rumors of Ottoman-Zionist talks again surfaced, anti-Zionist societies appeared in Haifa as well as Jaffa and Jerusalem.[68] These societies involved minute numbers, but they were drawn from the small politically conscious group in Palestine and, in particular, from a cross section of the Arab elite.

Of greater importance for the spread of political ideas in Palestine was the formation of newspapers, of which at least a half dozen appeared after 1908.[69] Najib al-Nassar founded *al-Karmil* in Haifa in late 1908, with an anti-Zionist but, originally, pro-C.U.P. editorial policy. Nassar was a Protestant convert from Greek Orthodoxy, who had worked for fifteen years in the Free Church of Scotland's missionary hospital in Tiberias. After a brief period as a land agent for a Jewish colonizing society, he turned against the Zionists and helped Amin Arslan fight the Sursuq land sale of 1901. After the Young Turk coup, Nassar turned to journalism as the most effective means to express and expand popular distrust of the Zionists. He also published *al-Sahyuniyah* (Zionism) in 1911, the first book-length analysis of Zionism to be written in Arabic. It consisted of an essay by Nassar and excerpts from the *Jewish Encyclopedia*, selected so as to prove that the Zionists sought a Jewish state in Palestine and also had ambitions in Syria and Iraq.[70]

Other anti-Zionist newspapers included *Filastin* and *al-Asma'i* in Jaffa, the former published by the Orthodox Arab 'Isa al-'Isa,[71] and *al-Quds* and *al-Muntada* in Jerusalem. The newspapers printed translations of Zionist statements in Europe, including reports on the 1913 Zionist congress. They carried editorials that criticized landowners for selling land to Zionist companies, and they published articles by Arab students in Istanbul on Zionist activities in the capital. Two such correspondents were Jamal al-Husayni and 'Arif al-'Arif, twenty-year-old law students in Istanbul.[72]

A brief attempt to reach an Arab-Zionist detente in the spring of 1914 illustrated the depth of difference and suspicion between the two peoples.[73] A Muslim Arab engineer from Jerusalem who worked in Beirut, Nasif al-Khalidi, proposed to Zionist leaders that a joint conference be convened that would seek an accommodation between them. Although Nasif al-Khalidi was interested in promoting an accord, most of the Arabs who agreed to participate were known to be outspoken opponents of Zionism. They included Jamal al-Husayni and the editors of *Filastin* and *al-Karmil*. Moreover, the agenda specified that the Zionist delegates "should explain, as far as possible by producing documentary evidence, the aims and methods of Zionism" and "thereafter the Arabs will formulate their demands, acceptance of which would determine whether the [Zionist] movement could be considered harmful to the Arabs or not."[74] It was apparent that the "documentary evidence" would indicate that the Zionists did not intend to integrate with the local population and that they sought a Jewish state in Palestine. Unwilling to participate in a hostile gathering, the Zionist leaders sought to postpone the meeting, which was finally set aside when the empire plunged into World War I.

By the close of the Ottoman Empire, the Arabs had experienced a growing awareness as a community set apart from the Turkish rulers and in potential conflict with the European powers and the Zionist movement. Fear of the Zionists accelerated the organization of an Arab political movement in the districts that comprised Palestine. It also hastened the establishment of a vigorous, highly politicized press that played a key role in articulating the Arab grievances and in spreading these views beyond the small Arab elite. Finally, the Arabs who led the national movement in the 1920s and beyond were the same people who had gained their initial experience in organizing and writing against Zionism in the 1900s and 1910s.

1. For an overview of the movement in the 1920s and 1930s, see the author's "The Palestine Arab Nationalist Movement under the Mandate," in William B. Quandt et al., *The Politics of Palestinian Nationalism* (Berkeley, Calif., 1973).

2. Neville Mandel, in "Turks, Arabs, and Jewish Immigration into Palestine, 1882–1914" (*St. Antony's Papers*, no. 17 [1965]), argues persuasively that the outlines of the later national movement are discernible before 1914.

3. James Finn, *Stirring Times, or Records from Jerusalem Consular Chronicles of 1853 to 1856* (London, 1878), 2:384, 394.

4. James Parkes, *A History of Palestine from 135 A.D. to Modern Times* (New York, 1949), pp. 239–40; Finn, op. cit., 1:29; Sir Anton Bertram and Harry Charles Luke, *Report of the Commission Appointed by the Government of Palestine to Inquire into the Affairs of the Orthodox Patriarchate of Jerusalem* (London, 1921), pp. 13–15, 229; Elie Kedourie, "Religion and Politics: The Diaries of Khalil Sakakini." *St. Antony's Papers* 4 (1958): 82–84.

5. Laurence Oliphant, *Haifa or Life in Modern Palestine* (New York, 1887), pp. 282–84; also pp. 19–24, on the establishment of the Templar colonies.

6. Finn, op. cit., 1:300 ff.; 349 ff.; 2:34, 218, 258.

7. Oliphant, op. cit., pp. 48–49.

8. Finn describes the conditions in the old Yishuv and Montefiore's efforts (op. cit., 1:101–32; 2:56–82, 320–35); Moshe Ma'oz, *Ottoman Reform in Syria and Palestine, 1840–1861: The Impact of the Tanzimat on Politics and Society* (Oxford, 1968), pp. 205–9.

9. See, for example, a letter from a young settler in 1882, quoted in David Ben-Gurion, *My Talks with Arab Leaders* (New York, 1973), p. 2.

10. Oliphant, op. cit., pp. 62, 288.

11. Mandel, op. cit., pp. 80–83.

12. Ibid., p. 86.

13. Oliphant, op. cit., pp. 191, 109.

14. Mandel, op. cit., p. 85.

15. Ibid., p. 84; Yaacov Ro'i, "The Zionist Attitude to the Arabs, 1908–1914," *Middle Eastern Studies* 4 (April 1968): 222.

16. Mandel, op. cit., p. 86.

17. Oliphant, op. cit., pp. 59–60.

18. Mandel, op. cit., p. 96.

19. Ben-Gurion, op. cit., p. 3.

20. Oliphant, op. cit., p. 21.

21. Marvin Lowenthal, ed., *The Diaries of Theodor Herzl* (New York, 1962), passim, on Herzl's negotiating efforts.

22. Ro'i, op. cit., pp. 203, 206; Walter Laqueur, *A History of Zionism* (New York, 1972), pp. 218–19.

23. "The Truth from Palestine" (1891), quoted in Clement Leslie, *The Rift in Israel* (New York, 1971), pp. 31–32.

24. Ro'i, op. cit., pp. 198–99.

25. Ibid., pp. 208–10.

26. Ibid., pp. 205, 210.

27. Ibid., p. 224.

28. Ibid., pp. 215, 219, 231–32, 236.

29. Kemal H. Karpat, "The Transformation of the Ottoman State, 1789–1908," *International Journal of Middle East Studies* 3 (July 1972): 279, 281, notes that secular Turkish nationalism was born over two decades before the 1908 *coup d'état*, but it took the open manifestation of Turkish nationalism after 1908 to undermine pan-Islamism and hasten Arab separatism.

30. Zeine N. Zeine, *The Emergence of Arab Nationalism* (Beirut, 1966), pp. 90–93.

31. C. Ernest Dawn, *From Ottomanism to Arabism* (Urbana, Ill., 1973), pp. 129–30.

32. Dawn analyzes the ideas of Muhammad 'Abduh, Rashid Rida, and 'Abd al-Rahman al-Kawakibi (ibid., pp. 133–40).

33. Ibid., pp. 125, 146.

34. Sa'id was hanged as a traitor in 1915.

35. Zeine, op. cit., pp. 94–98. 'Awni 'Abd al-Hadi (b. 1889), a law student in Paris, also attended the Arab congress in 1913. He was later Amir Faysal's legal adviser at the 1919 Paris peace conference and was active in the Palestine national movement in the late 1920s–40s, partly as the founder of the Istiqlal party. Rafiq al-Tamimi (b. 1890) became a secondary school principal in Palestine, participated in Istiqlal, and wrote about the Arab resistance against the Crusaders.

36. Ibid., pp. 132–33; Dawn, "The Rise of Arabism in Syria," *Middle East Journal* 16 (1962): 152, 159.

37. No military conscription was imposed during the Crimean War for fear of a revolt (Finn, op. cit., 2:316). A tax increase in 1824 resulted in a bloody rural uprising (see S. N. Spyridon, "Annals of Palestine, 1821–1841," *Journal of the Palestine Oriental Society* 18 (1938): 73–82, an abridged translation of the diary of a Greek Orthodox monk, Neophytos, from the Mar Saba collection of manuscripts).

38. Ibid., pp. 89–119, on the 1834–35 revolt, and pp. 127–30 on Ibrahim Pasha's subsequent enforcement of conscription and his loss of Palestine in 1839–40; see also Ma'oz, op. cit., pp. 4–11, on pre-1831 Ottoman rule in Palestine, and pp. 12–20 on Ibrahim's era.

39. Elias N. Haddad, "Political Parties in Syria and Palestine (Qaisi and Yemeni)," *Journal of the Palestine Oriental Society* 1 (1921): 210.

40. Ibid., p. 213; Ma'oz, op. cit., pp. 118–22.

41. Haddad, op. cit., p. 212; Finn, op. cit., 2:194.

42. Finn, op. cit., 2:431, 434, 437, 441; Spyridon, op. cit., p. 106; Ma'oz, op. cit., pp. 113–18.

43. Finn, op. cit., 2:5, 153; Ma'oz, op. cit., pp. 130–34, 147, 164.

44. Finn, op. cit., 2:178; Ma'oz op. cit., pp. 166–68.

45. Oliphant, op. cit., pp. 23, 208, 286, 341; Shimon Shamir comments on the

relatively greater public security and economic advancement in Palestine and Lebanon in contrast to Syria, in "The Modernization of Syria: Problems and Solutions in the Early Period of Abdülhamid," William R. Polk and R. L. Chambers, eds., *Beginnings of Modernization in the Middle East: The Nineteenth Century* (Chicago, 1968), p. 367.

46. Ibid., pp. 341–43; Adnan Mohammad Abu Ghazaleh, "Arab Cultural Nationalism in Palestine, 1919–1948" (Ph.d. diss., New York University, 1967), pp. 23 24.

47. Oliphant, op. cit., pp. 59–60.

48. Ibid., pp. 319–24.

49. Ibid., pp. 60, 63–66, 289, 342.

50. Parkes, op. cit., p. 221.

51. Zeine, op. cit., p. 29; Yehoshua Porath, "Al-Hajj Amin al-Husayni, Mufti of Jerusalem," *Asian and African Studies* 7 (1971): 126; P. M. Holt, *Egypt and the Fertile Crescent, 1516–1922* (Ithaca, N.Y., 1966), p. 242.

52. Haddad, op. cit., p. 213.

53. Muftis from the Husayni family were Mustafa, his son Tahir, Tahir's son Kamil (d. 1921), and Kamil's step-brother al-Hajj Amin. Mayors from the family included Salim (in the 1870s), his son Husayn Salim (d. 1918), and the latter's elder brother Musa Kazim Pasha (Porath, op. cit., pp. 124–25).

54. Raghib al-Nashashibi (1880–1952) was mayor from 1920 to 1934. The family became the principal rival of the Husaynis in the 1920s and 1930s. In 1949 Raghib became military governor of the West Bank, under Jordanian control.

55. Ruhi al-Khalidi was elected to parliament in 1908 and 1912; Sa'id al-Husayni in 1908 and 1914; Ahmad 'Arif al-Husayni and 'Uthman al-Nashashibi in 1912; and Raghib al-Nashashibi and Faydi al-'Alami (d. 1924) in 1914. 'Alami's son Musa (b. 1897) was a lawyer in the British administration (1922–37) and then a leading independent politician.

56. For the names of other prominent leaders see Y. Porath, *The Emergence of the Palestinian-Arab National Movement, 1918 1929* (London, 1974), p. 13. Musa Kazim Pasha (1848–1934) was mayor of Jerusalem during 1918 20, president of the Arab Executive from 1920 to 1934, and led several Arab delegations to London, as titular head of the Palestine national movement. Ruhi 'Abd al-Hadi (b. 1885) served in the British administration in Palestine through the 1940s. Haydar Tuqan supported the Zionists in the 1920s and was active in municipal politics in Nablus.

57. Some Muslim Arab children attended the English schools in Jerusalem, in particular. Jamal al-Husayni (b. 1893), Husayn Fakhri al-Khalidi (b. 1894) and his brother Ahmad Samih al-Khalidi (b. 1896) attended St. George's School. Jamal al-Husayni was a leading nationalist in the 1920s 40s; Dr. Husayn Fakhri was mayor of Jerusalem (1935 38) and a respected doctor and politician; Ahmad Samih was principal of the Government Arab College from 1925 to the 1940s.

58. Bertram and Luke, op. cit., pp. 26–29, 250–71; Parkes, op. cit., p. 241; Kedourie, op. cit., p. 86. Kedourie also analyzes the reasons for Orthodox Arab adherence to Arab nationalism in Palestine (ibid., pp. 77–79, 92).

59. Porath, *Emergence of the Palestinian-Arab National Movement*, pp. 7–8.

60. Mandel, op. cit., p. 86.

61. Ibid., pp. 89–90; Herzl replied on behalf of Kahn, that immigration would benefit the local economy and settlers would not displace the indigenous population (Ro'i, op. cit., p. 200).

62. Mandel, op. cit., pp. 92, 102. See footnote 55 for the names of the successful candidates from Jerusalem.

63. Ibid., p. 102; Porath offers a similar quotation in *Emergence of the Palestinian-Arab National Movement*, p. 27.

64. Ro'i, op. cit., pp. 224, 228. Shuqayri was a leading opponent of the Husaynis in the 1920s and 1930s. His son, Ahmad Shuqayri, headed the Palestine Liberation Organization from 1964 to 1968.

65. Mandel, op. cit., p. 94.

66. Ibid., p. 97.

67. Ibid., p. 98. He was an active politician and newspaper editor until his death in 1939. A consistent opponent of Hajj Amin al-Husayni, he also turned against the British in the 1930s.

68. Ibid., p. 102.

69. Ibid., pp. 92–95, on the press.

70. Ibid., p. 97; N. Mandel, "Attempts at an Arab-Zionist Entente: 1913–1914," *Middle Eastern Studies* 1 (1965): 263. He continued to edit the newspaper and oppose Zionist land purchases under British rule.

71. 'Isa al-'Isa (b. 1880) was a Greek Orthodox Arab, educated at the American University in Beirut, who founded *Filastin* in 1911 at age 31. After a period in exile during World War I, he resumed publishing the newspaper, which served as an influential, moderate organ in the 1920s–40s.

72. See note 57 above on Jamal al-Husayni. 'Arif al-'Arif (1892–1973) was the son of Ahmad 'Arif al-Husayni, parliamentary delegate in 1912–14. He was accused of inciting violence at the 1920 riots in Jerusalem, but subsequently became an official in the British administration in Palestine and confined his political activities to historical studies of Arab ties to Palestinian towns.

73. Mandel, "Attempts at an Arab-Zionist Entente," describes several abortive efforts that took place outside Palestine, largely involving the Decentralization party in Cairo. He details the 1914 effort, pp. 257–64.

74. Ibid., p. 260.

Notes on the Contributors

William W. Haddad is an associate professor of history at Illinois State University. He is the author of several articles that have appeared in Arabic as well as English.

Roderic Davison teaches in the Department of History at George Washington University. His most recent work is *Turkey* (Englewood Cliffs, N.J., 1968).

Alan Fisher teaches in the Department of History at Michigan State University, and is the author of *The Russian Annexation of the Crimea* (Cambridge, 1970)

Carole Rogel is associate professor of history at the Ohio State University.

William Spencer is a member of the Department of History at Florida State University and the author of, among other works, *The Land and People of Tunisia* (Philadelphia, 1972).

William Ochsenwald teaches in the Department of History at the Virginia Polytechnic Institute and State University.

Caesar Farah is a member of the Department of Middle Eastern Languages at the University of Minnesota, and the author of *Islam: Beliefs and Observances* (Woodbury, N.Y., 1973).

Russell Yates Smith received his doctorate under Professor Fisher, and taught in the Department of History at Capital University, Columbus, Ohio.

Rashid Khalidi is a member of the Department of History at the Lebanese University.

Suleiman Mousa resides in Amman, and is the author of *Al-Harakah al-'Arabiyah* (Beirut, 1970).

Ann Lesch is a Middle East representative of the American Friends Service Committee in Jerusalem, and coauthor of *The Politics of Palestinian Nationalism* (Berkeley, Calif., 1973).

Index